Data Privacy for the Smart Grid

Data Privacy for the Smart Grid

Rebecca Herold • Christine Hertzog

CRC Press
Taylor & Francis Group
Boca Raton London New York

CRC Press is an imprint of the
Taylor & Francis Group, an **informa** business
AN AUERBACH BOOK

Reprint 2019

CRC Press
Taylor & Francis Group
6000 Broken Sound Parkway NW, Suite 300
Boca Raton, FL 33487-2742

ISBN: 978-0-367-24039-4

Library of Congress Cataloging-in-Publication Data

Herold, Rebecca.
Data privacy for the smart grid / Rebecca Herold and Christine Hertzog.
pages cm
Summary: "The Smart Grid is a convenient term to describe the modernization of electric, natural gas, and water grid infrastructures. The term encapsulates the convergence of remote monitoring and control technologies with communications technologies, renewables generation, and analytics capabilities so that previously non-communicative infrastructures like electricity grids can provide time-sensitive status updates and deliver situational awareness. While initially and mostly focused on electricity, many of the same technologies, particularly in information and communications technologies or ICT apply to natural gas and water grids. This book addresses privacy in all three of these consumables, but electricity occupies a unique place by virtue of the fact that we can produce it as well as consume it. In addition, existing technologies make it easier to get many more measurements about electricity than gas or water. These two unique qualities about electricity have very interesting ramifications for privacy, and therefore, this book will refer to electricity and electricity use cases because that provides the best framework for discussion of this important topic"-- Provided by publisher.
Includes bibliographical references and index.
ISBN 978-1-4665-7337-6 (hardback)
1. Smart power grids--Security measures--United States. 2. Public utilities--Security measures--United States. 3. Consumer protection--United States. 4. Privacy, Right of--United States. 5. Records--Access control--United States. I. Hertzog, Christine. II. Title.

TK3105.H46 2015
363.60285'58--dc23 2014030904

Visit the Taylor & Francis Web site at
http://www.taylorandfrancis.com

and the CRC Press Web site at
http://www.crcpress.com

Printed and bound in India

For sale in India, Pakistan, Nepal, Bhutan, Bangladesh and Sri Lanka only.

Dedication

A huge thank you to Mom and Dad (may they rest in peace) for always expecting me to do my best, and telling me I could accomplish anything, no matter what it was. They never put limitations on me because of my gender; I have only encountered that from others since starting my career. I am grateful my parents taught me that such gender-based limitations were ridiculous.

To my wonderful sons, Noah and Heath. You are both the apples of my eyes and the joys in my life.

To my husband, Tom, even though he will never read a book like this.

To Rich O'Hanley, for giving us the opportunity to write this book, his always unwavering patience while we finished this book, and his continuing support and confidence throughout these many years. Thank you!

To Laurie Schlags, for being patient, professional, and going out of her way to assist us in getting everything necessary completed for this book. Thanks!

To Christine Hertzog, for asking me to write this book with her. Thank you! It's been great working with you. Thank you for putting up with some of my Sheldon Cooper tendencies. We did it!

To those who read these types of books, and appreciate the work that goes into them, thank you. If you find the information we provide useful, please let us know.

To Stephen Colbert and Jon Stewart, because I really think they should read this book and then talk about it and Smart Grid privacy on their shows!

Rebecca Herold

I dedicate this book to my mother, who taught me that common sense and determination are never overrated.

Christine Hertzog

Contents

Preface

So why did we write this book? In short, we wanted to have a book that covers Smart Grid privacy more thoroughly than the others that were available. Additionally, we wanted to provide a book that also represents two different approaches on the topic, one from a Smart Grid sector expert and one from a privacy expert. We also wanted to show how the convergence of the two results in not only more effective privacy actions, but also more proactive business decisions. We each had different, but in many ways similar, motivations and goals.

Rebecca Herold

I became interested in the privacy issues of the Smart Grid after I led the very first ever Smart Grid privacy impact assessment (PIA). I've been addressing privacy within business since 1994, when I was given the responsibility of establishing privacy requirements for one of the very first online banks. This was in addition to my responsibility of creating the information security requirements. There were no privacy laws at that time, so the lawyers in the large organization where I worked said they were not obligated to determine privacy requirements when I asked them if they could get involved. However, I strongly believed it was important, so I convinced my senior vice president at the time to let me take on that responsibility. Since then

I've welcomed the opportunity to identify privacy risks in new technologies and practices, in the absence of any laws or regulations, in a wide range of industries.

I firmly believe that if you wait until there are laws in place to protect privacy for specific types of technologies, information, etc., that can reveal information about people's lives, you will be too late in being as effective as you can be to help prevent privacy problems. In my experience, I've seen that data protection laws always lag behind technology advances by many years. I've been gratified to see this trend changing in some areas, though. For example, laws are being established more closely to the launch of new technologies in the Smart Grid in part by the work of my NIST SGIP SGCC Privacy Group. This is evidenced, as one example, by California being the first state to implement smart meter privacy law just several months, instead of years, after my group released to the public the first version of NISTIR 7628 Rev. 1: Guidelines for the Smart Grid Cybersecurity: Volume 2–Privacy and the Smart Grid as a draft in 2010. The law closely mirrors many of the recommendations from NISTIR 7628 Rev. 1.

Since 2009, my NIST SGIP SGCC Privacy Group has created a lot of really valuable work products, not only both versions of NISTIR 7628 Rev. 1, but also additional work products that those who will be working in the Smart Grid environment need to know about so they can use them to help support their privacy efforts. I am happy to have a chance within this book to point to them.

I met Christine when she led the privacy use cases subteam within the NIST SGIP Privacy Group, and I had the opportunity to work closely with her as a member of that team. When Christine approached me with the idea to write a book about Smart Grid privacy, I looked at the other books available on this topic. There weren't many at that time. However, those that did have both *Smart Grid* and *privacy* in the title had very little actual privacy discussion beyond the mention of encryption within the text! And none of them mentioned privacy principles to use, or privacy impact assessments that could be performed. They were, instead, overwhelmingly about cyber security controls, a great injustice to the readers who actually expected privacy to be discussed in detail, and comprehensively. Our book looks at the Smart Grid, and describes in detail how practitioners and those building portions of the Smart Grid can address privacy.

I also have been increasingly frustrated by those who claim that addressing privacy (and information security for that matter) is bad because it prevents innovations. Poppycock! I agree that the Smart Grid holds great promise for inspiring significant innovations, improving upon all sectors of organizations, and bringing true benefit to individuals in possibly unlimited ways. However, organizations that are part of the Smart Grid, including those that create devices and software for use within it, must determine the associated privacy and information security impacts before they actually put software and hardware into use. By doing so, you are actually improving upon innovation, because the resulting products will have the privacy baked in, which is much more effective than trying to latch something on to an existing product later.

I want this book to be read by three primary audiences: (1) those building and architecting the many different components of the Smart Grid, to help them to build in effective privacy controls; (2) those who are or will be using smart meters, smart appliances, and generally living within the Smart Grid in one or more ways, so they know the true privacy risks, and also the ways in which those risks can be mitigated; and (3) those who are interested in knowing more about the Smart Grid and privacy and want to get objective, factual information. I am concerned about privacy, and I am interested in identifying and mitigating privacy risks within Smart Grid technologies to the extent possible. While most in the energy industry want to identify privacy risks and mitigate them appropriately, I know from direct experience that there are still a few who do not want to have privacy discussed for stated fear that it will harm consumer adoption or "thwart innovation." I want to provide the facts without having the risks downplayed to meet the interests of those few who want to only provide positive information about the Smart Grid. There are also groups, some of whom have contacted me directly, who want to scare consumers into not using smart meters for a very wide variety of reasons. I want to provide the facts and analysis about Smart Grid privacy that can be used to allow readers and consumers to recognize when sensational, exaggerated warnings are made about privacy that are not based upon any research or facts.

We address the legal issues without getting into legal jargon. We address the technical aspects without getting deep into the weeds of technical details. We point out the privacy topics without providing the information in an academic research paper type of narrative. In short, we are striving to make this book usable by anyone concerned about privacy within the Smart Grid and who wants to know the facts, in addition to providing practical privacy safeguards and guidance for those entities within the Smart Grid.

Christine Hertzog

The Smart Grid is a convenient term that describes the collection of technologies, policies, and financial innovations that are spurring the modernization of our electrical, natural gas, and water infrastructures. The Smart Grid consists of multiple machine-to-machine (M2M) applications that are characteristic of the Internet of Things (IOT). The Smart Grid produces significant amounts of data and can also create new types of data. Data can be created in timescales that range from milliseconds to hours to days, and it can also be event driven.

Smart meters are one of the most visible M2M applications for many consumers, but hardly the only one in the Smart Grid sector. While the focus of this book is on the Smart Grid, it also addresses the data generated at its periphery—such as in the connected home and in automobiles (and not just the electric ones). Every business sector is deploying technologies that are capable of collecting and communicating new and more data about performance, use, and status.

My focus on privacy came about from my work as the team leader for the NIST SGIP SGCC Privacy Group's work on privacy use cases and the results we published in NISTIR 7628 Rev. 1. Ongoing observations about the quality and level of discussion about what is actually transmitted as data by different Smart Grid technologies and applications prompted this book. The word *convergence* is often used in reference to Smart Grid topics. It was only logical to apply that practice to writing this book to leverage the knowledge of two different experts.

Intelligent investments in Smart Grid infrastructure are best made with accurate information. The same can be said for development of policy and law. This book offers a clear and concise explanation of the Smart Grid and provides a solid foundation to understand the problems being addressed and proposed solutions. It describes the most important technologies, policies and trends, and the impacts that the transformation to a modern grid will have on stakeholders like consumers, utilities, regulators, and lawmakers, and businesses that sell grid-related products and services to stakeholders. Most importantly, it addresses these topics through the lens of data privacy and the considerations for privacy of individuals and organizations.

This book educates readers about data that is created by the Smart Grid and Smart Grid technologies, as well as some other M2M applications. My objective is to help educate readers to develop informed opinions and meaningful contributions to legislation, policy, and hardware and software technologies to preserve and protect privacy for individuals and entities. In other words, let's generate light instead of heat on the topic of the Smart Grid and privacy.

Acknowledgments

- Tanya Brewer, Marianne Swanson, Vicky Pillitteri, and Amanda Stallings provided great support and did a lot of work for my NIST SGIP SGCC Privacy Group. Much of that is reflected in this book. My thanks to them.
- Dr. Ken Wacks and Dr. Jim Kirtley, both from MIT, provided valuable information about the first "smart" electricity meter, along with a great explanation for how it came to be, and how the patented design worked. My thanks to them.
- Klaus Kursawe from ENCS in the Netherlands provided important information about his smart meter privacy research. My thanks to him.
- Gal Shpantzer originally got me involved with the NIST CSWG Privacy Group. I'm grateful to him for that. My thanks to him.

Rebecca Herold

I am grateful for the assistance of my colleagues who generously gave time and information in conversations and reference materials that contributed to this book's content. The following individuals provided valuable background, ideas, and perspectives:

- Chris Kotting, Executive Director at the EIS Alliance
- Ed Beroset, Director of Technology and Standards at Elster Solutions
- Dave Krinkel, Principal at EnergyAI
- Chris Villareal, Senior Regulatory Analyst at California Public Utilities Commission

Thank you for serving as sounding boards and sharing your expertise and knowledge.

A very special thank you to Rebecca Herold, my co-author, and the publishing team at Taylor & Francis Group. We had a vision, we created a schedule, we put words to paper, and we got it done. And we did it as a team.

Christine Hertzog

About the Authors

Rebecca Herold has over 2½ decades of information privacy, security, and compliance expertise. Rebecca is CEO of Privacy Professor® and owner/partner for SIMBUS® and has led the NIST SGIP Smart Grid Privacy Group since June 2009. She has been an adjunct professor for the Norwich University MSISA program since 2005 and has written 17 books and hundreds of published articles. Rebecca is invited to speak at a wide variety of events throughout the United States, and other worldwide locations such as Melbourne, Australia, Bogotá, Colombia, and Ireland.

Rebecca is widely recognized and respected, and has been providing information privacy, security, and compliance services, tools, and products to organizations in an extensive range of industries for over two decades. Just a few of her awards and recognitions include the following:

- Named in the Top 2 Female Infosec Leaders to Follow on Twitter in 2014 by Information Security Buzz.

- Named to the ISACA International Privacy Task Force in 2013.
- Named on Tripwire's list of InfoSec's Rising Stars and Hidden Gems: The Top 15 Educators in July 2013.
- Named one of Information Security Buzz's list of Top 5 Female Infosec Leaders to Follow on Twitter in 2013 and 2014.
- Has been named one of the "Best Privacy Advisers in the World" multiple times in recent years by *Computerworld* magazine, most recently ranking number 3 in the world in the last rankings provided.
- In 2012 was named one of the most influential people and groups in online privacy by Techopedia.com.
- In 2012 was named a privacy by design ambassador by the Ontario, Canada, data privacy commissioner.

Rebecca is an owner and partner for the SIMBUS services for healthcare organizations and their business associates to meet their HIPAA, HITECH, and other legal requirements, with more industries added in late 2014. She is also a partner for the Compliance Helper services and has been leading the NIST SGIP Smart Grid Privacy Group since June 2009. Rebecca is a member of the IAPP Certification Advisory Board, and is an instructor for the IAPP's CIPM, CIPP/IT, CIPP/US, and CIPP Foundations classes.

She currently serves on multiple advisory boards for security, privacy, and high-tech technology organizations. Rebecca is frequently interviewed and quoted in diverse broadcasts and publications such as *IAPP Privacy Advisor*, *BNA Privacy & Security Law Report*, *Wired*, *Popular Science*, *Computerworld*, IEEE's *Security and Privacy Journal*, NPR, and many others. Rebecca regularly appears on the Des Moines, Iowa-based Great Day morning television program on KCWI to discuss and provide advice for information security and privacy topics.

Born and raised in Missouri, she has degrees in math, computer science, and education. She has lived in Iowa on a farm with her family for the past couple of decades, where they raise corn, soybeans, sunflowers, and make hay. They are currently renovating a house, over 100 years old, that had previously been occupied by raccoons and chipmunks for several years. See more about Rebecca, her work, services, and products at:

Rebecca Herold, CIPM, CIPP/IT, CIPP/US, CISSP, CISM, CISA, FLMI
Owner and CEO, The Privacy Professor (http://www.privacyguidance.com and http://www.privacyprofessor.org)
Partner, SIMBUS (http://www.HIPAAcompliance.org)
Adjunct professor for the Norwich University Master of Science in Information Security and Assurance (MSISA) program (http://infoassurance.norwich.edu/)
Twitter ID: PrivacyProf (http://twitter.com/PrivacyProf)

Christine Hertzog is the founder and managing director of the Smart Grid Library and SGL Partners, delivering consulting and information services about Smart Grid and Smart Infrastructure technologies, services, and solutions. Her firm provides pragmatic guidance to global vendors, governmental entities, and utilities covering a broad range of needs, such as strategic corporate and market insights and design and deployment of prosumer-centric utility operations.

Ms. Hertzog is the author of the *Smart Grid Dictionary* that defines the jargon, acronyms, and terminology about technologies, international standards, and organizations associated with the Smart Grid and Smart Infrastructure. She is the coauthor of *The Smart Grid Consumer Focus Strategy*, which identifies consumer/utility challenges and methods to ensure successful prosumer operations and interactions. She is a recognized thought leader and regular speaker at industry conferences and writes a syndicated blog about Smart Grid and Smart Infrastructure topics.

Based in Silicon Valley, Ms. Hertzog serves as an advisor to Smart Grid start-ups and industry associations and publications, including The Energy Collective, ElectricityPolicy.com, *Energy Post*, Agrion, and IBCon. She has a master of science degree in telecommunications from the University of Colorado–Boulder. See more about Ms. Hertzog at www.SmartGridLibrary.com.

1

The Smart Grid and Privacy

What Is the Smart Grid?

The Smart Grid is a convenient term to describe the modernization of electric, natural gas, and water grid infrastructures. The term encapsulates the convergence of remote monitoring and control technologies with communications technologies, renewables generation, and analytics capabilities so that previously noncommunicative infrastructures like electricity grids can provide time-sensitive status updates and deliver situational awareness.

While initially and mostly focused on electricity, many of the same technologies, particularly in information and communications technologies (ICTs), apply to natural gas and water grids. This book addresses privacy in all three of these consumables, but electricity occupies a unique place by virtue of the fact that we can *produce it* as well as *consume it*. In addition, existing technologies make it easier to get many more measurements about electricity than gas or water. These two unique qualities about electricity have very interesting ramifications for privacy, and therefore this book will refer to electricity and electricity use cases because they provide the best framework for discussion of this important topic.

Changes from Traditional Energy Delivery

One of the other critical ramifications of the Smart Grid is that it changes the supply chain. The traditional view is that electricity, gas, or water is supplied by a utility to consumers, and on a periodic basis, your consumption is metered and you pay a bill for the amount you consume, typically at a flat rate. Many technologies in the Smart Grid now make consumption a new point in the supply chain, and when it comes to electricity, new technologies make it a value chain. Electricity has a special distinction in the Smart Grid.* Consumers can become prosumers—producing consumers—of electricity. We can generate electricity on our rooftops or backyards and sell kilowatts back to a utility or use it ourselves to reduce the amount we buy from a utility. We can also participate in programs that encourage us to reduce our electricity use, thereby generating negawatts, or watts of energy saved through a reduction in energy use or increase in energy efficiency.†

We don't have the same range of possibilities to create water or natural gas, which is why electricity occupies the unique status of elevating us to prosumers. Water and gas meters are much simpler in design and metrology (what is measured) than electricity too. However, Smart Grid technologies definitely change what can be determined about our consumption of electricity, natural gas, and water. Think about it this way. Suppose you went to a grocery store and just walked out of the store with a reusable canvas bag full of items every day. At the end of the month, you received a bill with a single-line descriptor for "groceries" and a total amount of money owed. That's it. No identification of how many quarts of milk, pounds of bananas, or boxes of cereal that you consumed that month. That's how we currently get electricity, gas, and water bills.

Smart Grid Possibilities

Now consider the possibilities with Smart Grid technologies. This is a new situation. We're accustomed to significant reporting of our lives in other aspects—we get detailed bank information identifying dates and times of deposits and withdrawals from specific accounts. We

* Definition from the *Smart Grid Dictionary* (http://www.smartgridlibrary.com/shop-smart-grid-library-books/smart-griddictionary_new/): "Bi-directional electric grids and communication networks that improve the reliability, security, and efficiency of the electric system for small- to large-scale generation, transmission, distribution, storage, and consumption. It includes software and hardware applications for dynamic, integrated, and interoperable optimization of electric system operations, maintenance, and planning; distributed energy resources interconnection and integration; and feedback and controls at the consumer level."

† Ibid.

get detailed credit card summaries every month listing business, date, time, and total of each purchase. And with the introduction of many Smart Grid technologies, we have the opportunity to have similarly granular, time-stamped data about our use of electricity, gas, or water, in addition to information about the devices using such items from those device vendors. In the special case of electricity, that data can include our generation of electricity from solar panels on our rooftops, kitchen appliance usage, or location and duration of charging electric vehicles (EVs), just to name a few.

Not every Smart Grid technology that is deployed in an electricity grid creates, monitors, transmits, or stores data about individual consumption of electricity (or gas or water). And sometimes, the entity collecting data is not a utility or affiliated with a utility. This book focuses on those technologies that do have impacts on personal privacy. Chapter by chapter, we'll describe these technologies, existing policies and practices, and areas that require careful consideration for policy makers, privacy officers in utilities and the companies that provide solutions, and citizens. Our identification of these technologies and their associated privacy risks is not a condemnation of them. We see these technologies as very useful tools. But any tool, used incorrectly, can be dangerous. Recognizing the privacy implications surrounding the new data that is created, collected, aggregated, analyzed, reported, or anonymized is key to building the solutions, policies, and processes that deliver generally accepted levels of privacy.

Business Model Transformations

But there's another angle to this discussion, and it's about transformation of business models. It's likely that businesses other than utilities may manage electricity-generating assets or water conservation equipment. Depending on regulatory environments, businesses other than utilities might even sell electricity, or collect energy usage* or energy

* Energy usage data is data that shows how much energy is used at the consumer's location, such as by the consumer's computers, mobile devices running smart energy apps, third-party energy management services, smart appliances, and other types of devices associated with that consumer. The data may also include the associated operational and other types of metadata.

production* data directly from consumers. Utilities may also get into new services outside of their traditional areas of business activity. Indeed, a recent publication titled *Reforming the Energy Vision* from the New York Department of Public Service,† the state regulatory agency responsible for oversight of investor-owned electric utilities, makes this point. The report describes the evolution of today's utility business model from a linear supply chain of centralized electricity generation from a few players with unidirectional electricity transactions to multiple consumers. The future utility business model will accommodate decentralized electricity generation and bidirectional electricity transactions between prosumers (producing consumers), multiple energy service providers, and utilities. Smart energy device manufacturers and vendors may also be brought in to the mix. Businesses may form new and different collaborations to exploit data about consumption or use. However, these transformations will sometimes blur the lines of responsibility for privacy protection. This book will highlight a few of those boundary-bending trends to help readers develop plans and policies to incorporate the appropriate actions to protect and maintain personal privacy.

Emerging Privacy Risks

Easy and quick access to energy consumption, energy usage, and energy production data has potential for benefiting consumers and utilities, just to name a few, to help conserve energy, keep costs as low as possible, and discover more ways to make energy delivery more efficient. Along with these benefits come risks related to how that energy

---

* Energy production data is data that identifies the flow of electricity for a device that generates or discharges electricity.

† This report was produced by the New York State Public Service Commission and is part of an initiative that will "lead to regulatory changes that promote more efficient use of energy, deeper penetration of renewable energy resources such as wind and solar, wider deployment of 'distributed' energy resources, such as micro grids, on-site power supplies, and storage. It will also promote greater use of advanced energy management products to enhance demand elasticity and efficiencies. These changes, in turn, will empower customers by allowing them more choice in how they manage and consume electric energy." From the commission's website: http://www3.dps.ny.gov/W/PSCWeb.nsf/All/26BE8A93967E604785257CC40066B91A?OpenDocument.

usage data, and the information associated with it, are used, shared, stored, and otherwise accessed.

Utilities, consumers, Smart Grid vendors, and other types of organizations using Smart Grid devices, applications, systems, and other types of technologies need to be aware of these new privacy risks, as well as those that will inevitably emerge as the Smart Grid matures.

Interconnected networks and devices (for example, smart phones with apps that can control energy settings within the home from remote locations) expand the scope for privacy risks within the Smart Grid. Many of these risks are not unique to the Smart Grid, but they introduce new types of threats and vulnerabilities to address within the Smart Grid. As new and emerging technologies and activities are deployed, they will likely introduce even more, and different, privacy challenges. Privacy risks, and ways to mitigate them, are covered in Chapter 7.

The Need for Privacy Policies

Organizations need to establish internal privacy policies and supporting procedures for their personnel to follow to provide direction on how to effectively and consistently protect consumer and energy usage data, energy consumption data, and energy production data. Such policies should span a comprehensive set of topics, such as how the information should be retained, distributed internally, shared with third parties, and secured against breach. There must also be not only online training and awareness policies and procedures, but also regular employee training and ongoing awareness communications sent to employees to help keep them aware of privacy risks and how to mitigate them.

Similarly, Smart Grid services and products recipients should be provided with a privacy notice that describes the information the organization is collecting and how that information will be used, shared, and secured.

Privacy policies and notices are described in detail in Chapter 7.

Privacy Laws, Regulations, and Standards

Privacy laws and regulations vary greatly throughout the world. There are generally four approaches in the United States to protecting privacy by law:

- Constitutional protections and issues. These are general protections provided by the First (freedom of speech), Fourth (search and seizure), and Fourteenth (equal protection) Amendments, which cover personal communications and activities.
- Statutory, regulatory, and case law, at both the federal and state levels. There are growing numbers of Smart Grid privacy laws at the state level. The first Smart Grid privacy law was issued on July 29, 2011, when the California Public Utilities Commission (CPUC) established new rules* to protect information about consumer use of smart meter energy provisioning services. The California rule established Fair Information Practice (FIP) requirements, including a consumer right of access and control, data minimization requirements, use and disclosure limitations, and data quality and integrity requirements. Electric utilities and their contractors, as well as third parties who receive electricity usage data from utilities, must comply with these rules.
- Data-specific or technology-specific protections, including direct regulation of public utilities by state public utility commissions. These protect specific information items such as credit card numbers and social security numbers (SSNs), or specific technologies such as phones or computers used for data storage or communication, or customer-specific billing and energy usage information used by public utilities to provide utility services. Other federal or state laws or regulations also exist that provide privacy protections to information within specific industries (e.g., Gramm–Leach–Bliley Act,† Health Insurance Portability and Accountability Act,‡ etc.).
- Contractual and agreement-related protections and issues: specific protections. These are protections specifically outlined within a wide range of business contracts, such as those between consumers and businesses, businesses and their

* See the full text of the California rules at http://docs.cpuc.ca.gov/WORD_PDF/FINAL_DECISION/140369.pdf.

† See the regulatory text at http://www.hhs.gov/ocr/privacy/hipaa/administrative/combined/hipaa-simplification-201303.pdf.

‡ See the regulatory text at http://www.gpo.gov/fdsys/pkg/PLAW-106publ102/pdf/PLAW-106publ102.pdf.

contracted vendors, etc. The privacy risks within the Smart Grid will necessitate such contracts for all entities that have access in some way to the associated customer and energy usage data.

Privacy-Enhancing Technologies

A wide range of existing privacy-enhancing technologies (PETs) can be engineered within the many technologies of the Smart Grid to support privacy protections. A few examples of PETs* include:

- Encryption: Encryption is a cryptographic process used to encode (scramble) data in such a way that only authorized parties can read it.
- Steganography: Steganography is a method used to conceal a message, image, or file within another message, image, or file.
- Aggregation† methodologies: Within the energy industry, data aggregation refers to methodologies that remove personally identifiable information from collections of energy usage data. (Other industries and groups define this term differently.)
- De-identification‡ methodologies: These are methodologies that remove all data necessary to keep the data from being analyzed to identify individuals.
- Access control systems: These are technical, administrative, and physical controls implemented to ensure only those individuals with a business need can gain access to confidential information or restricted areas.
- Privacy seals for websites: These are third-party validations that a specific scope of the associated business has been reviewed and determined to meet appropriate levels of privacy protections.

* Taken from Rebecca Herold, *Managing an Information Security and Privacy Awareness and Training Program*, 2nd edition, CRC Press, Boca Raton, FL, 2010. http://www.crcpress.com/product/isbn/9781439815458.

† This will be covered in detail in Chapter 7.

‡ This will be covered in detail in Chapter 7.

- Spam filters: A spam filter is a program that is used to detect unsolicited and malicious email, such as phishing messages that can collect personal information, or keystroke loggers, which can capture all information types and prevent those messages from getting to a user's inbox.

New Privacy Challenges

A variety of Smart Grid technologies are making more data available to utilities today. But beyond electric, gas, and water operations, many other business sectors are impacted by the same technologies. Sensors gathering more and new types of data, inexpensive data storage making it possible to keep data indefinitely, the increasing use of mobile devices, as well as smart devices,[*] for data collection and use, and the growth of reliable and robust communications networks—mostly wireless—contribute to business opportunities in machine-to-machine (M2M) applications and the Internet of Things (IOT).[†]

IOT

The Internet of Things (IOT) generally means the computing devices and gadgets to generate data, and then to be connected to other gadgets to share and use that data. Such devices include smart phones, laptops, and tablets. Also included are increasingly computerized things that can generate data, take actions based upon automatic analysis of that data, and automatically store data. The possibilities are endless. Already there are computer-enabled cars, wearable technologies, smart thermostats, medical devices, kitchen appliances, water treatments, baby

[*] As defined in the Q2 2014 issue of *Protecting Information Journal* (http://hipaaprivacy.org/product/protecting-information-journal/), "smart devices, are items that typically have existed for a very long time with no computing capabilities that are now being created with data collection, transmission, and/or processing capabilities built into them. All connect, in some manner, to the Internet to enable sharing of that data."

[†] As defined in the Q2 2014 issue of *Protecting Information Journal* (http://hipaaprivacy.org/product/protecting-information-journal/), "the Internet of Things (IoT) refers to uniquely identifiable objects and their virtual representations in an Internet-like structure."

monitors, clothing items, trash cans, stoplights, and the list goes on. Such computerized gadgets are typically referenced as "smart" devices. Just a few examples of some smart devices in the Smart Grid include:

- Electric vehicle charging stations
- In-home energy management displays
- Load control switches
- Wi-Fi range extenders
- Thermostats
- Smart meters
- Voltage regulators
- Smart phone apps
- Data concentrators

Big Data

All the data collected from the Smart Grid and the Internet of Things can become "big data" and characterized by the four Vs: volume, variety, velocity, and veracity. We can install sensors that remotely monitor and control devices that previously did not have these capabilities. That leads to increasing volumes of data. In many cases, sensors are providing new types or varieties of data. For example, wearable devices offer a wealth of data that weren't available before—new variety. Communications networks make data available for real-time or near-real-time consumption—increasing its velocity. Veracity addresses the accuracy of data. Inaccurate data can be benign or have serious impacts. Just ask anyone who had inaccurate financial data downgrade a credit score—the impacts can mean more expensive capital for everything from credit cards to mortgages.

However, big data offers a tremendous amount of potential and positive impacts for families, communities, business, governments, and everyone as inhabitants on planet Earth. In May 2014, Dr. Ernest Moniz, the secretary of the Department of Energy (DOE), spoke at the White House Energy Datapalooza* and stated that "freely available government data about energy is a national resource" to be leveraged to help mitigate climate change impacts

* https://www.youtube.com/watch?v=NpcStxOq2Ug&feature=youtu.be.

and improve electric grid resiliency. There are many interesting initiatives to make data open and accessible, all the while acknowledging the need to maintain privacy of data. However, as with any beneficial new technology, big data also brings with it privacy risks* that must be mitigated.

* See a summary of 10 common big data privacy risks at http://privacyguidance.com/blog/10-big-data-analytics-privacy-problems/.

2
What Is the Smart Grid?

Before launching into the Smart Grid and considerations of privacy, it is helpful to understand the traditional electricity grid structure in the United States and what makes the Smart Grid different from the existing grid. The electric sector is best described from regulatory, market, and technology perspectives. Our discussion scope is focused on the United States since regulatory and market structures, and even privacy legislation, differ by nation. However, the grid technologies are applicable everywhere.

Market and Regulatory Overview

Traditional Electricity Business Sector

The traditional electricity business sector consists of power generators and transmission and distribution operators, as illustrated in Figure 2.1. Depending on the region of the United States, all of these functions may be performed by one company—known as a vertically

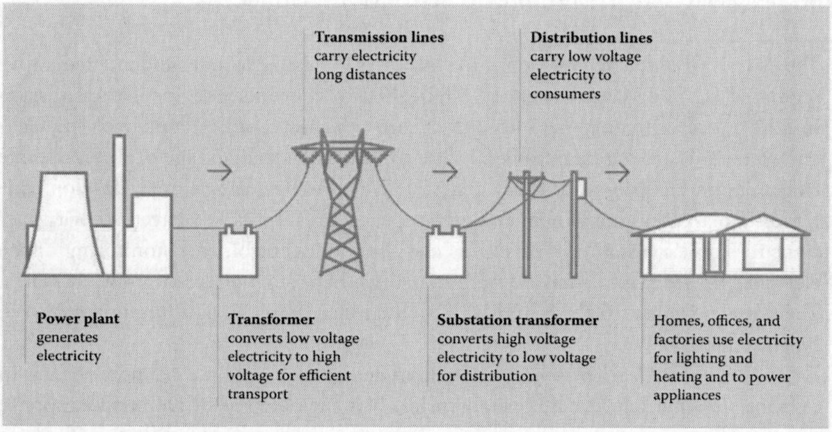

Figure 2.1 The traditional electricity supply chain. (Courtesy of Energy Efficiency Exchange (EEX), http://eex.gov.au.)

integrated utility. In other regions, generation, transmission, and distribution may be operated by different companies, reflecting different approaches to deregulation of the electric utility sector. From a supply chain perspective electricity is supplied by centralized, large, or utility-scale generation and delivered via high-voltage (69 kV and up) transmission lines connecting to low-voltage (4 to 35 kV) distribution lines or grids.

The Electricity Open Market

Historically, electric utilities typically have had a monopoly status at the distribution grid level—there's only one wire that connects to a meter attached to a building or other end point, not multiple lines from competing suppliers.

Many regions of the United States have entities called independent system operators (ISOs) or regional transmission operators (RTOs).* They ensure that all qualified power sellers (generators) have opportunities to get their electricity to buyers (utilities) by coordinating regional transmission. In the past, generation meant the creation of megawatts or kilowatts of power. There is growing interest in leveraging negawatts† as equal market participants. The Smart Grid can help enable more negawatts to be created and managed at the bulk market level. Later in this chapter there will be discussion of how the Smart Grid can help facilitate a market for generation of kilowatts and negawatts at the retail or distribution grid level.

---

* The *Smart Grid Dictionary* definition of an RTO is: "An independent, federally-regulated (U.S. or Canada) entity established to coordinate regional transmission in a non-discriminatory manner and ensure the safety and reliability of the electric system. These organizations monitor system loads and voltage profiles, operate transmission facilities and direct generation, define operating limits, develop contingency plans, and implement emergency procedures. ISOs also have authority over transmission expansion projects. This coordination, control, and monitoring of the electrical power system may be within a single U.S. state or across multiple states. There are currently 10 ISOs and RTOs (Regional Transmission Organizations) in North America."

† From the *Smart Grid Dictionary*: "Watts of energy reduced on a temporary basis in response to a market signal—usually price. It is the outcome of Demand Response programs that aggregate a number of these actions to represent reductions of energy use from kilowatts to megawatts. A permanent negawatt reduction is achieved through energy efficiency programs and actions."

At a federal level, there is oversight of the bulk or wholesale power market to ensure grid reliability. The North American Electric Reliability Corporation (NERC) is "an independent, self-regulatory, not-for-profit organization whose mission is to ensure the reliability of the bulk power system in North America. It monitors the bulk power system; develops and enforces reliability standards; assesses future adequacy of electricity; audits owners, operators, and users for preparedness; and educates and trains industry personnel."* The critical importance of its responsibilities received international attention after the August 2003 Northeast blackout that affected 50 million people in the United States and Canada.†

Classifications of Utilities

There are over 3,000 electric utilities in the United States. These fall into one of four classifications:

- Federal utilities like Bonneville Power Administration or Tennessee Valley Authority
- Investor-owned utilities (IOUs), which have shares bought and sold in stock exchanges and have operating territories that can be intra- or interstate. Examples include Duke, ComEd, or Southern California Edison.
- Municipal (munis) utilities, which are owned by local communities and their governing agencies and operate in those jurisdictions' boundaries. Examples include LA Department of Water and Power or the Electric Power Board of Chattanooga.
- Cooperative (coops) utilities, which are member-owned nonprofit utilities that typically serve rural areas. Examples include Bluebonnet Electric Cooperative and Sawnee Electric Membership Cooperative.

* Definition from the *Smart Grid Dictionary.*

† http://www.scientificamerican.com/article/2003-blackout-five-years-later/.

IOUs operate as monopolies and are regulated by state agencies.* In the United States, that translates into 50 regulatory commissions plus agencies for the District of Columbia, Puerto Rico, and the U.S. Virgin Islands. These commissions oversee electric, gas, and water utilities as well as telecommunications. At a high level, regulators are responsible for ensuring that the consumers they represent are receiving services (electric, gas, and water) at fair, just, and reasonable rates.

Munis and coops are generally not regulated by state regulatory agencies. However, these utilities track regulatory policy trends and rulings, and their operations and future plans may be influenced by these decisions. As businesses, they are bound by laws enacted in their home states, which can have important ramifications for privacy topics.

Rate-Making Processes

Ensuring fair, just, and reasonable rates in a monopoly environment has resulted in regulators and utilities relying on tariff or rate-making processes that guarantee a rate of return or profits to utilities to cover their fixed and variable costs. Figure 2.2† breaks down a complex process that varies by state and utility into its simplest factors.

Cost of fixed equipment
× Allowed "Rate of Return"
Profits
+ Grid Operating Costs
+ Cost of Generation
Revenue Requirement
/ kWh Sales
Retail Rate per kWh

Figure 2.2 Simple breakdown of tariff-setting process. (Courtesy of Chris Kotting, ckotting.com.)

* Common names include public utility commissions, commerce commissions, corporation commissions, and public service commissions. In some cases, regulators are appointed by governors; in other states, regulators are elected representatives.

† Tariff-setting processes are very complex and vary by jurisdiction, but this graphic provides a good generalized description at a high level.

Today's tariffs are fixed fees for electricity. While that provides predictability for the average consumer to budget his or her electricity use, it also shields consumers from the fact that electricity is traded like a commodity. Just like coffee, gold, or natural gas futures rise and fall, so too do electricity prices. Electricity prices can vary based on time and type of generation source. Electricity purchased during a period of high demand costs more than electricity purchased during a lull in needs.

Electricity Consumers

Consumers fall into categories that are typically organized as residential, commercial, industrial, and agricultural. Depending on the utility, there may be other specialized distinctions or subgroupings based on type of business or amount of electricity purchased. These consumer groups typically have some sort of representation with regulatory agencies and utilities. For instance, the California Public Utilities Commission has an Office of Ratepayer Advocates (ORA) with a statutory mission to "obtain the lowest possible rate for service consistent with reliable and safe service levels. In fulfilling this goal, ORA also advocates for customer and environmental protections."*

Regardless of the type of utility, for decades the business model has been consistent—there is one provider of electricity to consumers. At the time of this writing, 16 states, such as Texas and Pennsylvania plus the District of Columbia, have deregulated the market at the distribution grid level. This is often referred to as the retail electricity market or level, in contrast to the bulk or wholesale markets addressed by ISOs and RTOs. Residential (or in some cases, commercial) consumers in these states may choose their retail electricity provider. There is still just one wire and meter (smart or traditional) that connects a consumer to the distribution grid, but there are multiple companies competing for consumer business based on price of electricity plus additional services. Twenty-two states have deregulated gas.

This utility business model will continue to change, and deregulation policies are in some ways a minor influence compared to some transformative technology and financial drivers. These drivers include

* http://www.ora.ca.gov/default.aspx.

the astonishing growth of solar photovoltaic (PV) systems on residential and commercial rooftops and the proliferation of financial tools that reduce the cost of capital to deploy these systems.* The end result is that electricity revenues, the main source of funding for utilities, are slowing and even decreasing. We'll examine this in more detail later in this chapter.

Electricity Technology Overview

Thomas Edison and Alexander Graham Bell were contemporaries in the late 1800s and celebrated for their respective inventions that became the electrical grid and the telecommunications network. Mr. Bell would not recognize today's telecom operations because equipment has undergone multiple evolutions and upgrade iterations. Today's smart phone is radically different from the fixed devices that he invented. However, Mr. Edison would recognize many elements of an electric utility substation. There have been updates and upgrades, but many utilities have been encouraged to operate in a "run to failure" mindset and only replace equipment once it is past repair. There have not been any significant, industry-wide technology migration initiatives until the Smart Grid.

The power grid we enjoy today is a complex and marvelous machine, but it is definitely replete with aging infrastructure. Many of the transformers in the distribution grid are past their manufacturer-warranted lifetime. According to the Galvin Electricity Initiative, the average transformer age is 42 years on equipment designed for a 40-year life span. Some utilities still have operating infrastructure that was installed during Edison's lifetime. For instance, a senior executive for National Grid noted at a recent industry event that the utility had a line in upstate New York that was installed by Thomas Edison. Imagine a stretch of road lasting that long—it would be in need of significant overhauls and upgrades too.

This power grid operates as a just-in-time supply chain. What this basically means is that Americans have been conditioned to expect as much power as they need whenever they need it. There's no advance

* Interstate Renewable Energy Council, U.S. Solar Market Trends 2012 Year in Review, http://www.seia.org/research-resources/us-solar-market-insight-2012-year-review.

scheduling or reservation of kilowatts to coincide with usage changes. System operators at the ISO and utility planners carefully project electricity needs and then schedule for that, with room to spare. When they don't match supply to demand, the results are voltage sags or surges that can have very serious consequences for sensitive electronics equipment, especially for commercial and industrial operations that require steady power quality. Even worse, a mismatch of supply and demand can cause blackouts. In 2000–2001, California experienced "rolling blackouts"* that were found to be the result of illegal market manipulations in the wholesale power grid.

Electricity Supply Chain Vulnerabilities

This supply chain is extremely fragile. While the California rolling blackouts were caused by criminals manipulating markets, other regions of the country experienced severe power disruptions from extreme weather events, which will become more common as a result of climate change. The supply chain of centralized generation—transmission at long distances to substations that then convert the power to lower voltages suitable for movement along the distribution grid to consumers—lacks resiliency to quickly recover from these types of incidents. There is significant concern expressed within utilities and at the highest levels of government that the grid is also exposed to attacks. These attacks can be physical† or cyber based.‡ The electricity supply chain's weakest links are in its transmission and distribution grids. There are 200,000 miles of high-voltage transmission lines§ and 2.2 million miles of lines in the distribution grids. Most of these assets consist of overhead wires and equipment, not underground facilities.

---

* http://www.pbs.org/wgbh/pages/frontline/shows/blackout/california/timeline.html.

† PG&E announced a $250,000 reward for information leading to the arrest and conviction of the perpetrator(s) who fired gunshots that caused extensive damage to its Metcalf transmission substation near San Jose in 2013.

‡ In May 2014 the Department of Homeland Security (DHS) noted that an unidentified utility's control system network had been penetrated and compromised via an Internet connection and a weak password system.

§ Edison Electric Institute.

The costs of electric service disruptions are staggering. Estimates of the damage done to the U.S. economy range from $104 billion to $164 billion annually.* Service disruptions also have enormous impacts on our quality of life as well as our essential health and safety. There are no substitutes for electricity.

Magnifying these vulnerabilities caused by inherent supply chain fragility, traditional grids provide very little information to their utility operators about their status. For the most part, the grid has been uncommunicative about what is going on within its lines and equipment. How does the typical electric utility learn about a power outage? When you call to complain about your lack of service. Then, the utility narrows down suspected failure locations based on the addresses of complaints. Finally, repair teams are dispatched to search out the failure point, and hopefully have the right training and right equipment to repair the failure and restore service.

The situation is only slightly better in the traditional transmission grid. The 2003 blackout started with transmission lines sagging in the heat of an August day and touching tree branches. What should have been an outage limited to one utility became a multistate problem because of human error and a lack of situational awareness. Existing technologies provided status updates every 4 seconds. That may sound like a reasonable rate of data, but electrons move much faster than that. We don't recommend that you experiment with this illustration of the problem, but think of it in terms of driving a nonautonomous car on a highway. Can you imagine how much you miss if you close your eyes for 4 seconds as you're hurtling along at 65 miles per hour, briefly open them, and then shut them for another 4 seconds? That's how we managed the high-voltage transmission grid.

The Smart Grid

The Smart Grid promises significant changes to every facet or domain of the electricity grid sector. The simplest distinction is that the Smart Grid delivers bidirectional energy and information, in contrast to the single directional flow of electricity and minimal flow of information

* Electric Power Research Institute (EPRI), The Cost of Power Disturbances to Industrial and Digital Economy Companies, 2001.

that exists today. Smart Grid technologies can deliver significant amounts of data to create extraordinary situational awareness at every stage of the supply chain.

There are a couple of game-changing technologies that appear in the Smart Grid—primarily in renewable energy generation and energy storage. However, many Smart Grid technologies are merely deployments of established telecommunications and data analytics technologies that are already in use in other business sectors, like finance, consumer goods, and healthcare. They may be new to the utility sector, but they are not new technologies.

Some Smart Grid technologies are directly visible to consumers. You can see the smart meter that is installed on the side of a building. But many of the technologies adopted by utilities to modernize their grids are invisible to consumers. Again, that's no different from how our wireless carriers, our banks, or our stores upgrade the infrastructure that helps them improve the delivery of whatever service they are providing to consumers. But unlike those sectors, the consumer-utility relationship will undergo dramatic disruptions. Consumers will have many of their own energy usage, production, and management devices on their premises, some of which may connect to utility meters, and others that may connect to the Internet. In some situations, the disruptions caused by adoption of Smart Grid technologies will be driven by consumers rather than utilities or regulators. It will be extremely important to understand privacy impacts as a result of consumer-utility relationship changes.

Market Changes in the Smart Grid

Figure 2.3 is a graphic visualization of the Smart Grid. Here, the traditional supply chain of generation, transmission, and distribution is fully and securely connected, and most importantly from a privacy perspective, the consumer is now a full participant in that supply chain. Consumers transform into prosumers,* or producing

* From the *Smart Grid Dictionary*: "A term coined by Alvin Toffler to describe a producing consumer. From a Smart Grid perspective, it would apply to distributed energy resource situations in which the owner of electricity production or storage assets may also have a consumer relationship with a utility, aggregator, or other energy services provider."

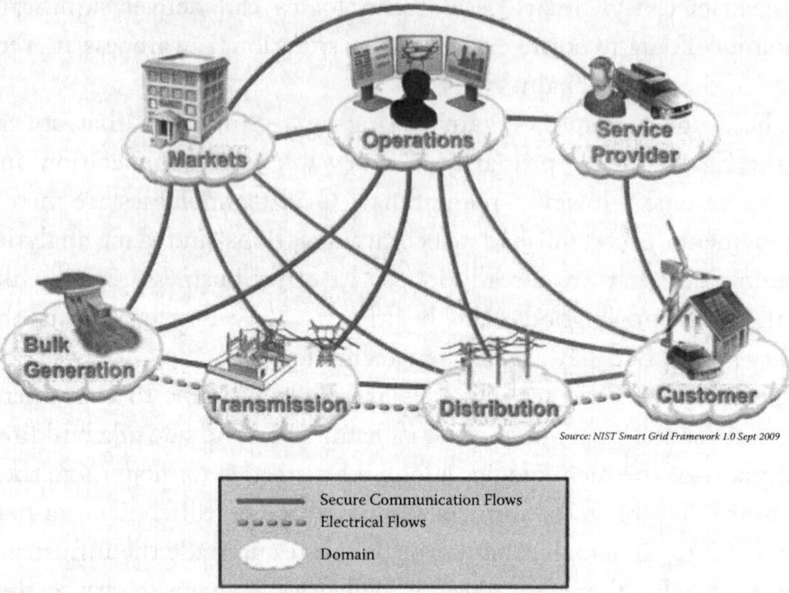

Figure 2.3 The new electricity value chain. Consumption becomes prosumption. (Courtesy of National Institute of Standards and Technology (NIST).)

consumers, who can create electricity (typically from clean renewables such as solar PV, wind generators, etc.) to sell back to the grid, or consume their self-generated electricity and only draw power from the grid if needed, or produce negawatts through reductions in electricity use that are sold back to the grid.

We see the first instances of this in states that have net metering* tariffs and feed-in tariffs† (FiTs). These tariffs either credit the solar PV or wind generator asset owner for electricity generated (an avoidance of electricity otherwise sold by the utility) or publish a price at which excess electricity is sold back to the utility.

* From the *Smart Grid Dictionary*: "The capability for residential and C&I (Commercial and Industrial) customers to generate electricity and sell back excess power to the utility, essentially offsetting their future purchases of utility power. Net metering uses either a single, bi-directional electric meter or two meters to separately measure in and out electricity flows at a customer's location. Net metering is currently implemented on a state-by-state basis with significant variation between states."

† From the *Smart Grid Dictionary*: "An energy supply policy that encourages new renewable power generation and attempts to provide investor certainty with guarantees of payments in dollars per kWh for the full output of the system for a guaranteed period of time."

Prosumer Evolution

This early prosumer example will evolve and repeat over time as more technologies like energy storage become commercially available or as electric vehicles (EVs) can support smart charging applications in which they can charge and discharge power with the grid. Prosumers will have a variety of energy services providers (ESPs) to choose from. ESPs offer solutions that typically incorporate some management of a prosumer's consumption or production of electricity. For instance, Solar City and Tesla are collaborating to offer a bundled solar PV generation and energy storage solution for residential prosumers. They will offer third-party ownership and management of the solution on the prosumer's behalf. Other ESPs aimed at the residential consumer market include AT&T, Comcast, and many smaller companies with products and services that bundle home security and home energy management with broadband communications. There are entire ecosystems of different ESPs that target their products and services to the commercial, industrial, and agricultural market segments. ESPs have the potential to intermediate the traditional direct relationship that consumers have with utilities. As the intermediary between the electricity consumer and the electric utility, ESPs could own the consumer relationship. Intermediation has very interesting implications for privacy.

Other Relevant Market Changes

There are other relevant market changes that can only occur as Smart Grid technologies are deployed by utilities, ESPs, or prosumers. Some state regulatory agencies and their regulated utilities are planning to convert today's fixed residential tariffs to time of use* (TOU) electricity rates in the future, which would reflect the price changes in electricity over a 24-hour time period. Prices for watts of electricity purchased during periods of peak demand would be higher than the

* From the *Smart Grid Dictionary*: "A rate structure with different unit prices for electricity use in a 24-hour time frame, generally to encourage use during periods of lower demand. This phrase applies to a time of use price, rate, or tariff and is a dynamic price scheme typically used with non-dispatchable demand response programs. Also known as time of day pricing."

prices for those same watts purchased at off-peak times. For TOU to work most effectively, consumers and prosumers benefit from Smart Grid technologies that help them manage production or consumption of electricity to "buy low and sell high" instead of operating within an artificially fixed and static market construct. It's a step toward the transactive energy market that is described later in this chapter.

A Smart Grid, with its ubiquitous and reliable communications capabilities, can enable electricity consumption based on price signals. Consumers can better manage their electricity consumption with Smart Grid technologies, and thus have better control over their electricity bills. But there's an existential threat here for utilities. Their revenues from electricity sales can flatline or shrink. That's already happening, as charted in Figure 2.4.

Simultaneously, utilities need to upgrade aging infrastructure and modernize into the Smart Grid, so their costs are increasing. These dual trends exert significant pressure on the existing business model. There's a colorful term for it—the utility death spiral. The death spiral goes as follows. Regulated utilities will receive decreasing electricity sales revenues as more consumers become prosumers. Some prosumers may completely disconnect from the utility's grid, but will maintain a connection as insurance in case their self-generation and energy storage equipment fails. Utilities are mandated to deliver electricity to everyone, and will have to maintain these connections and ensure that they have purchased adequate megawatts of power in the bulk market

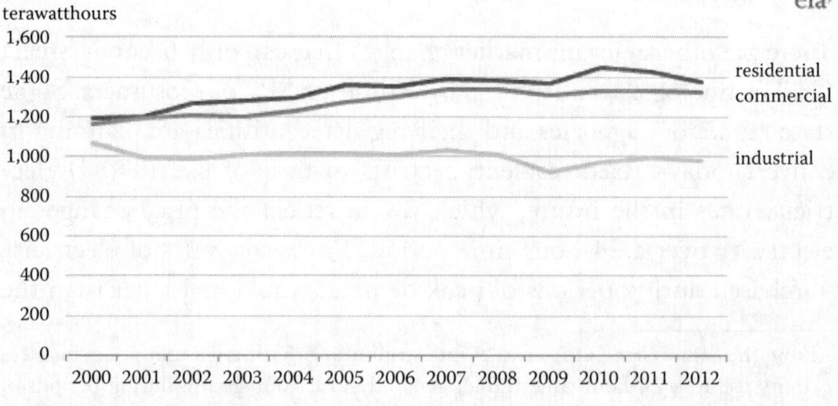

Figure 2.4 Retail electricity sales trends in the United States. (Courtesy of Energy Information Administration.)

just in case it is needed for these occasions. Their costs are fixed regardless of the number of electricity buyers. In turn, the utility increases rates on the remaining consumers still buying electricity in order to cover these costs. Those price increases motivate even more consumers to defect to self-generation, and the revenues shrink even more.

A 2014 report titled "Reforming the Energy Vision," released by the New York Department of Public Service, the state regulatory agency responsible for IOU oversight, is a policy game changer.* The report describes the evolution of today's utility business model from that linear supply chain of centralized electricity generation sold by a few players in unidirectional electricity transactions to multiple prosumers participating in a reorganized electricity market. This report envisions a future utility business model with decentralized, renewable electricity generation and bidirectional electricity transactions between prosumers, multiple energy service providers, and utilities. This new business model addresses the utility death spiral by proposing new service opportunities for utilities to survive and thrive in more open and intermediated scenarios.

Buildings as Prosumers

Intermediation is already happening and is most evident in the commercial consumer sector, focused on buildings. Buildings use 40% of the nation's energy. From an energy efficiency perspective, the National Academy of Sciences noted in a study† that the "full deployment of cost-effective energy efficiency technologies in buildings alone could eliminate the need to construct any new electricity-generating plants in the United States" until 2030.

A building operating as an electricity prosumer goes well beyond energy efficiency reductions. Energy efficiency is a passive tactic that delivers permanent energy reductions in electricity or gas. While building owners can justify investment decisions on energy savings as well as sustainability values, there are two other opportunities for building

* Download the report at http://www3.dps.ny.gov/W/PSCWeb.nsf/All/26BE8A93967E604785257CC40066B91A?OpenDocument.

† Report of the Building Energy Efficiency Subcommittee to the Secretary of Energy Advisory Board, http://energy.gov/sites/prod/files/Building%20Efficiency%20Report.pdf.

owners to invest in technologies that reduce energy use and deliver self-sufficiency to temporarily reduce consumption or produce their own electricity. The first reason involves demand response (DR) programs.*

The most common manifestations of today's DR programs are voluntary reductions in energy use within commercial buildings, often accomplished by modulating heating, ventilation, air conditioning (HVAC) temperatures, or interior lighting. These reductions are spurred by requests from utilities or ESPs that aggregate the actions of multiple DR participants to address times of peak demand for electricity. These situations are usually seasonal and predictable—often happening during the hottest or coldest times of the year. Upon receipt of a request, a building manager may manually adjust thermostats or take other measures to reduce electricity use (produce negawatts) for the requested durations of time. One of the authors participates in a residential demand response program offered by a utility and enjoys a year-round rate reduction in exchange for voluntary electricity reductions on selected days that correspond to heat waves in the region. Other programs offer payments based on the total amount of electricity reduced.

Industrial and agricultural businesses are also potential participants in DR programs. Their participation hinges on the type of operations and the flexibility to reduce electricity use at times when an ESP or a utility requests it.

The advent of more embedded intelligence and Smart Grid technologies in the forms of sensors and actuators with remote communications can create more opportunities for participation from greater numbers of buildings. Automated demand response (ADR) technologies enable buildings (commercial, industrial, agricultural, and

---

* From the *Smart Grid Dictionary*: "Utility programs designed to change on-site demand for energy through changes in prices, load control signals, or other incentives to customers. The programs are activated at times of peak usage or when system reliability is jeopardized. Demand response programs fall into two general categories known as price-based programs or capacity-based programs. Price-based programs include dynamic pricing/tariffs, price-responsive demand bidding, and critical peak pricing structures that let users voluntarily reduce their electricity use. Capacity-based programs include contractually obligated reductions and direct load control/cycling. Utilities use these programs to address system reliability, asset use efficiency, and market conditions; and avoid investments in new T&D (Transmission and Distribution) assets, peaker plants, or expensive peak power purchases."

residential) to produce negawatts on an as-needed basis without the need for human intervention. The eventual goal is that equipment or the systems that manage buildings will respond automatically to price signals, not just special requests to reduce energy use. Smart Grid technologies make it feasible for DR programs to work with energy storage to firm renewable energy like solar and wind, which are intermittent by nature.

Automated Demand Response and the OpenADR Initiative

Automated demand response (ADR) applies remote monitoring and control technologies to automatically modulate the HVAC, lighting, or other systems where it is deployed. This convenience factor is very important to the success of ADR. This factor is sometimes called "set and forget," and it eliminates the need to individually contact each DR participant with requests to make a change to a thermostat setting or another manually operated control.

For building owners and managers, DR program participation delivers payments for reductions in electricity use or lower rates throughout the year—nice impacts to their operating costs. Another potential benefit is to offer Leadership in Energy and Environmental Design (LEED) credits for participation in ADR, which means that buildings will receive sustainability recognition too. For utilities, DR benefits include the ability to avoid purchasing peak power, which is generally the highest priced electricity. Of course, it helps if a utility is decoupled,* but there are other reasons to embrace DR. It does have significant potential to help integrate intermittent renewables into the grid without impacts to reliability or power quality. For consumers, utility avoidance of purchases of the most expensive electricity or

* From the *Smart Grid Dictionary*: "A regulatory and market strategy that allows utilities to invest in and profit from efficiency-based capacity by assuring them a return that is equivalent to sales of electricity. This policy decouples utility fixed-costs recovery from electricity sales. Utilities collect revenues based on the amount determined by their local regulatory agencies, usually calculated on a per-customer basis. Periodically, revenues are reviewed for rate adjustments to ensure the pre-determined revenue requirement. This strategy is deployed in 17 states at the current time with several other states in the process of setting up utility mechanisms to support decoupling."

avoidance of investments in new grid capacity helps keep electricity tariffs from increasing. The growth of DR programs will almost certainly trigger new business opportunities for ESPs to develop services that appeal to specific verticals within consumer segments. These ESPs may intermediate the direct relationship that currently exists between the consumer and the utility. That means that parties other than a utility may be working with a consumer's energy data.

The OpenADR* initiative is focused on standardizing, automating, and simplifying demand response programs and technologies. It's the most comprehensive and widely used Internet Protocol (IP)-based communications standard for electricity providers and system operators to exchange DR signals with facilities and equipment within buildings.

As noted earlier, buildings and industrial and agricultural operations can play important roles as prosumers for two reasons. The first reason is participation in demand response programs. The second reason is to address the increasing vulnerability of the electrical grid to momentary and sustained power outages to both natural and human causes.

Microgrids

Buildings and their occupants as well as industrial and agricultural operations are impacted by power outages. The negative impacts range from reduced work productivity and decreased occupant safety and health to reductions in lifestyle standards. Just like real estate values are higher for green buildings with LEED recognition, in the future, buildings that are self-sufficient from an energy perspective may command premium prices because they preserve delivery of services regardless of the status of the electric grid. Buildings that incorporate energy resiliency into their infrastructure will be increasingly popular over time. Would you rather live in a high-rise apartment building that guaranteed it could generate or store enough power during outages to run elevators and water, or one that couldn't deliver on those desirable services?

---

* http://www.openadr.org.

Microgrids* are receiving significant attention from consumers ranging from the military and industrial operations to commercial property managers and individual homeowners who want full or partial functionality during grid outages. The Smart Grid offers opportunities to build microgrids that can operate independently of the grid as well as integrate to it. San Diego Gas and Electric (SDG&E) has demonstrated that a microgrid can be used to energize the primary distribution system. Using microgrids as energy sources to return power to the utility distribution grid points to new possibilities to engineer more resiliency into electric grids, and requires innovative new services that have interesting financial implications.

Buildings and industrial/agricultural operations that deploy microgrids are operating as prosumers and will have profound impacts on utility business models and market structures. Microgrid owners (residential, commercial and industrial (C&I), and agricultural) will accelerate the shift of power from concentration in the hands of utilities as the sole generators/distributors of electricity to prosumers on a distributed and decentralized basis.

The Smart Grid enables compelling new value propositions for prosumers. It also enables new market participation roles for residential, commercial, industrial, and agricultural consumers. But new market participation can only occur when the traditional power market structure has evolved to accommodate more sources of kilowatts and negawatts from many more prosumers. Microgrids will also bring with them unique privacy issues that must be addressed. This is discussed in Chapter 7.

* From the *Smart Grid Dictionary*. A small power system that integrates self-contained generation, distribution, sensors, energy storage, and energy management software with a seamless and synchronized connection to a utility power system, and can operate independently as an island from that system. Generation includes renewable energy sources and the ability to sell back excess capacity to a utility. On-site microgrid management software includes controls for the power generation, utility connect/disconnect, distribution, and energy storage equipment along with building energy management applications for industrial, commercial, or home use. CERTS (Consortium for Electric Reliability Technology Solutions) has documented a microgrid concept.

The Future Smart Grid

The Smart Grid of the future will support a vast marketplace that operates like a stock market where any participant can buy or sell electricity with confidence that transactions are managed through enforceable rules that apply to all. This market structure is called transactive energy. Transactive energy enables an active prosumer market, where prosumers include buildings, EVs, wind generators, distributed energy resource (DER)* assets, or microgrids owned by the consumer segments named above. Simply put, the current market that exists at the wholesale or bulk electricity level will be mirrored downstream at the distribution grid. It is a significant change from today's electricity markets, which are only available to qualified suppliers able to trade in large quantities (megawatts and negawatts) of electricity. But it will take time for the market to restructure into a transactive energy format.

What happens in the meantime? There's no one-size-fits-all scenario that perfectly addresses all the possible model and market transformation alternatives in the United States, where we have a balkanized regulatory structure. It is easier to track the technology trends and make some predictions.

Technology Changes

The Smart Grid has three innovation drivers: technology, policy, and money. There's been no shortage of technology innovations, which sometimes means that grid modernization isn't an evolution, but a revolution. That's particularly true regarding generation. Generation shifts from highly centralized to highly decentralized or distributed. It moves from large-scale production to mid- and small-scale production that is suitable for the voltages commonly found in distribution grids. Generation ownership transforms too, and this is primarily due to the rapid advances in renewable energy technologies.

These technologies—particularly solar PV or wind deployments in the low-voltage or distribution grid—are game changers for the

* From the *Smart Grid Dictionary*: "Grid-connected or stand-alone generation, energy storage, or negawatt assets that are deployed in the distribution grid. DER assets can substitute for or supplement grid-supplied power."

electric grid. Utilities and independent power producers have focused on large-scale solar and wind generation projects that resulted in 2,847 MW of PV and 410 MW of concentrating solar power (CSP) deployed in 2013*—usually sited for high-voltage transmission. Commercial and residential building owners have enjoyed falling costs, increasing choices, inexpensive financing, and new third-party ownership options for rooftop PV installations that are sited in the distribution grid. Consider these two trends. From 2007 to 2013, the costs of solar panels dropped from $3.40/watt to 80 cents/watt, and PV deployments in the United States increased from 735 MW to 7,200 MW. Solar generation is intermittent—the sun obviously isn't around at night, and weather can impact its generation abilities. However, advanced data analytics solutions hold promise to improve forecasts of solar availability and management, and Smart Grid technologies improve distribution grid operations to manage the voltage fluctuations on a real-time basis.

Energy Storage

Energy storage is another game-changing collection of technologies involving different chemistries and uses.† Affordable and scalable solutions are considered by some to be the holy grail of the Smart Grid. We predict that fast iterative innovations in technologies and financing options will create the same trends that continue the rapid expansion of solar PV systems. Energy storage has intriguing synergies with intermittent renewable generation too. The SDG&E microgrid demonstration project referenced earlier included energy storage to firm the intermittency exhibited by large numbers of rooftop solar PV systems. Energy storage performed very well in dealing with rapid fluctuations in power. As energy storage evolves, related privacy issues will also be created. Some of those possibilities are discussed in Chapter 7.

Generation and storage comprise two of the three categories of distributed energy resources (DERs). The third category addresses

---

* Solar Energy Industries Association (SEIA).

† Examples include backup power and grid stabilization, which require different types of batteries.

negawatt production through participation in DR programs. One of the most interesting plays in DER is the use of bundled solutions that combine solar generation with energy storage. For instance, an elevator company just introduced the first solar-powered elevator system—one that can operate even during grid blackouts. It includes battery storage, so it operates at night too.

A recent poll* of utility executives identified that the strong growth of distributed generation or DER would result in grid integration issues and represent the top challenge to utilities in the next 5 years. DER is relatively new, and there will be a range of possibilities for different ownership and service models. Here are a few options:

- DER assets may be owned and managed by individuals or businesses.
- DER assets may be leased by individuals or businesses but owned and managed by another entity.
- DER assets may be owned by one party, leased to another, and managed by still another entity.

DER management includes services that maintain the optimal performance of equipment and services that monitor bidirectional payment transactions. While the most popular ownership and service models have to be identified, it's clear that there will be new data about energy production, probably new data about energy consumption, and data regarding financial transactions that will be created as a result of DER assets. Some of this data may be personally identifiable information or have other sensitivities, such as financial data. There are limited guidelines regarding energy data, and those that exist primarily define how regulated utilities must treat energy data from consumers and prosumers. We'll discuss data ownership relationships later in this chapter and drill down into the technologies that are most likely to touch data that merit privacy protections.

Transmission Grids

From the revolutions occurring in generation, we follow the supply chain into transmission. Here the word is *evolution*. The transmission

* DNV GL, Utility of the Future Pulse Survey, 2014.

grids in many regions are deploying advanced sensor networks through participation in an initiative called the North American SynchroPhasor Initiative (NASPI).* While there are other technologies that increase voltages and reduce line losses, the significant modernization effort leverages sophisticated sensors and high-speed communications. The NASPInet effort and other investments in phasor technologies offer unprecedented monitoring and control capabilities for our electric superhighways. There are massive amounts of new data produced from these technologies, but they are not in need of privacy protections.

Why do we make this statement? These advanced sensor networks deliver wide-area situational awareness of grid stability.† The phasor technologies convert the standard three-phase analog signal of voltage or current into time-tagged measurements that result in real-time snapshots of the transmission system. The data that is collected includes location, time, frequency, current, voltage, and phase angle relative to some known reference point on the grid at a frequency of 30 times per second (hence the volumes and velocity of data are massive) to offer early warning of any disturbances in system conditions for immediate corrective actions. Remember the 2003 Northeast blackout mentioned earlier in this chapter? That grid catastrophe could have been avoided with these monitoring and control devices. The data is also valuable for diagnostic analyses to understand problem causes and develop better protocols to avoid future operational issues in the high-voltage transmission grid.

---

* From the *Smart Grid Dictionary*: "A collaborative initiative between the DOE (Department of Energy), NERC (North American Electric Reliability Corporation), and electric utilities, vendors, consultants, and researchers. It receives funding from the DOE, NERC, and industry. Its mission is to improve power system reliability and visibility through wide-area measurement and control, using the precise, synchronized measurements of Synchrophasor technology as a diagnostic tool. Synchrophasor measurements will assist in wide-area monitoring, real-time operations, power system planning, and forensic analysis of grid disturbances. Phasor technology is expected to help integrate renewable and intermittent resources, automate controls for transmission and demand response, increase transmission system throughput, and improve system modeling and planning. The DOE has several grant programs for large-scale prototypes, regional demonstrations, and Smart Grid/PMU (Phasor Measurement Unit) deployments."

† The North American SynchroPhasor Initiative offers additional explanation about the devices and the value of data collected by them. See https://www.naspi.org.

There's another reason that there are no privacy concerns regarding this data. Phasors measure sinusoidal waveforms, which are comprised of streams of electrons. Electrons are not tagged with unique identifiers to indicate that they originated at your solar panel or are heading to my meter.

The distribution grid is undergoing multiple upgrades, but it is a much needed evolution with Smart Grid technologies, instead of a revolution in this part of the supply chain. The traditional distribution grid, according to some industry experts, has been the laggard in investments and grid modernization. The American Recovery and Reinvestment Act (ARRA) of 2009,* commonly called the Stimulus Act,† spurred significant investments in distribution grid technologies. There are many technologies that improve distribution grid operations. The most visible of these technologies to consumers that are provided by utilities is the smart meter. This technology will be discussed in detail in Chapter 4. At a high level, a smart meter is a specialized measurement device that includes wired or wireless communications capabilities, and just like any phone, it relies on a network to transmit or receive data. These bidirectional networks are part of the advanced metering infrastructure (AMI).‡

Data Volumes within the Smart Grid

There is a tremendous amount of new data and, in some cases, increasing volumes of traditional data. Most of this data helps grid operators monitor and react to real-time grid conditions, improving overall service reliability to consumers. In other situations, analysis of historical data reveals previously hidden information about equipment that is trending to failure. Smart Grid technologies—primarily sensors

---

* See http://www.gpo.gov/fdsys/pkg/BILLS-111hr1enr/pdf/BILLS-111hr1enr.pdf.

† See more about the Stimulus Act activities at http://www.recovery.gov/Pages/default.aspx. For information specific to the Smart Grid, see http://www.recovery.gov/arra/News/featured/Pages/Nation%E2%80%99s-Electric-Grid-Gets-Smart.aspx.

‡ From the *Smart Grid Dictionary*: "Electricity meters, bi-directional communications network hardware and software, and associated system and data management software that measures and records usage data at set intervals, and provides usage data to consumers, utilities, and other parties at set intervals. The set intervals are specified by regulatory agencies."

gathering data; robust and reliable communications networks, usually wireless; and back-end data analytics—are essential to help integrate renewables into the distribution grid. Smart Grid technologies help manage intermittent renewable energy sources and maintain stable, reliable, and safe delivery of electricity. Smart meter data has significant implications to privacy, because this data can become information about consumption patterns and behaviors of occupants within specific locations via data analytics. We'll explore smart meter data in more detail in Chapter 4.

The Smart Grid revolutionizes consumption. Consumers become prosumers and have a range of innovative solutions that help them manage energy consumption, generate their own electricity, or schedule when their EV battery should be charged. Before we launch into an overview of some important Smart Grid technologies in the consumption part of the electricity supply chain, it is useful to review the roles of data owners, data custodians, and data managers because the proliferation of companies that have a solution that impacts consumption can make it confusing to understand what role each company plays. The topic of data ownership is also hotly debated and lends itself to privacy as it relates to consumers being able to control the data that applies to them.

Data Owners, Data Custodians, and Data Managers

The concepts discussed here are framed in energy usage, consumption, and production data, but could have equal relevance to data created for other purposes, such as vehicle telematics or personal health monitoring. These concepts are focused on data ownership, data custodianship, and data management.

Data ownership identifies the owner of data, the entity that has ultimate control and decision-making authority over the data. In California, for example, customers own their energy consumption data derived from smart meters.* This is a critically important designation and bears repeating. In some states, utility customers are explicitly identified as the owners of their energy consumption data.

* This is the published final decision of the CPUC that outlines, among other findings, that customers own their energy consumption data, and that utilities may not sell this data. http://docs.cpuc.ca.gov/PUBLISHED/FINAL_DECISION/140369.htm.

However, with regard to energy usage data, from such things as smart devices (smart refrigerators, home energy management tools, and apps running on the smart devices), the answer has not been explicitly stated at the time of this writing. The ownership of energy production data also has not been explicitly determined by any laws at the time of this writing. California has often set precedents for privacy law. Appendix B contains a list of significant legislative and regulatory agency privacy decisions with impacts on energy usage data in the state of California.

The investor-owned utilities (IOUs) that are regulated by the California Public Utilities Commission (CPUC) are designated as data custodians. Custodians are charged with ensuring the secure transmission, handling, and storage of data. Data managers* can be data owners or data custodians. Utilities function as both custodians and managers in their roles of collecting consumption data and billing customers based on that data. Data managers can also be third-party companies† that are authorized by the data owner to have one-time or ongoing access to that owner's energy consumption measurements. Data managers typically manipulate data into information. That could be as simple as a visual display or graphic about home energy use, or a more sophisticated analysis of energy use data combined with other outside sources of data.

Data owners have many good reasons to voluntarily share their energy consumption data with data managers. However, and this is a big caveat, once data leaves the custodianship of a utility, the data is at the risk of the third party's safeguards and practices. For example, the legal responsibilities of the utility for security incidents and privacy breaches that occur within their contracted vendors will depend upon the utility's published privacy notice (also often called privacy policy). If the utility makes commitments to protect data, then it may be held liable for any harm that occurs to the data,

---

* These are also known as third parties or energy service providers (ESPs). We use the term *data manager* to clarify data relationships.

† Third-party companies are the entities contracted by the custodians or the data owners to access or process in some manner the energy data.

and associated individuals, as a result of the vendors it contracts.* However, if consumers are passing their energy usage data directly on to other entities themselves, then they are at the mercy of the safeguards and practices of that entity. Call it the data equivalent of *caveat emptor* (buyer beware). Data owners who value their privacy as it relates to energy usage data will need to exercise caution by carefully reading the privacy policies of the third parties they authorize to be data managers or custodians of that data.

Here's another caveat. The description above about data owners, custodians, and managers applies to the state of California. The United States has a fragmented regulatory structure for energy, and each state has responsibility for developing any privacy requirements for any energy data on behalf of its citizens. At the time of this writing, some states had not elaborated a policy or position about privacy for energy consumption, production, or usage data.†

Energy Consumption

Let's look at some of the revolutions occurring in the electricity supply chain's final destination—consumption at an end point. Utilities traditionally supplied electricity to a meter and owned all the equipment leading to that device, including the meter. The other side of the meter—the breaker box, the interior electrical wiring, and all the devices plugged into a residential or commercial building—is outside

* This is the explicit case in some industries, such as healthcare under the Health Insurance Portability and Accountability Act (HIPAA). However, the Federal Trade Commission (FTC), which has broad consumer oversight across all industries, has made many statements that businesses and other types of organizations will bear some responsibility for ensuring the security and privacy of data they outsource to other entities. State Attorneys General offices also have interest and have taken action to hold organizations accountable for breaches that occur in their outsourced vendors. As one representative example, per legal analysis from Microsoft (accessed from http://technet.microsoft.com/en-us/magazine/hh994647.aspx on June 27 2014): "In the United States, both federal and state government agencies such as the FTC and various attorneys general have made enterprises accountable for the actions of their subcontractors. This has been replicated elsewhere, such as in the EU with the data protection agencies."

† To see the latest activities by each state regarding energy laws and related activities, see http://www.ncsl.org/research/energy/energy-environment-legislation-tracking-database.aspx.

of the utility's jurisdiction. Very little was known about consumption. A meter was read by physically going to the meter once a month, or sometimes with less frequency, so it was virtually impossible* to tweeze out when, why, or what was consuming electricity. This is another lack of situational awareness. The Smart Grid completely revolutionizes the ability for consumers to acquire detailed knowledge about electricity consumption, as well as energy usage data that could reveal performance of their other types of smart devices, such as a smart refrigerator. This ability to acquire detailed knowledge is a significant privacy concern; to be able to protect privacy, there need to be controls on the entities that have access to this data that can reveal such detailed knowledge about the associated individuals. This is discussed in more detail in Chapters 4 to 7.

Smart Grid Privacy Risk Examples

We will explain in more detail privacy risks throughout the remainder of this book. However, here is a sampling of a few of the most apparent areas where privacy risks exist within the Smart Grid.

1. Energy management systems and area networks for buildings. More granular energy consumption data, along with the related metadata, such as the GPS, date, and time,† from smart meters can be useful for many entities beyond the data owner for a number of reasons, but the nature of usage or consumption data can reveal much more about what happens inside the walls of a home or office building. Two of the enabling technologies to collect, analyze, and communicate electricity

* Elias Leake Quinn detailed in his report "Smart Metering and Privacy: Existing Law and Competing Policies" (Spring 2009, p. 3) how he had set up surveillance to continuously monitor a traditional meter to determine activities. However, this would require a separate monitoring device to accomplish the insights that he obtained. Read more about this at http://www.dora.state.co.us/puc/DocketsDecisions/DocketFilings/09I-593EG/09I-593EG_Spring2009Report-Smart GridPrivacy.pdf. *Note*: A hob heater is a top-of-stove cooking surface.

† Metadata describes other data. It provides information about a certain data item's content. For example, energy usage data from a smart device may also have accompanying it metadata that indicates the time, date, and location for when the energy usage occurred, along with other types of data associated with the energy usage.

consumption data are home energy management systems (HEMSs) and home area networks (HANs). A HAN is on "the other side of the meter" and serves as a communications network within the walls of a house, apartment, or other type of residence. HEMSs are software products that gather/analyze/display information about a home's energy consumption and sometimes provide control capabilities for devices managed by them. Many solutions in this category are using apps loaded on smart phones and tablets as the primary display and control device, but there are also dedicated devices being used as well. This is a meaningful distinction, because that means that energy data has crossed the boundaries from utility custodianship and is now managed by another entity, most likely not bound by the same regulatory or other legal requirements.

Commercial and industrial consumers have similar solutions that are tailored to their unique needs. There's more maturity to this market segment, with a number of well-known vendors that include Honeywell, Johnson Controls, Siemens, and IBM offering solutions to help commercial facility managers and occupants monitor and control energy consumption for heating, ventilation, air conditioning (HVAC), lighting, and other plug loads. Privacy concerns exist here too, but differ from residential ones. Consumption data is generally aggregated or grouped together for purposes of improving building management, reducing costs, or improving occupant comfort and safety. Data owners are building or property managers working in conjunction with authorized data custodians such as ESPs. Data owners are typically more concerned about protecting their energy consumption data from a competitive differentiator perspective than a privacy perspective.

The associated risks, and possible risk mitigation actions, for HEMSs, HANs, and commercial and industrial buildings will be discussed further in Chapter 7.

2. Electric vehicles and charging stations. The Smart Grid enables a proliferation of data about electric vehicles (EVs), particularly when charging stations are involved. The convergence of location-based information, electricity consumption, times, dates, and personal identity in vehicles creates a wide

range of fascinating privacy considerations and challenges. EV charging stations are immature products, but the trends are clear—businesses that make charging station management software have the most to gain or lose in privacy rules, which in some cases may be established by the public utility commissions that regulate electric utilities or state lawmakers. We'll discuss this more in Chapters 6 and 7.

3. Smart appliances. The smart or connected home and the Smart Grid intersect in smart appliances. Like smart meters, a smart appliance has communications capabilities so that it can interact with other devices, directly to vendors, such as Whirlpool's 6th Sense Live, the electric grid, and the Internet. Some of the new devices data reports energy usage or consumption data, but other new data can conceivably communicate status about device performance, including how and when it was used.* There are many beneficial possibilities for consumers with this new data, but careful attention will have to be given to clearly identify ownership of this data. We'll discuss this further in Chapters 5 and 7.
4. Consumer to prosumer transformation. We previously described the revolution in energy generation at the start of our supply chain discussion. That same revolution exists at the termination point—consumption. Renewable generation options—particularly rooftop PV—are proliferating for all electricity consumer categories. But there's more to being a prosumer than production of kilowatts via solar, wind or other power. In the future EV owners may sell excess energy stored in a battery back to the grid, making EVs earn money for owners. This setup has already been successfully tested in a small pilot.

The ability to reduce electricity use by participation in DR programs is a form of negawatt generation, and transforms a consumer into a prosumer. Smart appliances or HEMSs may be instructed to automatically operate based on price signals, and thus shift operations. The bottom line is that these Smart Grid

* There are smart phones and other types of mobile smart devices that indicate GPS locations. However, for the typical smart appliance that was in use at the time this book was written, they were not enabled with any location-based services.

technologies revolutionize consumption. These technologies also create new data that assists in energy management and financial transactions. There may be many intermediaries between a consumer or prosumer and a utility, and that "chain of data custody"* needs to be understood at each transaction point to ensure that desired or required levels of privacy are maintained.

Energy Regulation

Every discussion about privacy in the Smart Grid is complicated by the United States regulatory ecosystem. States have regulated monopolies or investor-owned utilities (IOUs) that are governed by public utility commissions (PUCs). There are also publicly owned utilities or municipal utilities and cooperatives that are not as highly regulated as IOUs, but often align to the policies enacted for IOUs. What this means is that there is no one-size-fits-all policy for privacy in the Smart Grid. You might find consensus around some statements, such as "consumption data is owned by the customer," or not. Since the Smart Grid offers some early examples of machine-to-machine (M2M) applications, the government policies that are devised for regulated utilities could be copied for unregulated businesses, or then again, perhaps they won't be adopted outside of this unique category of businesses. There are huge implications to this statement, and government policy makers are well advised to consider how their decisions about using consumption data impacts consumer privacy, and could or should be applied to products and services focused in vehicle telematics, digital health, or wearable sensors.

Smart Grid, Smart Infrastructure

Just as there is much excitement about how communications technologies are revolutionizing utility operations and creating new product and service opportunities, the same interest levels exist in Smart

* The chain of data custody or chain of custody borrows from the justice system's procedures to document each transfer of evidence. For privacy purposes, it documents each transfer point where data has privacy sensitivities and notes the privacy guidelines in effect.

Infrastructure. Government agencies, businesses, and consumers are realizing that Smart Grid technologies can have broader applications in all sorts of infrastructure with significant beneficial impacts.

Some favor the term *Smart City*, but that artificially limits the thinking to urban scenarios. We use the term *Smart Infrastructure* to describe the bigger picture. Infrastructure is inclusive to urban, suburban, and rural settings. For instance, the technologies that make the electric grid smart have proven benefits to rural distribution grids. Remote monitoring and control capabilities offer new capabilities for utilities to predict equipment wear and tear and proactively repair or replace failing assets, thus avoiding a service disruption. Even when lightning strikes, Smart Grid technologies can result in faster services restoration to far-flung communities and consumers.

From a Smart Infrastructure perspective, many utilities own the streetlights in cities and towns. These streetlights consume a considerable amount of electricity, and over the years, utilities have been converting to more energy efficient lamps to save money. But smart streetlights go one step further—they are starting to function as communications antennas and relay stations to convey wireless signals for a variety of public and private uses.

Traffic lights and cameras can now be networked with streetlights, and use motion sensors to detect the presence of moving vehicles or people. One of the most interesting applications concerns smart parking. Some estimates claim that 30%* of the traffic in any city is focused on finding a parking spot. If empty spots could communicate their status to nearby vehicles and reduce time to park, that would reduce street congestion and avoid emissions produced in searches for elusive parking spots. What if cash-strapped municipalities could do a better job of finding the parked cars that overstayed their welcome at parking meters? These scenarios are not far-fetched future possibilities—the technologies are being deployed now, and all rely on data. The bottom line is that a city can't really be smart without a Smart Grid, and a Smart Grid can enhance, and be enhanced by, a city that intelligently manages its consumption of energy and water. All these beneficial possibilities must address the associated privacy risks that exist as a result of collecting and analyzing all this data.

* From IBM study: http://www-03.ibm.com/press/us/en/pressrelease/35515.wss.

Smart Grid technologies, policies, and financial innovations are disrupters to the energy status quo. Disruptions are nothing new to business and society—until it happens to your chosen business sector or consumer group. The telephone disrupted the telegraph. The automobile disrupted horse and buggy services. But for every loser, there can be multiple winners. Sometimes innovations create new value where none existed before. That's one of the overlooked aspects to the Smart Grid. The modernization and transformation of the electricity infrastructure to integrate renewables resulted in significant job growth for solar panel sales, design, and installation. Designing privacy controls into these devices from the initial design stage will be more cost effective than trying to retrofit privacy within a device that is already deployed.

The bottom line is that we now have technologies—renewables coupled with energy storage, inexpensive sensors coupled with wireless networks, and analytics coupled with cost-effective data storage—to convert a fragile grid into an agile grid. An agile grid relies on highly distributed energy assets (generation, demand response, energy efficiency, and storage) with highly distributed intelligence. We all win when our energy infrastructure is safe, reliable, resilient, cost-effective, and based on clean power. However, to be successful and have the public embrace such technologies, the entities using these components, as well as the agencies governing the various portions of the Smart Grid, must demonstrate that privacy risks have been identified and appropriately and effectively addressed.

Key Points for Smart Grid Technologies

The Smart Grid relies on communications and data. Here are three main takeaways about data that are generated by Smart Grid technologies and the associated policies that utilities, regulators and legislators, product and service vendors, and ESPs should consider:

1. There will be new data about transactive market participants as consumers and prosumers, and some of this data will have sensitivities that require secure transport and storage as well as privacy protections.
2. There will be new relationships beyond the traditional consumer-utility relationship. New intermediaries that negotiate

on the consumer's behalf may not be bound by the same privacy requirements that are in place for utilities—if indeed those exist. All entities involved with collecting and using energy data must address privacy to mitigate risks appropriately, even in the absence of legal requirements.

3. If the question about who owns the consumer's data that is generated by Smart Grid technologies, applications, and service providers has not been answered, it must be, and soon, to protect privacy. However, this is a hotly debated topic, and we don't expect that there will be any fast or easy decisions.

3

What Is Privacy?

What Is Privacy?

The term *privacy* is a subjective term. There is not a single, universal definition for privacy. Let's consider some modern history of the word.

In the 1890 issue of the *Harvard Law Review* an essay entitled "The Right to Privacy" by Samuel Warren and Louis Brandeis defined privacy as "the right to be let alone." What inspired Warren and Brandeis to write such an essay? They were concerned about a new-fangled technology/gadget—the Brownie camera—a new technology at that time period that was starting to be widely used by the general public to capture images not only in private residences, but also in public venues. It reportedly greatly disturbed in particular Samuel Warren that journalists were now taking photos with this new-fangled privacy-invading gadget whenever they had the opportunity. Some say the essay was inspired by a specific incident in which journalists were intruding on a society wedding by taking photos.* However, others claim the inspiration was from a more general coverage of intimate personal lives, increasingly including photos, within the society columns of newspapers.† Regardless of the original definition, the definition now goes far beyond that original simple concept. One thing that is the same, though: emerging new technologies, such as those found within the Smart Grid, are creating new privacy concerns in ways similar to the little Brownie camera.

Privacy also is not simply defined by laws. Laws always lag far behind technology use and human practices, and address a small

* See, e.g., Dorothy J. Glancy, The Invention of the Right to Privacy, *Arizona Law Review*, 21(1), http://digitalcommons.law.scu.edu/cgi/viewcontent.cgi?article=1318&context=facpubs (accessed June 13, 2014).

† Ibid.

fraction of the actual privacy risks that exist, and that are created by new technologies.

Instead of thinking about privacy as one definition, it is more useful to think about privacy as a concept that involves revealing details about individuals in some manner, along with controlling how that information is used and shared, and the access individuals have to the associated information.

Categories of Privacy

There are four categories of privacy* that must be considered and addressed, both with security controls and with appropriate privacy practices.

- *Information privacy* is concerned with establishing rules that govern the collection and handling of personal information. This is the most commonly considered type of category to have privacy implications that involve protecting specifically referenced information items. A few examples include financial information (such as bank account numbers), medical information (such as health insurance account numbers), government records (such as social security numbers), and records of a person's activities (such as through access logs) on the Internet.
- *Bodily privacy* is focused on a person's physical being and any invasion of the body. Some examples include genetic testing, drug testing, body cavity searches, information about surgeries, and Transportation Security Administration (TSA) scans at U.S airports.
- *Territorial privacy* is concerned with placing limits on the ability to intrude into another individual's environment. The environment is not limited to the home; it also includes the workplace and public spaces. Invasion into an individual's

* See Roger Clarke, What's Privacy? http://www.rogerclarke.com/DV/Privacy.html. Clarke makes a similar set of distinctions between the privacy of the physical person, the privacy of personal behavior, the privacy of personal communications, and the privacy of personal data. Roger Clarke is a well-known privacy expert from Australia who has been providing privacy research papers and guidance for the past couple of decades.

territorial privacy typically takes the form of monitoring such as video surveillance, drones, ID checks, and use of similar technology and procedures. Having others take an individual's photo or record individuals out in public with their smart phones or wearable computers is included in this category.

- *Communications privacy* involves protection of the ways in which individuals correspond with others. Examples include postal mail, telephone conversations, email, Skype and similar types of voice-over Internet protocol (VoIP) solutions, and other forms.

What's the Difference between Security and Privacy?*

In many organizations the people responsible for privacy are completely separated from and in entirely different departments from the people responsible for security. Often these departments do not communicate, or even acknowledge or understand the compelling relationship that essentially exists between the two. Too often privacy is considered a purely legal issue, the responsibility for which is often handed to organizational legal counsel. Or, it is ignored altogether as a separate issue, and management assumes it will be addressed by all the various business units during the course of doing business. Security is too often viewed as a purely technical issue, and the responsibility for security is more often than not placed within the information technology or networking support area—often buried beneath several layers of management. And the twain never meet. Security personnel must be actively involved in privacy issues and crafting privacy policies, and privacy personnel must be actively involved in security issues and crafting security policies.

So, to the crux of this topic: How is security different than privacy? It is really pretty simple; you must implement security to ensure privacy. You must use security to obtain privacy. Security is a process, privacy is a consequence. Security is an action, privacy is a result

---

* This section is an updated version of the passage from an essay written by Rebecca Herold for a Computer Security Institute publication in 2002 (http://www.privacyguidance.com/downloads/privacyandsecurity.pdf), recently published in Rebecca Herold and Kevin Beaver, *The Practical Guide to HIPAA Privacy and Security Compliance, Second Edition,* Boca Raton: Auerbach Publications, 2014.

of successful action. Security is a condition, privacy is the prognosis. Security is the strategy, privacy is the outcome. Privacy is a state of existence, security is the constitution supporting the existence. Security is a tactical strategy, privacy is a contextual strategic objective. Security is the sealed envelope, privacy is the successful delivery of the message inside the envelope. The bottom line: enterprise privacy management strategies and security management architecture must be effectively and actively integrated.

What is a common mistake an organization can make that can lead to potentially devastating public press, irreversible damage to personal lives, and huge fines and lawsuits? Often when the privacy responsibility lies in a different part of the organization from the security responsibility, or the two areas do not communicate, privacy policy notices are issued, but no security policies, procedures, or mechanisms are implemented to ensure the now-published privacy policies are enforced. These published privacy policies are in effect a contract with your patients, customers, and consumers. The privacy policies are often the first and main point of contact between the public and your organization. If an organization tells customers that it is performing certain activities to ensure their privacy, that organization had better well make sure its personnel know what they have committed to, whether or not they were involved with the privacy policy creation.

Privacy with respect to many of the current legislated regulations means people are able to make informed choices when seeking care and reimbursement for healthcare based on how protected health information (PHI) may be used, or are able to make choices about how their personally identifiable financial information is used and shared by the organizations with which they do business. Privacy enables patients to find out how their information may be used and what disclosures of their information have been made. Privacy enables consumers to find out how financial information is going to be protected and know that the people handling their information have been properly trained to protect their privacy. Privacy limits release of information to the minimum reasonably needed for the purpose of the disclosure. Privacy gives people the right to examine and obtain a copy of their own personal records and request corrections.

Security with respect to these same regulations constitutes those reasonable and prudent policies, processes, safeguards, controls, steps, and tools that are used to maintain confidentiality, integrity, avalability and privacy. It involves all methods, processes, and technology used to ensure the confidentiality and safety of the once private information that has been entrusted to a third party by the consumer, customer, or patient.

Bottom line: You must implement information security controls to have privacy.

Data Types

Many types of information can be considered to be personal information. Generally any data that can reveal information about an individual or an individual's life activities, whereabouts, etc., could be considered to be personal information. In some locations of the world, business-related employee information is also considered to be personal information. Some of these types of personal information are more sensitive than others. Table 3.1 lists some common personal information items.

Table 3.1 Personal Information Examples

GENERAL TYPES OF PERSONAL INFORMATION ITEMS
• Name
• Gender
• Age and date of birth
• Mailing address
• Email address
• User IDs
• Marital status
• Citizenship
• Languages spoken
• Veteran status
• Disabled status
• IP address (some jurisdictions)
• Dozens (hundreds?) more
ORGANIZATIONAL INFORMATION CONSIDERED PERSONAL INFORMATION THROUGHOUT THE WORLD
• Business and personal addresses
• Business and personal phone numbers
• Business and personal email addresses
• Internal identification numbers
• Government-issued identification numbers
• Identity verification information

Table 3.2 Examples of Sensitive Types of Personal Information Items

UNITED STATES

SENSITIVE PERSONAL INFORMATION

- Social security number
- Financial information
- Driver's license number
- Medical records
- Etc.

WITHIN THE U.S. AND OTHER COUNTRIES

SPECIAL CATEGORIES OF DATA (WHICH ARE CONSIDERED TO BE SENSITIVE)

- Racial or ethnic origin
- Political opinions
- Religious or philosophical beliefs
- Trade union membership
- Health or sex life
- Criminal convictions or offenses
- Etc.

Generally, the more personal information items you have, the more risk that is generally associated with that personal information. One of the best and simplest ways to lessen privacy risks is to collect and store less personal information.

That said, there are increasingly more types of personal information being created. Every organization must be aware of the data they are collecting, or creating, that could be associated with individuals. Such information would likely be considered as personal information, even if the data is not formally defined in a law or book somewhere (Table 3.2).

Smart Grid data, such as data collected from smart meters, when collecting energy usage data frequently enough, can create an electricity usage "fingerprint" that can be associated with specific households. How frequently meter reads are really needed to improve energy usage, without having this data reveal too much about personal activities, is a question that utilities are trying to answer.

Not all personal information is equal, and so there must be varying degrees of safeguards around certain categories, based upon sensitivity, risk, and applicable legal requirements.

Smart Data Privacy Implications

The data collected throughout the Smart Grid, from smart meters, smart appliances, apps, and many other types of grid-connected gadgets, can potentially reveal much about the lives of individuals, leading to privacy invasions and breaches. Table 3.3 provides 15 specific

Table 3.3 Privacy Concerns for Smart Grid Information Disclosure and Misuse

PRIVACY CONCERN	DISCUSSION
1. Identity theft	Specific combinations of personal information may be used to impersonate a utility consumer, resulting in potentially severe impacts, such as negative credit reports, fraudulent utility use, and other damaging consumer actions.
2. Determine personal behavior patterns	Access to data use profiles that can reveal specific times and locations of electricity use in specific areas of the home can also indicate the types of activities or appliances used. The information revealed could be considered a new type of surveillance. The data could be (mis)used by other entities to do target marketing, by governments to try and tax specific activities and uses, and by persons with malicious intent.
3. Determine specific appliances used	Energy usage data could be used to track the use of specific smart appliances that are programmed to communicate with smart meters or Internet of Things (IOT) applications. Appliance manufacturers may want to get this information to know who, how, and why individuals used their products in certain ways. Such information could impact appliance warranties. Insurance companies may want to use this information to approve or decline claims. And there is an unlimited number of other possible uses as yet not imagined that these data could provide.
4. Perform real-time surveillance	Access to real-time energy usage data could reveal if people are in the residence, what they are doing, where they are in the residence, and so on. This not only presents a safety risk, with burglars and vandals using it to their destruction, but also could be used to do target marketing based upon home energy use behaviors.
5. Reveal activities through residual data	If the data on the metering devices is not effectively or completely removed when the home resident no longer needs to use them, the residual data may possibly reveal to the new meter user, or entity that possesses the meter, the activities of the former owner. Not only does this present similar concerns to those listed in the first three concern topics, but it also could be used by activists or others who have agendas to reveal what they view as a lack of social responsibility. However, to prevent any tampering of historical data and to satisfy the size constraints for the new meters—providing more functionality in the same physical meter box—the data are not likely to be stored within the smart meter itself. But, the possibility of storing data within residential meters should be considered in any meter functionality plans so that if it does become possible to store personal information in smart meters, the privacy issues will be appropriately addressed.

(continued)

Table 3.3 Privacy Concerns for Smart Grid Information Disclosure and Misuse (continued)

PRIVACY CONCERN	DISCUSSION
6. Target home invasions	Malicious use of meter data for specific consumers could lead to a wide number of problems, such as physical invasions to the home because crooks could tell when residents were away, whether or not they have an alarm system, and so on.
7. Provide accidental privacy invasions	Combinations of meter data, analyzed for one purpose, could reveal unexpected information about the residents that is then used to the detriment of the residents.
8. Activity censorship	The meter data could reveal resident activities or uses that utility companies may then subsequently decide are inappropriate or should not be allowed. Without restrictions, if this information could then be shared with local government, law enforcement, or public media outlets, the residents could suffer embarrassment, harassment, loss of vital appliances, or any number of other damaging actions.
9. Decisions and actions based upon inaccurate data	With meter data being stored in potentially many locations, accessed by so many different individuals and entities, and used for a very wide variety of purposes, it is a significant risk that the personal information data could become inappropriately modified. Not only could automated Smart Grid decisions made for home energy use be detrimental for residents (e.g., restricted power, thermostats turned to dangerous levels, and so on), but also decisions about Smart Grid power use and activities could be based upon inaccurate information.
10. Reveal activities when used with data from other utilities or third parties	Even more personal activities and derived personal information could be revealed if the power meter personal information was combined with the personal information from other utilities and utility meters, such as those for gas, water, and so on, or third parties (e.g., data brokers, energy service providers, vendors, etc.). As the use of big data analytics increases and becomes more powerful, this is made more likely.
11. Profiling	Profiling may be possible in ways that were previously not possible, or not as easily possible. What can you tell about what you can see from energy usage? For example, if the consumers are straight or gay? Terrorist profiles? Affairs? Illegal activities? Will access to do data mining for investigations put people on terrorist watch lists, etc.? Will politicians want to use data for potential activity taxation? Performing a gap analysis could point out scenarios and associated risks.
12. Unwanted publicity and embarrassment	Embarrassment and other negative impacts resulting from unauthorized disclosure or publication of household or electric vehicle use.
13. Tracking behavior of renters/leasers	When a different individual owns and pays the utilities other than the resident, such as in the case of a rental unit, room subletting, leasing, and so on, the landlord or property owner could have access to the smart meter data and potentially track the residents' activities. Rent decisions could be made based on past power usage history. Power usage profiling could follow individuals and impact a wide range of decisions.

(continued)

Table 3.3 Privacy Concerns for Smart Grid Information Disclosure and Misuse (continued)

PRIVACY CONCERN	DISCUSSION
14. Behavior tracking	Will there be any items within the smart meters that can act in ways similar to browser/document cookies or web bugs? If so, these items could potentially be misused in ways similar to how cookies and web bugs are currently misused. Perhaps radio frequency identification (RFID) tags can be used in some smart appliances? Perhaps GPS types of technologies?
15. Public aggregated searches revealing individual behaviors	What kind of Smart Grid data search engines will there be? What discussions or plans have occurred around this possibility? What information would be involved? What control would consumers have to not have their data included in such searches? The privacy issues would be similar to the privacy concerns that currently exist with Internet search engines, only the implications could be more wide reaching because the data would be based upon individuals' actual daily living activities, and not upon what they consciously choose to put onto the Internet.

Source: Rebecca Herold, Smart Grid Privacy Concerns, October 2009, http://www.privacyguidance.com/files/SmartGrid_PrivacyHeroldOct2009.pdf.

ways in which Smart Grid data could be used to reveal information about the lives of those using or associated with all these gadgets if proper controls are not applied.

It is important to note that each of the potential privacy risks can be sufficiently mitigated with the appropriate technical, administrative, and physical controls.

Data Communications Privacy Concerns

The manner in which Smart Grid data is communicated can also present privacy risks. There are a large number of possibilities for how Smart Grid data may be transmitted.

- The data from smart appliances, smart meters, apps, and other devices may be transmitted through utility-owned networks.
- Smart Grid device data may be sent through third-party networks via Wi-Fi, broadband, public carriers, or private licensed networks.
- Energy consumers' home area networks (HANs) and home energy management (HEM) systems may be used to send data directly to appliance vendors, energy management vendors, utilities, and Internet sites.

Each of these methods has privacy risks that must be mitigated through a wide range of controls, such as authentication, encryption, access controls, and physical controls, just to name a few. Privacy impact assessments (PIAs) should be done to determine the associated risks in each situation where energy usage data that can be attributed to specific individuals or households will be transmitted. Appropriate controls can then be implemented to address the risks. See Chapter 7 for information about mitigating privacy risks within the Smart Grid.

The Smart Grid is only smart because of the deployment of a wide range of sensors and actuators to remotely monitor and control equipment coupled with a variety of communication networks. Each network option has its pros and cons from cyber security perspectives to discourage data interception during transmission. There are many technologies, policies, and practices that can reduce the risks of unauthorized access to stored data. There are also many books already written on these topics.

In the subsequent chapters, we'll explore the most important end points and devices where energy usage data is created and privacy implications for this data. We like the concept of data owners, data custodians, and data managers* as convenient ways to think about energy usage data and other data in general, but it's important to note that this concept is unique to energy consumption data that is generated from select utilities in one state.

Customers are identified as data owners for energy usage data in a number of states. But after that, at the time this book was written, there was no standard approach or definition that describes overall privacy rights and responsibilities.

---

* In the privacy profession, and in various data protection laws throughout the world, the following terms are commonly used:

  Data protection authority (DPA): A supervisory entity chartered to enforce privacy or data protection laws and regulations.

  Data controller: An organization or individual with the authority to decide how and why information about data subjects is to be processed.

  Data processor: An organization or individual that processes data on behalf of the data controller.

  Data subject: An individual about whom information is being processed.

However, the terms shown in the text are the terms used by the California Public Utilities Commission (CPUC), and within some other parts of the U.S. energy space, so we are using them in this book instead.

Energy usage data puts significant challenges on territorial or spatial privacy. But as we'll explore in this book, the Smart Grid is just a collection of machine-to-machine (M2M) and Internet of Things (IOT) technologies and applications. Many other M2M and IOT applications create even more opportunities for risking the loss of privacy. In particular, the connected home, vehicle telematics, and location-based services on mobile devices also have real privacy implications. Some of these applications have an association with the Smart Grid, such as monitoring energy usage in the connected home, or electric vehicle (EV) charging, but other applications may have no data creation or exchange relationship to the Smart Grid, other than to draw power from it.

4

Smart Meter Data and Privacy

Meter Comparisons

Traditional meters, such as the one shown in Figure 4.1, measure electricity, gas, or water use. The most sophisticated metering technology goes into electric meters. The metrology for gas and water meters is much simpler. Why? It's a matter of power. Gas and water meters rely on battery power, and therefore are less complex in terms of the amounts of data they collect and transmit. Electric meters can

Figure 4.1 Traditional electricity meter. (From First Energy Corporation, https://www.firstenergycorp.com/content/customer/help/billingpayments/meter_reading_schedule/reading_your_meter.html.)

draw the power they need to operate from the electrified wire they are connected to. More complexity in collecting and processing data means more power is needed to perform these functions. The metrology in electric meters is based on sensors that detect current and voltage. Utility meters are considered revenue grade, meaning they are accurate enough to be trusted for financial settlements by supplying the data used to calculate consumption of what is measured for billing purposes. In other words, a meter—smart or not—is a cash register. It is the trusted transaction point for your purchase of electricity, gas, or water from a utility.

Traditional meters require a visit from a meter reader to jot down the difference in gauges (those dials shown at the "mechanical register" in Figure 4.1) from their last trip. That means someone from a utility drives up to your home, dashes over to the meter clamped on the side of your house, on a pole in your yard, or in your house or building, reads the register, jots down numbers on a chart or computer, and then dashes off again. The family dogs sometimes went ballistic over these invasions of their territory.

From a historical perspective, it is interesting to note that while smart meters may seem like new technology, the first meter designed for measuring consumption in real time to accommodate dynamic pricing was invented in the 1970s. James Kirtley and Thomas Sterling of the Massachusetts Institute of Technology (MIT) filed a smart meter patent application in November 1979 and were granted a patent in February 1982.[*] The patent was for a meter that would calculate the cost of the energy consumed over short time intervals.

In one author's (Rebecca Herold) discussion with Dr. Kirtley,[†] she discovered there were a couple of inspirations for the invention at that point in time.

1. The leader of the MIT research group, Dr. Fred Schweppe, was concerned with privacy, and indicated a desire that any real-time pricing meter should limit the ability of utilities to accumulate detailed consumption data for each time interval.

---

[*] See http://patft.uspto.gov/netacgi/nph-Parser?Sect1=PTO1&Sect2=HITOFF&d=PALL&p=1&u=%2Fnetahtml%2FPTO%2Fsrchnum.htm&r=1&f=G&l=50&s1=4317175.PN.&OS=PN/4317175&RS=PN/4317175.

[†] In a phone discussion with James Kirtley and Ken Wacks on April 4, 2014.

2. Dr. Kirtley indicated he was thinking more about issues related to data rates than about privacy. There was no widespread Internet in 1978, and available communications technologies were very immature. The smart meter invention allowed time-varying rates for electricity to be downloaded into the meter by the utility. The meter measured consumption during the time interval when a rate was in effect and applied that rate to calculate the cost. The reason for doing the calculations in the meter was to minimize data traffic, which was relatively expensive then.*

See the first of four diagrams of the invention in Figure 4.2. When asked how the invention was received at that time by the utilities, Dr. Kirtley told Rebecca, "The industry folks said, uniformly, that we were idiots, because they thought it [the meter invented] wasn't usable." As we can see now, it took close to 30 years before a smart meter would be practical and deployed for residential use.

One of the authors, Christine Hertzog, lives in a neighborhood that has had smart electric and gas meters since 2009. There's no meter reader entering the backyard anymore to conduct a monthly read. The water meter, which is definitely not smart, still requires someone to come out to the sidewalk meter vault, lift a heavy cover, and peer down to read consumption information. That cover isn't secure, so anyone could lift it and read the numbers.

AMR Metering

Meter technology called automated meter reading (AMR) is one evolutionary step away from smart meters. AMR enables specially equipped vehicles to pick up stored data that is transmitted wirelessly to the vehicle driving by or an individual walking by to create the bills for usage. Collection of data only occurs when the right receiver is within the physical range of meter transmitters equipped to communicate with that receiver. Each meter has to be "polled" to transmit the latest consumption data, which cover the time period since the last poll.

---

* See more about the concept in a paper by the inventors entitled "Impact of New Electronic Technologies to the Customer End of Distribution Automation and Control" (Kirtley et al.).

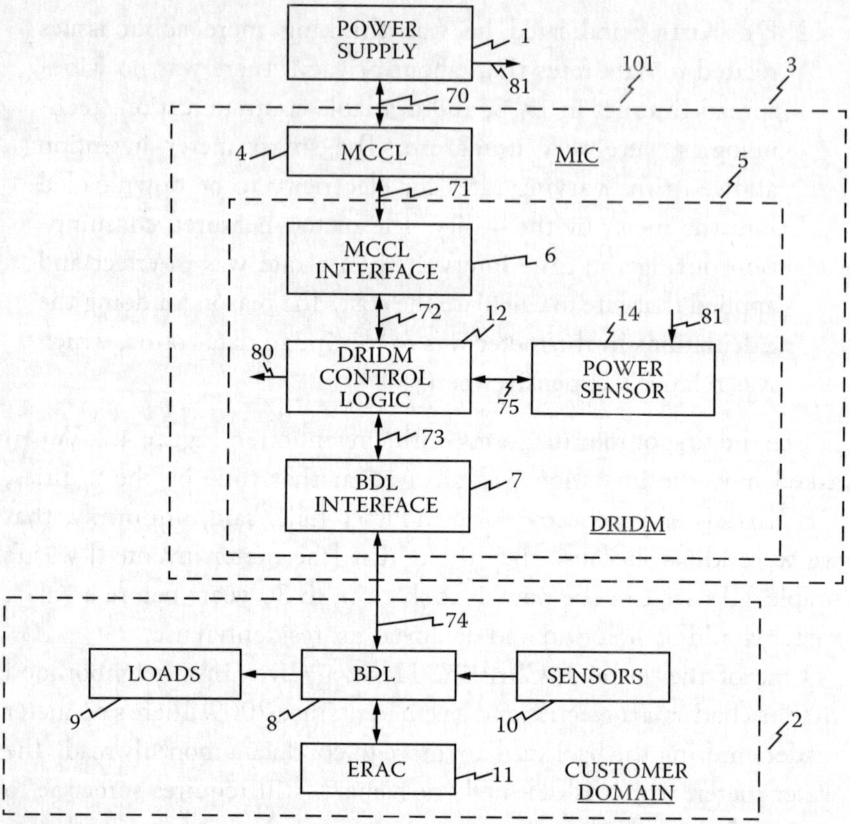

Figure 4.2 The first of four diagrams in the first "smart meter" patent by Kirtley and Sterling. (See all four meter diagrams from the patent filing at http://www.google.com/patents/US4317175, and also at http://patft.uspto.gov/netacgi/nph-Parser?Sect1=PTO1&Sect2=HITOFF&d=PALL&p=1&u=%2Fnetahtml%2FPTO%2Fsrchnum.htm&r=1&f=G&l=50&s1=4317175.PN.&OS=PN/4317175&RS=PN/4317175.) (From U.S. Patent US 4317175 A.)

Smart Meters Overview

Smart meters have communications technology—wired or wireless—that can transmit data on a more frequent basis than once a month or whenever a drive-by AMR-style meter read takes place. This communications technology accompanies the same metrology that existed in traditional, electromechanical meters. Smart meters are part of an advanced metering infrastructure (AMI) that includes the revenue-grade meters, data collection equipment, and communications equipment needed to exchange data with a utility. Figure 4.3 shows an example of a typical smart meter.

Figure 4.3 Smart meter example. (From PG&E, see http://www.pgecurrents.com/2012/06/12/pge-catches-wave-on-smartmeter-deployments/.)

The time and fuel savings eliminated in manual or AMR meter reading is significant.* It results in reduced miles driven and subsequent reductions in carbon emissions as well as improved productivity, as meter readers can focus on the "outlier" meters.

Smart meters can provide more data than previously collected by traditional electromechanical meters as kilowatt-hours (kWh) or consumed electricity. The typical residential smart meter gathers the following data:

- Instantaneous voltage
- Instantaneous current
- Peak voltage/current
- System frequency
- Root mean square (RMS) voltage/current
- Phase displacement

* Examples of utility savings: http://www.clarkpublicutilities.com/index.cfm/payment-options/about-your-bill/meter-reading/remote-meter-reading/ and https://smartgrid.gov/sites/default/files/doc/files/Central%20Maine%20Power%20Case%20Study_0.pdf.

- Power factor
- Instantaneous apparent power
- Instantaneous real power
- Instantaneous reactive power
- Energy use/production
- Harmonic voltage distortion
- Total harmonic distortion*

Smart meters are collections of sensors with some data storage and communications capabilities. They measure the current coursing through a wire, record readings at specific time intervals, store some meter usage data (from 1 day to 1 month is typical in the United States), and communicate the meter data, along with the code that represents the meter, to utilities.

Smart meters can also be enabled to communicate on the "other side of the meter," or inside a home or business. For residential environments, some typical protocols for a home area network (HAN) are ZigBee, Z-Wave, or HomePlug. There is a variety of communications protocols in place for communications with the other side of the meter for commercial and industrial environments too. We'll briefly discuss some of the types of signaling that could occur from smart meters to devices in a home, but more substantial discussion will be reserved for Chapter 5 on the connected home.

Signaling Types

In the United States smart meters must comply with American National Standards Institute (ANSI)† C12.19 standards for meter data structure—in other words, establishing a common structure for what is collected. Meter data is typically defined in terms of tables. Different standards are in place for Europe (DLMS/COSEM) and

* http://breakingenergy.com/2013/07/24/the-true-roi-of-smart-meter-deployments/.

† The American National Standards Institute is a standards development organization (SDO) that creates standards through a consensus-based process. The C12.19 standard's participating entities included utilities, meter manufacturers, automated meter reading service companies, ANSI, Measurement Canada (for Industry Canada), National Electrical Manufacturers Association (NEMA), Institute of Electrical and Electronics Engineers (IEEE), Utilimetrics, and other interested parties.

Asia (DLT/645 is used in China), but with the same principle in mind—to structure the data tables.

Depending on the manufacturer, meters can also provide data about power quality or tamper detection. The list above describing smart meter data includes measurements for power quality, which helps identify power surges and sags that can be harmful to devices that rely on a steady source of power. It's a valuable source of data that was previously not available in the vast majority of meters since it can provide measurements more than once a month. This data can help utilities diagnose the "health of the grid" and, in particular, the flow of electricity into the smart meter.

Many utilities are utilizing smart meters to deliver much more granular sensing of voltages in their distribution grids. Commonly known as conservation voltage reduction (CVR) regulation, smart meters serve as the sensors to communicate voltage levels. Before smart meters, utilities had much less visibility into their distribution grid operations. They managed by oversupply to ensure that the last meter on a circuit had sufficient power. However, smart meters can communicate details about voltages, and this data allows utilities to modulate power in the grid much more effectively. Utilities can reduce overall power needs—often to the tune of millions of dollars in annual savings.*

The data about energy usage or generation is what is most visible and useful to consumers, since it supplies the data that measures kilowatt-hours (kWh) and is used for billing. Other specialized meters collect similar data about natural gas or water consumption.† Some of these are smart too—meaning they have the ability to remotely communicate measurements.

Smart Meter Communications Capabilities

Drilling down into the communications capabilities of the smart meter, there are a couple of deployment options that utilities consider.

* http://www.elp.com/articles/2013/09/report-smart-meters-offer-multiple-benefits-to-utilities-customers.html and https://www.smartgrid.gov/files/doc/files/SGIG_progress_report_2013.pdf and http://www.intelligentutility.com/article/13/06/time-take-second-look-conservation-voltage-regulation.

† Gas is typically measured in therms; water is measured in 100 cubic feet or CCF units.

Every smart meter has a communications card that connects to the external world via the utility's wireless or wired network that supports the distribution grid. The external communications connection can be wired using power line carrier (PLC) technology. This means that the communication signal is carried in the same wire that is supplying electricity. Smart meters also have the ability to communicate on the other side of the meter to a HAN, which is discussed in more detail in Chapter 5 on the connected home.

Smart meters are a collection of sensors. In addition to sensing voltage or current, smart meters can also serve as actuators, or devices that have a control capability. For instance, a smart meter can be remotely connected and disconnected and automatically send messages about service outages. That means that consumers with smart meters no longer have to wait for a field technician to arrive to turn electric service on or off for relocations; this can be done remotely by the utility. For utilities, smart meters can alert them to outages the moment they occur and reduce the time that homes and businesses are without electric service. With traditional meters, utilities don't know there's a problem until someone calls in with a service complaint. Smart meters collect much more data about usage because they have digital storage, and smart meters can provide data on a much more frequent basis than the traditional meter reads.

This increased data collection delivers more granular awareness about energy usage. What granularity really means is that you can obtain a more detailed graph of electricity usage over the course of an hour or a day or week than what would be available from a simple monthly read of total kWh. It's important to note that many of today's commercial meters installed on office buildings and factories have these communications capabilities and collect the same power quality data that is now collected for residential dwellings. These commercial meters have been "smart" for a number of years. But these are also more expensive meters because they typically are polyphase meters—measuring three phases of electricity. So are smart meters really new? The answer is yes when it comes to the meters now deployed in residential buildings, which are sometimes called single-phase meters. Because single-family homes and many multiunit residential buildings operate on a one meter per home allocation, the granularity of consumption (and production) data merits discussion about the privacy risks associated with the use of and access to that data.

Smart Meter Data Read Frequency

In the past, the typical U.S. electric utility collected consumption data from a meter 12 times a year—12 data points. Now, smart meters have the ability to collect and transmit data as often as once a minute or less.* Even at meter data collection at 15-minute intervals, a utility would gather 3,000 reads (or receipts of data) per meter per month. At the time of this writing, the authors could not find a U.S.-based utility that had shown an appetite for collecting data from every meter at more than a 15-minute interval, which would create significant strains on the communications infrastructure and internal utility systems to manage and store all this data.

However, it is possible that utilities would selectively and temporarily examine the power quality meter data on a more granular basis to conduct diagnostics for customers who experience service issues. More granular data could detect power surges or sags that can damage sensitive electronics in appliances and computers. It is also possible that utilities could schedule more granular meter reads for selected meters in order to obtain more fine-grained consumption knowledge. We'll explore that more in Chapter 5 on the connected home.

Smart Meter Data Granularity

The granularity of meter consumption data can create insights into activities within a dwelling. For instance, the well-known graph in Figure 4.4 offers an interesting distillation of appliance activity from a study done by Elias Leak Quinn where he established ongoing surveillance of a traditional electric meter. The attribution of specific appliance activity does not come from the meter itself, which collects

* Regulatory policies often dictate the frequency of data collection. In the United States, the typical utility collection frequency is around once per hour, although some utilities have permission to obtain data on 15-minute intervals. Realistically, any utility could overwhelm its data management capabilities if it sought to collect data on residential meters at a read per minute. Some utilities could have issues managing data collected on an hourly basis.

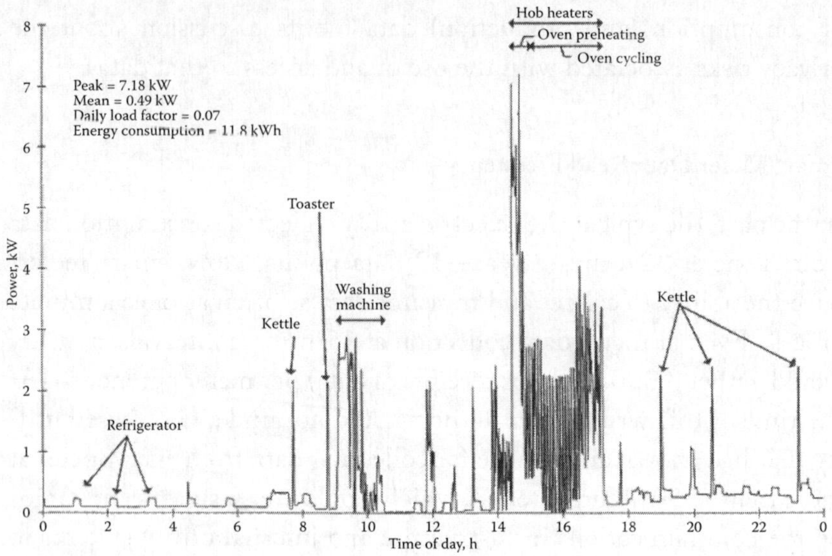

Figure 4.4 Activities shown by energy usage. (From Elias Leake Quinn, Smart Metering and Privacy: Existing Law and Competing Policies, Spring 2009, p. 3, http://www.dora.state.co.us/puc/DocketsDecisions/DocketFilings/09I-593EG/09I-593EG_Spring2009Report-Smart GridPrivacy.pdf.)

an aggregation of consumption data at the point of the meter outside of the house. The identification of specific appliance activity in this chart occurs because of specialized technologies or algorithms that *disaggregate* that electric current into the specific amounts used by them. This disaggregation is possible because each appliance has a unique electricity signature in the amount of power drawn from a meter. Without the technology or disaggregation algorithms, educated guesses would need to substitute for accurate appliance identification when working solely with smart meter data.

What's missing from smart meter data now? Personal information, such as the name of the person paying the bill associated with that meter, or the address of that person. Why? The reasons are not about privacy, although that is a welcome beneficiary of them. The reasons have to do with payload and relevance. Information theory* focuses on minimization of the amount of data that needs to be sent in a transmission. The most important data is the data that identifies a

* Claude Shannon's paper, "A Mathematical Theory of Communications," has been called the "Magna Carta of the information age." Read it at http://cm.bell-labs.com/cm/ms/what/shannonday/shannon1948.pdf.

change—such as the total kWh drawn or the price of electricity.[*] The bigger the message, the more power that's needed to transmit it, and the more capacity that is needed in the network. With apologies to Mr. Shannon, think of it as a transport decision. If you have to go to the grocery store to purchase a bar of soap and quart of milk, do you need a huge cargo truck or a smart car? Obviously, the smart car will take less energy to get to and from the store, and it takes up less space on the roads, which means more cars can also use the highway. This is a key practice in Shannon's information theory—keep the data to a minimum to optimize the bandwidth.

There's no provision in meter data standards for transmission of traditional personal information. A unique meter identification (ID) is associated with the person who has established a customer relationship with the utility. This unique meter ID is a code that serves as the shorthand identification of the customer. The unique meter ID is matched to data about the customer once it has been transmitted back to a utility's billing operations. It is extremely important that utilities protect the personal customer data that is collected for their operations, including the association between the meter IDs and customers, but this data is not contained within smart meter communications themselves.

There's another key point to the data that is collected and transmitted by smart meters. Most of the meter manufacturers operating in the United States have standard encryption capabilities for data. They use 128-bit Advanced Encryption Standard (AES-128),[†] which is also widely used in a variety of other products. A number of utilities note that they are encrypting meter data within the AMI networks, including Pacific Gas & Electric (PG&E), CenterPoint Energy, and Florida Power & Light (FPL).[‡] However, other countries may require

---

[*] Pricing information is useful for dynamic pricing and time of use (TOU) tariff structures. This information could be communicated via a meter to smart appliances.

[†] http://csrc.nist.gov/publications/fips/fips197/fips-197.pdf.

[‡] PG&E, http://www.pge.com/en/myhome/customerservice/smartmeter/howitworks/index.page; Centerpoint, http://www.centerpointenergy.com/staticfiles/CNP/Common/SiteAssets/doc/123062_%20SmartMeterDataSecurity.pdf; FPL, http://www.fpl.com/energysmart/pdf/facts_about_smart_meters_and_privacy.pdf.

encryption. For example, the Netherlands requires that selected smart meter data must be encrypted.*

Energy Savings Initiatives

The old adage that *knowledge is power* is literally true about the results of collection and feedback of consumption data on energy or water use. A number of studies† have shown that once people are aware of how and when they use electricity, they are more likely to take steps to reduce the use of it. This recognition of the power of knowledge coupled with a feedback loop spurred development of a couple of interesting initiatives that involve energy data owners, custodians, and managers. The bottom line is that data can be correlated from a number of sources and analyzed to create meaningful information for the owners of the energy usage data. As we'll discuss later, data has significant monetary value to many entities.

Green Button Initiative

The Green Button initiative leverages the purpose and use of smart meter data.‡ The objective of this 2011 federal government initiative is to offer utility customers easy access to their electricity usage data. It is modeled on the popular Blue Button§ program that first made military veterans' medical data easily available for them to download, view, and share with medical resources. The data is organized in a standard machine-readable file format that can be shared by the data owner with third-party entities (data managers) of the owner's choosing to turn into visual displays and applications that help the data owner manage his or her electricity consumption. The common data format lets application developers build one interface that will work

* See more about this in EN 13757-x at www.cenelec.eu, and also http://oms-group.org/en/standard-sources/.

† www.scientificamerica.com/article/do-smart-meters-mean-smart-electricity-use/.

‡ http://www.data.gov/energy/page/welcome-green-button.

§ http://bluebuttondata.org. Since its inception, a growing number of private sector organizations are also implementing similar programs for their medical services consumers.

with the energy usage data across all utilities that agree to participate in the Green Button program.

This data is available in some states now, and a growing number of utilities are supporting this initiative.* For consumers, detailed data about how and when they use electricity can influence decisions about how to save money on electric bills, identify appliances that are energy hogs and potential savings through use of more energy efficient models, or even build business cases for energy efficiency renovations or investments in distributed energy resources (DERs) like solar photovoltaic (PV). The granularity of this data is unique. Instead of a single number identifying the kilowatt-hours consumed last month, consumers can see usage at daily, hourly, or smaller increments of time.

Figure 4.5 shows the major classes of data supplied by meters in the Green Button format.

The Green Button initiative is based on the premise that energy usage data has real value to consumers. Each consumer's electrical usage data belongs to that consumer, and consumers may opt to share their data with companies (data managers) that offer information services or products. Information services may create comparisons

Data Class	Description
UsagePoint	The location of measurements—a meter or submeter, or individual load or appliance
ReadingType	The type of measurement contained in MeterReading
MeterReading	A collection of the same ReadingType measurements
LocalTimeParameters	A universally recognized time stamp to ensure time has the same meaning for all measurements
IntervalReading	A single measurement that may include cost or quality
IntervalBlock	A collection of IntervalReadings, usually by day, week, or month
ElectricPowerUsageSummary	A summary of measurements for a specific period of time
ElectricPowerQualitySummary	A summary of statistics about power quality for a specific period of time

Figure 4.5 Green Button data classes. (From http://en.openei.org/wiki/Green_Button.)

* http://en.openei.org/wiki/Green_Button.

of electricity usage with anonymous peers (usually based on demographic, geographic, and property information) or offer recommendations on how to reduce electricity use. The services include web-based and mobile apps, offering a wide range of information options for consumers. Products may include smart plugs or more energy efficient appliances.

The federal government has promoted private sector development of applications that leverage Green Button data through a challenge* in 2012 that offered monetary prizes to the best solutions. There's significant potential for applications that can go beyond simply tracking existing energy usage. Green Button data can be combined by authorized data managers with other data to analyze the value of rooftop solar panels or electric vehicles for individual consumers, or to identify local utility rebates that consumers can claim to help reduce overall energy costs through investments in energy-efficient appliances or building upgrades. Smart Grid-enabling technologies like smart meters and Green Button apps create new data, and new information based on this data. That information has value to consumers, utilities, and a range of other entities.

Perhaps energy usage data will enjoy an evolution similar to that seen for credit card data. Once upon a time, we simply received our monthly bill with itemized expenses. Then credit card companies started summarizing those monthly expenditures into categories, and sent annual reports about spending patterns. The summary reports helped consumers understand exactly how much money over the course of a year was spent on dining or entertainment or fuel. That is powerful information that can shape budgets and spending habits. The same logic can be applied to energy usage habits and decisions.

Green Button data also serves to illustrate the roles of data ownership, custodianship, and management. Green Button data is owned by the consumer. The local utility supporting Green Button is a custodian of this data. The investor-owned utilities (IOUs) follow the privacy and security mandates for this data as defined by their state regulatory agency. A third party or service provider selected by the data owner to receive Green Button data becomes a data manager.

* http://appsforenergy.challengepost.com.

A key point is that there is not one national data privacy policy that covers all the roles.

For instance, if the California-based author, Christine, chooses the Best Data Company to receive her Green Button data, that triggers notification to her local utility, the data custodian, that she authorizes it to allow Best Data Company to access and receive her data on a one-time or ongoing basis. Best Data Company is now a manager of her data. In California, even when the data has crossed the utility boundary to Best Data Company, the utility's data privacy policy is in force for her data. Her consumption data cannot be sold by Best Data Company. However, if she directly hands her data over to a third party without her utility's involvement, then these privacy safeguards no longer apply; but if the third party has a privacy policy in place, it will apply.

This is an important point: many consumers may not be aware this data can cross boundaries and be subjected to different public utility commission (PUC) privacy policies. California serves as a good example of requiring legal privacy protections for energy usage data. The California Public Utilities Commission (CPUC) has been very supportive of the Green Button initiative and a follow-on project called Green Button Connect, which we'll explore below.

Green Button Connect

Green Button Connect is an extension of the initial White House Green Button initiative.* The Connect project encourages utilities to make it procedurally and uniformly easy for consumers to provide authorization to release data to their selected third parties. Large organizations like utilities can create unintended complexity for consumers to complete a service request that authorizes their selected data manager to receive their Green Button data. Green Button Connect defines a standard process to request data and authorize data managers to access Green Button data on behalf of the data owner. Green Button Connect does not create new energy usage data; it makes it easier for consumers to get access to this data. However, as noted above, if the utility has not been involved as a data custodian, this data is now at the mercy of the

* See http://www.whitehouse.gov/blog/2013/12/05/expanded-green-button-will-reach-federal-agencies-and-more-american-energy-consumers.

privacy policy in place at the third party selected by the consumer (the data owner) and any other applicable privacy laws for that location.

The CPUC, in collaboration with its three IOUs and other interested parties, created Decision 13-09-025,* issued September 19, 2013, that requires that the third-party companies that seek to become Green Button data managers must comply with the same requirements for privacy and security that apply to the regulated utilities themselves. Utilities, as data custodians, have a defined process to follow if a third party is identified or suspected of data abuse. Most importantly, if a consumer believes his or her privacy has been compromised by a third party with access to the energy usage data, a request to the utility to terminate that third party's authorized access can occur immediately.

One California utility, San Diego Gas and Electric (SDG&E), relies on the TRUSTed Smart Grid Privacy Program† for the Green Button Connect program. TRUSTed is "a self-regulatory program that certifies that companies use responsible privacy practices as they collect and share consumer smart grid data." This program was developed by the Future of Privacy Forum in collaboration with TRUSTe‡ and is somewhat similar to an Underwriters Laboratories (UL) approval or a Good Housekeeping seal of approval. The privacy certification must be annually renewed. This program requires that data owners (consumers) be notified of any security incidents that could impact or result in a privacy breach.

Like any other data, energy usage data should have privacy protections. Given that this data is new and there's little experience with it, we should expect that consumers won't always know who is responsible for the security and privacy of the data that they have made available to utilities and third parties. Consumer education is essential to help data owners understand the chain of data custody and what privacy safeguards exist if data is transferred from a utility to a third party, or from the consumer directly to a third party without utility involvement.

---

* Available for download at www.cpuc.ca.gov/PUC/energy/smartgrid.htm.

† http://www.sdge.com/newsroom/press-releases/2013-01-27/powertools-app-helps-sdge-customers-manage-save-energy.

‡ See http://www.truste.com/privacy-program-requirements/TRUSTed-smart-grid/.

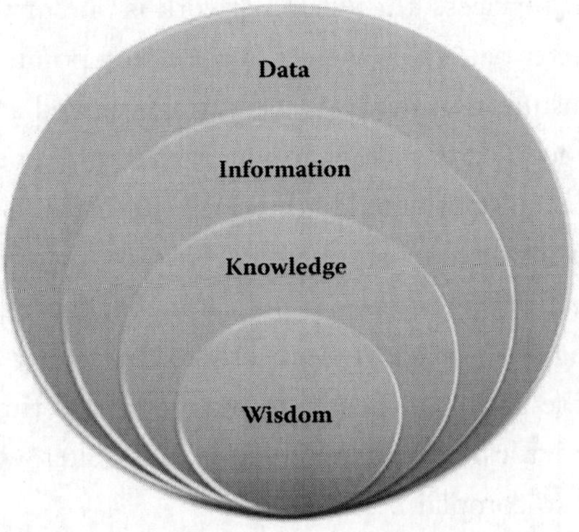

Figure 4.6 The value of data.

California is very interested in making energy usage data available for academic research. The CPUC is actively working on developing data practices and policies that make energy usage data available while protecting consumer privacy. The CPUC rules indicate that if data has identifiable characteristics removed, it can be available for research use without individual consumer consent. Data privacy practices of anonymization and aggregation will factor in to these policies and guidelines. As we noted before, knowledge is power.

Figure 4.6 puts it another way. Data is the starting point for us to learn how to manage our energy usage as intelligently as possible. Applications that illustrate when and what our energy usage is can be as helpful as reports that summarize spending categories and manage financial budgets.

AMI Networks

Let's briefly review the networks that transmit smart meter data. These are sometimes called advanced metering infrastructure (AMI)* networks. The typical utility has several networks that are deployed

* From the *Smart Grid Dictionary*: "Electricity meters, bi-directional communications network hardware and software, and associated system and data management software that measures and records usage data at set intervals, and provides usage data to consumers, utilities, and other parties at set intervals. The set intervals are specified by regulatory agencies."

for specialized services. The AMI network is one of them. It transports smart meter data from meters to collection points where routine data—like consumption data—is usually aggregated and then transmitted on a scheduled basis back to a utility's central operations. Some smart meter data is considered high priority and sent in real time back to a utility for immediate action. High-priority data includes a "last gasp" message from a meter—an indicator that there's a service disruption causing a cessation of electricity to that meter. Smart meters give utilities the ability to detect an outage in real time and initiate restoration activities immediately—not hours later when impacted customers call to complain.

AMI networks are bidirectional. Utilities can send messages or commands to smart meters as well as receive data. One useful command is to activate or connect a meter. This simple command eliminates countless hours spent waiting for the utility service representative to arrive and start the flow of electricity into a new home or apartment. This same functionality lets utilities determine if restoration services have been successful in returning all affected customers to full power.

This bidirectional network functionality has real promise for transactive energy. It is technically possible for a utility to send price signals to the meter, and then into a building to any appliances or other devices that are capable of receiving that signal. This "prices to devices" scenario is discussed as a means to automate decisions about when to use electricity. It is intriguing, but as of mid-2014, there were only a few pilots exploring this capability. There are a number of reasons, but from a technology perspective, it's a chicken-and-egg dilemma. If there isn't a communications capability from the utility, then there's no need for electricity-consuming devices to have communications functionality to a utility. And if the devices lack communications capabilities, there's no need to build utility networks that can send signals to them.

The introductions of smart appliances and smart plugs are changing this situation. However, in many instances, there's little or no reliance on a utility network to communicate pricing information. The communications are occurring over cellular, broadband, and Wi-Fi networks that may not belong to utilities. Smart meters could be one gateway to data exchanges of consumption data, but other gateways are proposed by companies including AT&T, Comcast, Google, and Apple.*

Smart Meter Data Summary

In summary, smart meters and their AMI networks do collect and transmit energy usage data and voltage measurements. Green Button data enables electricity customers to get more detailed information about their consumption that can help them save money. It's a voluntary, opt-in program where the customer controls who gets access to his or her data.

Once smart meter data is transmitted back to a utility, what happens to it? There are several utility software applications that use data from smart meters, as well as traditional, noncommunicating meters. Meter data management systems (MDMSs) are specialized software applications that handle the volumes of data that are derived from smart meters. At a high level, MDMS applications generally include a data repository that holds meter reads, events such as outage and restoration with time stamps, and support audit trails to document any data updates or changes. MDMS applications excel at managing large volumes of data, and smart meters can create significant amounts of data. As of mid-2014, no U.S.-based utility was collecting smart meter data at a smaller time increment than 15 minutes. That translates into 35,040 annual data collection events per smart meter.

MDMS applications also perform validation, estimation, and editing (VEE) of meter read data. These functions help ensure the accuracy of meter data, which is vital for utility bill calculations. Some MDMS applications offer additional analytics capabilities on energy usage data. Some MDMS applications have personal information, such as customer name or address; others just reference unique meter IDs to associate consumption with a particular meter.

* See their corporate websites for more information: https://my-digitallife.att.com/learn/ and http://corporate.comcast.com/news-information/news-feed/comcast-launches-new-xfinity-home-control-and-energy-management-service-2.

Other utility systems may not contain detailed energy usage data, but generally do contain personal information such as name, address, and even financial data. The customer information system (CIS) and customer relationship management (CRM) applications are a couple of these applications. Another is the utility billing application that generates the monthly bills consumers receive for electricity, gas, or water. These applications generally hold the customer name, address, and depending on which system is in play, financial information. Some utilities own these applications and keep all data within logical utility boundaries as defined by their data networks.

Utilities may outsource some of these capabilities to third parties and allow consumer data (that could range from smart meter data to automated payment data) to leave the utility's computer systems and communications networks and travel across public networks to non-utility destinations. To be clear, outsourcing functions like customer service or billing is a standard practice across many business sectors. Many businesses are migrating to cloud-based solutions that are definitely outside of their logical perimeters, meaning that sometimes sensitive data resides outside of their direct control. What we want to point out is that energy usage data could end up outside of a utility's controlled domain of computers and communication networks.

Smart meters produce more data, there's no question about that. Smart meter data has many privacy protections, with a number of states clearly stating that the consumer is the data owner of the data coming from the smart meters. This is not the case with most location-based services. There are legitimately beneficial reasons for consumers to have their energy usage data correlated with other data and analyzed to bring about changes in energy use that reduce costs and carbon footprints. However, to conform with generally accepted privacy principles, all entities accessing, using, and possessing smart data meters should be held accountable for protecting the data, and not using the data beyond what the data owner has authorized.

Utilities and any third parties that have custodianship or management of energy usage data or any other sensitive data, such as personal information, need to exercise all required precautions for physical and cyber security and privacy. Mapping and auditing the communications and computer facilities where data travels and resides is extremely important to ensure the privacy of the data owners.

5

The Connected Home

Smart Grid technologies embed new sensing, control, and communications technologies into utility networks and devices. The same technologies can also be incorporated in the networks and devices found in homes, businesses, and factories. In many cases, they already are. The *connected home*[*] is a convenient term to describe the burgeoning applications that can improve security and quality of life and reduce operating costs for people in a dwelling. Some people also call it a *smart home*. By either term, it consists of communications networks and communications-enabled devices or equipment, most notably appliances, electronics equipment, and sensored (sensor-equipped) home structures, and depending on the solution and degree of sophistication, it may be controlled remotely. Figure 5.1 illustrates the main consumption domains. This chapter focuses on the activity in the residential or home domain.

Home Area Networks

Commercial and industrial buildings have interior communications networks that serve the same purpose as home area networks (HANs).[†] A HAN, as its name describes, is a network in your home. It is also a gateway for connection to the outside world. You may have one today in the form of a wireless router that connects your laptops, printers, tablets, smart phones, and entertainment devices to the Internet. As

[*] See more about connected homes at http://solartoday.org/2014/06/interest-in-connected-home-and-alternative-energy-solutions-to-increase-six-fold-accenture-research-shows/.

[†] These may be specialized M2M networks called building automation systems (BASs) or energy management systems (EMSs) to manage HVAC, lighting, and other building services separately from networks that transmit human communications. In factories, these networks typically monitor and manage processes.

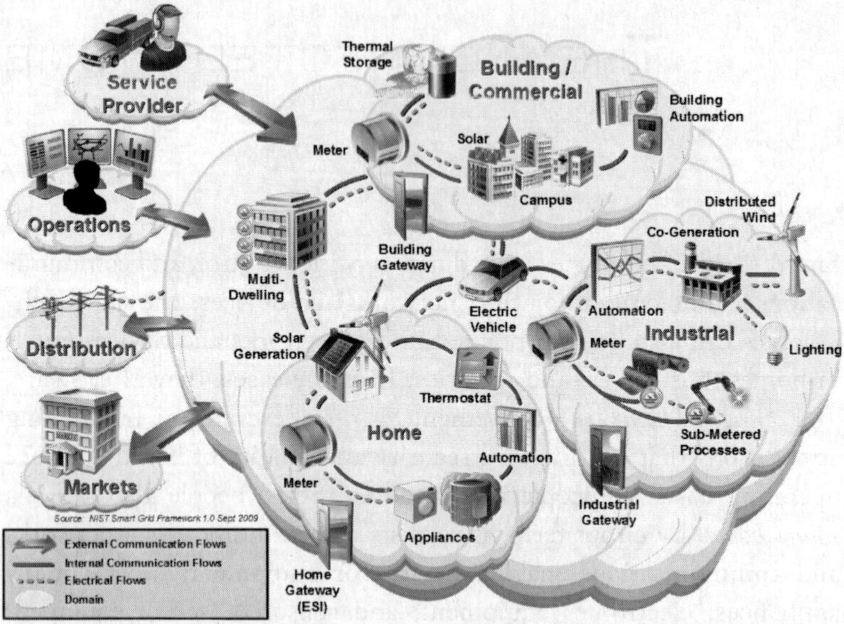

Figure 5.1 Smart Grid domains. (From Report to NIST on the Smart Grid Interoperability Standards Roadmap, Electric Power Research Institute (EPRI), Palo Alto, CA, 2009.)

(mostly) wireless technologies proliferate in North American homes* in the form of Wi-Fi† routers for computers, laptops, tablets, and other mobile devices, similar technologies can enable home thermostats, clothes dryers, hot water heaters, and other appliances outfitted to communicate within the home and with the outside world.

* Power line carrier (PLC) technology uses the electrical wiring to send communications. It is more commonly used in Europe than in the United States.

† From the *Smart Grid Dictionary*: "An IEEE (Institute of Electrical and Electronics Engineers) standard 802.11 that refers to a family of specifications developed by the IEEE for wireless LAN technologies that use unlicensed radio spectrum. The term Wi-Fi initially described operations in the 2.4-GHz band, but the term has also been applied to unlicensed wireless devices operating in the 5-GHz band in accordance with IEEE 802.11a. Wi-Fi technologies may also work in licensed spectrum. The FCC (Federal Communications Commission) does not require devices operating in unlicensed spectrum to meet the IEEE standards. The IEEE 802.11i standard addresses security issues with Wi-Fi."

HANs connect energy management devices (like programmable communicating thermostats (PCTs)*), consumer electronics, appliances, and energy management applications inside the home.† A HAN in a smart home logically connects devices that can be remotely monitored and controlled, and communicates status between devices and a homeowner. The key common capability is that all devices in a HAN are communications enabled or "smart." Therefore, a refrigerator may be drawing electricity, but unless it is equipped with an ability to transmit or receive communications through either "in skins" or built-in communication capabilities or an external smart plug,‡ it won't appear as a connected device in your HAN. Your HAN could be your gateway to the Internet for bidirectional communications to the rest of the world and will be discussed later in this chapter. Communication that occurs solely between devices is also known as machine-to-machine (M2M) communications, and in many aspects a HAN is an example of M2M.

This book won't explore the technological pros and cons of each HAN communications technology or protocol. Other books debate the distinctions between wireless and wired signaling technologies for home automation.§ Regardless of the communications scenario, here's a key point. There is data that can be created by devices and carried by a HAN. Communication options and their standards and protocols offer different degrees of security of data, and different mechanisms (technical, physical, and administrative) for securing the data. While good security is integral to data privacy protection, our discussion in

* From the *Smart Grid Dictionary*: "A thermostat that controls HVAC components based on consumer time and temperature preferences. It may communicate with a smart meter or a smartphone. PCTs may be used to deliver automated participation in demand response programs."

† From the *Smart Grid Dictionary*: "A network of energy management devices, digital consumer electronics, signal-controlled or enabled appliances, and applications within a home environment that is on the home side of the electric meter. It is similar to a home-based LAN, but it connects more than personal electronics like computers, printers, and TVs. HAN specifications include OSHAN, ZigBee, HomePlug, Z-Wave and Wireless M-Bus (a wireless variant of M-Bus)."

‡ From the *Smart Grid Dictionary*: "Hardware that enables remote monitoring and control of devices in homes or businesses. It retrofits existing 120V AC wall outlets with (typically wireless) communications capabilities."

§ Here are some of the other contenders for home automation: 6LoWPAN, LonWorks, Wi-Fi, FlexNet.

this chapter remains focused on the policies and practices that govern energy usage data. Chapter 8 includes discussion of the security methods that can be used to secure energy usage and production data. Key points to consider in any communications scenario are the ownership, custodianship, and management of energy usage data, because they have significant impact on the privacy risks accompanying this data, but are too often overlooked after the security controls have been established.

Communications Options

With regard to ownership, custodianship, and management of energy usage data, there are two primary communications scenarios to connect HANs to the external world. The first option is utility-based communications. In this scenario, utility networks carry data back and forth between the HAN and the utility head end.* Utility-based communications may use the smart meter as the transmitter and receiver to relay messages between the utility and the devices connected to a HAN (i.e., the gateway.) A smart meter that can serve as a gateway has two wireless radio communications chips. One chip enables communications between the utility and the meter. The second chip enables communications between the meter and the HAN, or directly with devices in the home that are enabled to transmit and receive data. At the time of this writing, only a small percentage of all the smart meters in the United States have an activated second chip. The vast majority of installed smart meters do not have an active communications channel established in the home.† Utility-based communications may also use some other communications platform. What makes them utility based is that the electric utility owns and manages the communications between the HAN and the utility.

The second category covers broadband service providers such as AT&T, Verizon, Comcast, and some alarm companies. These companies provide home automation services and home security services

* The head end is industry jargon to denote the centralized reception point for data that is behind the utility (or other entity's) logical firewall protecting its operations.

† The reasons are generally summarized as an absence of a predominant home automation standard and a paucity of utility services that can leverage communications capabilities inside residential dwellings.

along with their traditional voice, Internet, and cable TV services. You may have seen the ads about remotely monitoring or adjusting thermostats to enhance comfort or save money. The gateway device into the home that supports these capabilities is not a smart meter, nor is it owned and controlled by the electric utility. It is a broadband router or other network device that functions as a hub for these services in the home.

Home Energy Management Systems

Home energy management systems (HEMSs) are software applications that display information about a home's energy consumption and may also provide control capabilities for devices that are capable of being managed by it. Some HEMS solutions also bundle in specialized hardware such as programmable communicating thermostats (PCTs) or smart plugs. HEMSs leverage the communications capabilities of a HAN. HEMSs are fairly new solutions with little standardization, and there's a wide range of vendors that provide varying features and functionality. We'll discuss HEMS solutions in general terms and avoid any comparisons of them.

Your home might already have a programmable thermostat. You can define and modify the timing for heating or air conditioning to occur, and the temperature setting for that heating or cooling. With a PCT and an interface with a HEMS solution, you can do that programming from a laptop, tablet, or smart phone. Your connection could be a HAN, a utility-supplied interface with the local grid, or the Internet via a third-party solution from a cable provider.

HEMSs often start as a software solution that controls a PCT since heating, ventilation, and air conditioning (HVAC) is the largest use of electricity or gas in the average residential building.* The solution could be part of an offering from a company that you authorize to work with your Green Button data. HEMSs are targeted to residential buildings, and typically single-family use. Similar management systems called building energy management systems (BEMSs) or simply energy management systems (EMSs) provide similar functions

* HVAC loads are also predominant for most commercial buildings, but we'll focus on residential buildings in this discussion.

for commercial buildings or multifamily housing such as apartment buildings. Given the focus on the privacy risks related to energy usage data, most of our discussion will address HEMSs and the single- and multifamily residential market sectors, which have the most apparent privacy-related risks. However, there are still risks for other types of locations and buildings. These are discussed in the next sections of this chapter.

HEMS Adoption

Today, HEMS applications are still in early adoption stages. There are many reasons that these applications are slow to achieve mass popularity, but two important reasons are: (1) a lack of common communications standards or protocols between consumer products such as appliances and electronic devices, and (2) lack of common communications standards or protocols between those devices and the grid. According to Chris Kotting, executive director of the Energy Information Standards Alliance (EIS Alliance), "The development of a common expression of fundamental or abstract information for Home Energy Management Systems (HEMS) is crucial for manufacturers and service providers to develop systems that allow for different appliances, HVAC, lighting, entertainment and other home systems to work together. This is true not only for equipment entering the marketplace now [at the time this book was written], but for products still on the proverbial 'drawing board.' These systems may each use different ways of expressing information internally, and having a common expression all can refer to will allow them to communicate needed data, and only needed data, for intelligent coordination."*

Here's an easy way to think about it, and this is equally true about interoperability concerns for manufacturers of any Smart Grid technologies. For instance, some manufacturers may use yes/no to indicate if power is on or off in a device. Other vendors may program this status data as on/off. When converting back to binary machine code, everyone has to agree that if *yes* is the equivalent of *on*, and *no* equals *off*, then *1* now corresponds to the *yes/on* state and *0* corresponds to the

* http://www.eisalliance.org/index.php/press-releases/5-home-energy-management-systems.

no/off state. Simply put, different ways of saying the same thing prevent different companies' products from working together, and that increases costs and complexity for consumers.

Industry associations such as the EIS Alliance exist to encourage different systems and architectures from vendors to operate together in homes with appropriate communications and coordination. That means that consumers can install different vendors' products in homes with the confidence that the products can "play well together" under the monitoring and control of HEMSs and HANs. Just like we would like all the equipment in our entertainment centers to work with a single remote control, we will want one HEMS solution to be used for our kitchen, laundry, and electronics appliances and devices found in homes. As noted above, most communications service providers are bundling additional services, including healthy lifestyle applications, along with dedicated touchscreen displays that function as sophisticated remote controller devices.* Current trends point to the smart phone becoming a universal home controller via apps.† Whatever the type of app or device that is chosen, app developers, smartphone manufacturers, and communications service providers will need to ensure they engineer the apps and devices with privacy controls to address the associated risks if they hope to be well received by a privacy-breach-weary public. Additionally, the legal privacy protections regarding energy usage data vary based on the provider and the type of device that serves as the interface to a utility, a broadband or mobile carrier's network, or another service provider via the Internet.

HEMS Communications with the Smart Grid

Here's one scenario that describes how HEMS solutions or smart devices connected by a HAN can communicate with a utility or an

* As just one example, in Rebecca's home state of Iowa, Mediacom, a cable and telecommunications company, is seeking to become the home energy management solution of choice with its dedicated devices and apps that run on laptops, smart phones, and other types of devices. See more at https://mediacomcable.com/site/bundlesdg/home_security.html. See "HEMS Vendor Taxonomy" showing a wide range of the possibilities at http://www.greentechmedia.com/research/report/home-energy-management-systems-2013-2017.

† http://www.electricaltimes.co.uk/blogs/blog-entry/the-rise-of-home-automation.

ESP and become part of the Smart Grid. A homeowner has enrolled in a utility's program that asks customers to voluntarily reduce electricity use on specific dates and times.* These selected time frames typically occur on the days when a utility has the greatest demand for electricity. As noted before, wholesale electricity markets obey the laws of supply and demand. When demand is greatest, supply is most expensive. The utility wants to avoid buying megawatts of electricity at this most expensive peak price because it is regulated or managed to keep electricity rates as low as possible for consumers.

One way to avoid buying expensive electricity is to ask customers to voluntarily reduce their use. So on a very hot day in California when every air conditioner in the Central Valley is running full blast, the utility asks our hypothetical homeowner to cut back on electricity use. How does the utility do this? Some programs are set up so the homeowner gives permission for the utility to automatically raise the temperature on residential thermostats by a degree or two, or cycle AC unit compressors on and off.† The homeowner can opt out of participation if needed. Other demand response (DR) programs send a message by our homeowner's preferred means of communication—usually a text, email, or phone alert—requesting voluntary cutbacks in electricity use. These reductions in energy use are made by the homeowner—the consumer—not the utility. The reduction impacts are negligible to each participating homeowner, but on an aggregated scale, these actions add up to sufficient reduced electricity usage to avoid that purchase of the most expensive electricity. That has a benefit to the utility and to all customers by keeping electricity costs lower. Our homeowner enjoys a reduction in electricity rates or a rebate on the bill.

HANs and HEMSs offer interesting possibilities to expand the number of electricity-using devices that could automatically participate in these programs, increasing the potential for significant reductions in electricity during the times when it is most expensive. When

* These are usually known as demand response (DR) programs within utilities, and are branded by a variety of different names when marketed to utility customers.

† Programs operate today in this fashion without a HAN or a smart meter to support them. Simple radio controllers are affixed to outdoor AC units and these respond to signals from utility networks. Some other programs control residential pool pumps in the same fashion. These programs are effective, but require that each AC unit or pool pump have its own radio device co-located with it.

"smart" appliances, which have communications capabilities, are added to the equation, the hypothetical amounts of electricity consumption that can be avoided at certain times dramatically increase. Here's an example of how this might look in the future and on the path of a transactive energy future. If you have a HAN connecting your smart appliances and have designated that your thermostat, refrigerator's ice maker, clothes dryer, dishwasher, and electric hot water heater can participate in a DR program, each of these devices must have communications capabilities to receive and transmit data to your HEMS—which is mostly likely in a laptop, tablet, or smart phone. You would program settings for demand response, such as "don't make ice between 2:00 and 7:00 p.m." or "start a dishwashing cycle only after 6:00 p.m.," in order to avoid using electricity during the hours of greatest demand. Sure, you could run around the house and turn things off manually in response to an email or text, but there might come a day where you forget to adjust something and receive an expensive electric bill as a result of consuming electricity at the wrong time. This is why the concept of set and forget is very important to developers of connected homes, smart appliances, and HEMS solutions.

Continuing with this scenario, on those DR event days, your appliances would receive signals via your HAN that instructed them to operate with the restrictions you put in place on them. These signals could come from a utility and be sent via a smart meter, or they could be sent over the Internet to your HAN from the utility or from an energy services provider (ESP). This distinction becomes extremely important, as you'll learn later in this book. If you choose to override those controls, you can—so on that DR event day when you have a party planned for 50 people, you will have all the AC and ice you need, but it may cost you.

In this future scenario, here's where the granularity and value of data beyond energy management come in to play. The utility or ESP will need to know if you are complying with the electricity reduction request, and if not, how much variance there is in your electricity use. Depending on the turnaround times between their initial request and their checkup to see if your appliances are performing as expected, your utility or ESP might send a text alert to let you know that your home hasn't reduced electricity use as much as anticipated. Is this a problem? Maybe, maybe not. Perhaps your refrigerator compressor is failing, so it is running more than it should, and consumes more electricity as a result. Perhaps a device isn't programmed correctly. Perhaps you have out-of-town guests and overrode all appliance instructions while they are in town. All your utility or ESP can tell you is that you are using more electricity than you promised to use. Or is there more it can tell about your electricity use? Quite possibly yes, if it correlated this data with other energy usage data.

HANs Do Not Need Smart Meters

Here's a key point to remember: a HAN does not need a smart meter to perform as described here. It could work with an Internet connection—wired or wireless. This is the approach adopted by companies like Comcast or Verizon. It also requires a collection of smart plugs or appliances that can communicate across that HAN supporting a common protocol. Just like the wireless local area network (LAN) in your home can connect to all computers, entertainment displays, tablets, and smart phones that have communications capabilities, a HAN could connect smart appliances and other types of smart electronic devices. We'll discuss smart appliances in greater detail later in this chapter.

HANs as Communications Gateway Devices

A HAN could be the gateway device for communications "on the other side of the meter," meaning it could serve as the interface between utility or ESP equipment and smart devices in the home. However, its ability to function within a dwelling is unrelated to a connection to the outside world. HANs and HEMSs, like wireless modems, should have strong passwords to prevent unauthorized access to devices in your home. For instance, an article in *Forbes* magazine* detailed how that author hacked into several homes that deployed a device from an unnamed manufacturer—a device that had no password protections and no other security controls implemented. The author was able to obtain personal information, and remotely control devices like lamps that were connected to the hacked systems. No smart meter or HEMS solution was involved in this scenario, but without proper security safeguards, privacy and data

* http://www.forbes.com/sites/kashmirhill/2013/07/26/smart-homes-hack/.

integrity can be compromised. It is critical for each consumer to ensure all the appropriate security controls are implemented within his or her HAN to minimize the risk that unauthorized entities can gain access to the data within the HAN.

History just continues to repeat itself. Years ago, the examples of password carelessness concerned companies that installed expensive telecommunications equipment and never changed the default password of 1234 to something unique, exposing themselves to all sorts of nefarious havoc. More recently, the Department of Homeland Security encouraged transportation agencies to change default passwords for the digital signs that offer traffic advisories after a couple of quite visible hacks.*

Comcast was contacted as part of an inquiry to learn more about the home automation services, and in particular, ask questions about encryption of data and privacy policies. The answers, or rather the lack of them, reveal a great deal. At the time of this writing Comcast had not received too many questions about data privacy, and therefore didn't have much information about technologies and policies in this topic area. That's not a criticism leveled solely at Comcast. It's a cautionary message to all of us. However, we had to feel sorry for the contact center agent—she obviously hadn't been trained to address these questions and had no resources to turn to.† The investigating author, Christine Hertzog, asked about obtaining a copy of the data privacy policy for one of its home automation services that included home energy controls. The response was, "We'll get back to you in 3–5 days." Christine is still waiting for that information.

Privacy Risks within Rentals and Other Leased Spaces

The prior discussion focused on single-family residences. However, there are additional concerns with using HEMSs within rental

* http://www.torontosun.com/2014/06/06/after-godzilla-attack-us-warns-about-traffic-sign-hackers.

† An SGIP SGCC Privacy Subgroup training subteam led by Rebecca Herold created sets of "train the trainer" type of training slides for a variety of entities to use. Included in these was a set to train those who must answer such questions from customers. You can obtain the training slide sets at https://collaborate.nist.gov/twiki-sggrid/bin/view/SmartGrid/CSCTGPrivacy#Privacy_Training_Slides.

properties. Rent payments sometimes include utility services like electricity or water, particularly in properties where one meter is associated with all units. This creates the concern that the named party for the meter supplying a rental unit would then have access to detailed energy usage data for renters. Could tenants subsequently be discriminated against, evicted, or have their rent payments raised if the landlord determined the renter was using too much electricity? Would landlords be able to monitor tenant activities through their energy usage throughout the day and in various locations of their rented spaces? It is technically feasible, but not practically feasible, at least without some level of awareness on the part of the tenants. However, these privacy concerns need to be addressed as more laws mandating the reporting of energy usage are deployed in cities and states to drive energy savings and job creation.*

Utilities are struggling with how to provide energy usage reports to entities legally entitled to such information for residential rental units without infringing on the privacy of those living within them. For example, in January 2013, Xcel Energy asked Minnesota state regulators for guidance† on the minimum number of customers to include in aggregated energy usage data reports without infringing on the privacy of those whose data was being used. Could they aggregate total building energy usage data for a 50-tenant property without exposing any individual customer's information? The privacy risks of a building with just two or three renters would be more significant because of fewer tenants being involved—the ability to perhaps even intuitively guess at unit's energy usage data would be much easier to accomplish. Xcel Energy requested more legal guidance and state policy to protect consumer privacy to help utilities to make better decisions whenever aggregated energy usage data was evaluated with the goal of energy usage improvement.

* California's Assembly Bill (AB) 1103 mandates benchmarking at a whole building level of energy efficiency information for nonresidential buildings, which raises privacy concerns for commercial and industrial tenants. Resolution of these concerns is ongoing as of this writing. http://www.energy.ca.gov/ab1103/.

† See https://www.edockets.state.mn.us/EFiling/edockets/searchDocuments.do?method=showPoup&documentId={D3334DBB-4851-4606-BEEF-3D59B2DC711D}&documentTitle=20131-83405-01.

While current laws protect social security numbers (SSNs) and standards protect credit card numbers, at the time this book was written, no known laws or regulations existed to protect renters' energy usage data from building owners or landlords,* or indeed from being published for public review. Since housing trends are moving toward more multifamily and rental housing,† this area should be addressed sooner rather than later, given the associated privacy risks. Chapter 7 provides more discussion of the various privacy risks of renters, and Appendix A documents the privacy risk levels for energy usage data within privately owned dwellings and commercial and industrial sites.

Employee Privacy Risks within Commercial Buildings and Industrial Sites

Similar to the privacy concerns within residential rentals, there have also been concerns expressed about the privacy risks of HEMSs within commercial buildings and industrial sites. However, unlike residential dwellings, industrial and commercial facilities have historically not been locations where there is an expectation of privacy outside of locker rooms, bathrooms, or other personal care spaces. In 2010 one of the authors, Rebecca Herold, participated in a team that included a National Institute of Standards and Technology (NIST) representative and the security officer from a large Midwest utility that spent several months researching and discussing the possible privacy issues within commercial buildings and industrial sites. Appendix A documents the privacy risk levels for these areas. The conclusion was that since these areas have historically been subject to monitoring and surveillance for safety reasons, and because business owners typically have established policies that employees and others within the premises are subject to monitoring, and with consideration

* This scenario applies when a building owner, landlord, property management company, etc., pays for the utility bills.

† Fannie Mae report: http://www.fanniemae.com/portal/research-and-analysis/data-note-0312.html. For more discussion about the unique challenges of rental housing and the Smart Grid, see these blogs by Christine Hertzog: http://www.smartgridlibrary.com/2014/04/28/wanted-smart-grid-policies-for-14-million-homes/ and http://www.smartgridlibrary.com/2014/04/14/the-smart-grid-and-multifamily-dwelling-challenges/.

of the bulk electricity usage in commercial sites, there were minimal privacy risks within such locations specifically related to electricity usage. However, when considering the use of personally owned electric devices, plug-in electric vehicles (PEVs), and mobile devices with smart energy apps loaded on them that could reveal information about an employee's off-business-site activities, there are some privacy risks involved.

Chapter 7 provides more discussion of the various privacy risks of renters and employees.

Disaggregation Technologies

Disaggregation technologies use specialized current-sensing equipment and data algorithms to break down electricity use into individual device or appliance consumption. These technologies can be deployed at the smart plug level or at the electrical panel as a "whole home" solution. Here's a basic overview of disaggregation technologies. The associated privacy risks of disaggregation will be discussed in Chapter 7.

Hardware

One version of this technology deploys a smart plug that connects into the wall socket, and then the appliance or device to be studied is plugged into that smart plug.

Whole home disaggregation technology incorporates sensors at the electrical panel or breaker box* that samples the flow of household current and detects patterns of energy use that are common to a specific appliance, based on comparison of those patterns to a collection of other power consumption patterns. Those collections of patterns or signatures are usually derived from plug-level research. Each type of appliance has a unique signature, and if you collect enough examples of signatures, you could match electricity signatures the way crime technicians match tire or shoe treads. This could be useful for home energy audits, spotting appliance failures before they happen, or other

---

* The electrical panel box is also known as a fuse box, panelboard, circuit breaker box, and breaker panel.

helpful predictive uses, as discussed below. However, as with other benefits, this also brings insights into energy usage that create privacy concerns, as discussed in Chapter 7.

Software

There are disaggregation technologies that are software based too. These solutions take smart meter data and run sophisticated analyses of the energy usage data correlated with such things as weather data and even information gathered from queries with their customers. Typically cloud based, software disaggregation technologies also seek patterns based on large libraries of electricity signatures. The biggest distinction between the hardware- and software-based solutions is that the hardware solutions have much more granular data than software solutions, which are at the mercy of the utility's scheduled meter read. The difference can be 25 milliseconds (hardware) to 15 or 60 minutes (software).*

Here's an important point. Disaggregation technology was not installed in smart meters at the time this book was written, and meter manufacturers weren't too keen on installing this technology into their meters. Meter manufacturers and utilities want to keep meters focused on what they are meant to do—measure the electricity you use so they can send you an accurate bill. Loading a meter down with processor-intensive comparisons of electricity signatures, or consuming valuable utility network space to communicate to a cloud, just to learn what appliance is operating at any point in time, conflicts with the primary mission of keeping track of how much power is flowing through each meter.

In conclusion, disaggregation software and hardware technologies are opt-in technologies that are visible to homeowners (as hardware installed in the breaker box, or software feedback loops). So why would someone want this technology? The answer is that the ability to break down an electric current into the unique signatures of consumption

* See http://www.greentechmedia.com/articles/read/perfecting-energy-disaggregation-in-the-home for discussion of hardware. Software disaggregation technologies rely on the data transmitted by smart meters; thus, the interval is set by the utility. To date, utilities in the United States have not collected smart meter data in intervals less than 15 minutes.

by different devices is a powerful tool to assist consumers, utilities, and manufacturers in understanding energy consumption behaviors and patterns for appliances and electronics. There are a number of academic studies that demonstrate the value this data delivers to help consumers make informed and fact-based decisions about usage.* It could show a homeowner that a replacement of an aging appliance for a more energy efficient one is a great money-saving investment. From a utility perspective, this data could help formulate programs to encourage selection of more energy efficient appliances or target new categories of devices for demand response programs based on when they are used. Even from a market research perspective, this data could be quite valuable for manufacturers to influence product designs or future services. We emphasize the use of the word *could* here because the numbers of disaggregation devices were fairly low at the time this book was written, and much of the existing work with this data had been in academic research.

Disaggregation technologies eliminate the guesswork involved to see when the blender is whirring or the hot tub jets are bubbling, because "libraries" of electricity signatures can easily compare and match the signatures disaggregated from plug devices or technology at the electric panel.

However, while disaggregation activities bring benefits as described, they also bring significant privacy risks that must also be addressed. These risks and a few possible mitigation methods are discussed in Chapter 7.

Smart Appliances

Appliance is the generic term we use for kitchen equipment or white goods like refrigerators, stoves, microwaves, and dishwashers. It also covers laundry devices—washers and dryers. Electronic devices like TVs and receivers, hot tubs, smoke alarms, baby monitors, and closed-circuit TV (CCTV) surveillance systems can also be considered appliances. Finally, there's equipment that resides in a utility closet or basement or outside—the heating, ventilation, air conditioning

---

* This paper studies disaggregation and lists additional research. http://web.stanford.edu/group/peec/cgi-bin/docs/behavior/research/disaggregation-armel.

(HVAC) gear, water heaters, spas, and pool pumps. This last grouping has some special characteristics.*

A smart appliance is a device or appliance that can bidirectionally share data with a utility or service provider, and some even have data storage or data processing capabilities. It is also likely to contain more sensors than ever before to create new or more data. One of the authors would like to have a sensor or two in the oven to warn about possible overbaking before activating the sensor called the nose or the sensor called the smoke detector.

Connecting Home Appliances

As noted earlier in the discussion about HANs, there are two basic scenarios to deliver connectivity to home appliances. The first scenario is that selected smart appliances communicate with the electric grid via utility-owned equipment. The second scenario is that smart appliances connect to the Internet, and a hub or gateway within a residential dwelling is the communications manager. For the first scenario, that could be a HAN controller, and in the second scenario, it could be a Wi-Fi router or hub supplied by a telephone or cable service provider, or even an appliance manufacturer.† The connected smart appliances (in the future, to include EVs, energy storage, and private generation assets such as rooftop solar in this category) communicate with this hub or gateway, which in turn manages the connectivity to the utility or another vendor or energy services provider. It turns out there is a third scenario, in which smart appliances communicate directly to the cloud and use an operating system like Android or iOS and apps to deliver information to the appliance owners. And as our research discovered, this data was provided to the appliance manufacturers.

Increasingly more appliances, even a hairdryer or toaster oven, could be outfitted with communications capabilities. The annual

* Some of these devices are typically powered by natural gas rather than electricity. Particularly when it comes to furnaces or water heaters, the operations are already automated courtesy of sensors for temperature (air or water).

† http://www.greentechmedia.com/articles/read/whirlpool-launches-the-wi-fi-smart-appliance.

Consumer Electronics Show in Las Vegas highlights this trend. Here are some smart devices available when this book was written:

- A smart lock that can be controlled remotely and have a camera to record who is at your door*
- Smart appliances that may track energy usage, but can also provide detailed information about usage and have cameras built in to record those using them†
- Wi-Fi-enabled crock pots, and lightbulbs with remote control capabilities‡
- Thermostats that analyze heating and cooling settings to detect trends with remote monitor and control capabilities§
- Smart toothbrushes that collect data on your brushing habits, including duration, frequency, and neglected zones in your mouth, and then communicate with your iOS or Android smart phone via Bluetooth technology¶

From a utility perspective, appliances that consume the most electricity or gas are most important for DR programs. These appliances may have operational flexibility or discretionary use—meaning the device or appliance owner can postpone use to different points in time or modify parameters such as heating or cooling temperature, or even operate differently to provide other (somewhat esoteric) services back to the utility or ESP. For utilities, these are the appliances that make sense to enroll in demand response programs. These generally include HVAC equipment, clothes dryers, dishwashers, ovens, and hot water heaters—devices that tend to be the biggest energy users. These smart appliances must somehow connect to a utility or third party that manages DR programs to receive or transmit data.

* For example, see http://abcnews.go.com/Technology/ces-2014-smart-devices-mashed-home-appliances/story?id=21468578#1.

† For example, see http://abcnews.go.com/Technology/ces-2014-smart-devices-mashed-home-appliances/story?id=21468578#2.

‡ For example, see http://abcnews.go.com/Technology/ces-2014-smart-devices-mashed-home-appliances/story?id=21468578#4.

§ For example, see http://www.cnet.com/products/nest-learning-thermostat/.

¶ For example, see http://www.kolibree.com/.

DR Programs

DR programs are price based or capacity based. Price-based systems are precursors to future transactive energy markets and are predicated on the assumption that electricity (or gas or water in the future) is in some sense dynamic in price. Smart appliances could have the intelligence to be programmed or instructed to operate or not based on price signals. The programming is controlled by the appliance owner and, once in place, would automatically perform based on those instructions. Owners have the ability to override the usual programming for any special circumstance. This is the basic construct for OpenADR, an industry group that promotes an open protocol for all appliance and device manufacturers to adopt to readily accept utility price signals.

OpenADR, the acronym for Open Automated Demand Response, is an open standard for electricity providers and system operators to communicate DR signals over any existing Internet Protocol (IP)-based communications network like the Internet. It has support from a number of industry stakeholders, including appliance manufacturers, building managers, ESPs, and utilities who see the value in widespread adoption of the standard. We'll discuss OpenADR more in Chapter 9.

We alluded to data collection by appliance manufacturers a few paragraphs back, and this deserves careful examination. This is another new area of data collection. Some data is based on energy consumption, but most of the data collected today focuses on consumer use of appliances, and that concerns privacy. One of the pioneers in smart appliances is Whirlpool Corporation. At the time of publication, there were four electric appliances—a refrigerator, a clothes washer, a dryer, and a dishwasher—that were equipped with a technology called 6th Sense Live™,[*] and similar technology is embedded in some water heaters that are powered by natural gas.[†] This technology includes a platform for aggregated communications and control from a company called Arrayent.

Arrayent supplies the wireless communications platform to connect these Whirlpool appliances to the Arrayent cloud. The communications are bidirectional, meaning data can be sent to or received from a connected appliance. There can be benefits to that exchange of data.

[*] See http://www.whirlpool.com/smart-appliances/.

[†] See http://www.whirlpoolwaterheaters.com/learn-more/gas-water-heaters/6th-sense™/.

For instance, an appliance could submit data that assists in diagnosis of a problem and speeds repair time. A manufacturer could provide an over-the-air (OTA) update of software or firmware in an appliance, extending the useful life of that appliance. But manufacturers could also monitor use of an appliance. For instance, the Whirlpool refrigerator equipped with 6th Sense Live can send an alert to the owner's smart phone if the fridge door is open for 5 minutes. A sensor monitors appliance status, and then communicates this data to the Arrayent cloud. Arrayent's communications are encrypted, which is commendable. But who owns this data? It's not energy usage data, so it is not governed by state laws or utility policies that address energy usage data. This is data about how and when, and often where, an appliance is used.

The view of data custodianship gets even murkier. A consumer buys the product from Whirlpool. He or she might assume that the privacy policy on Whirlpool's website covers his or her purchase. That would be a mistaken assumption, because website privacy policies typically cover use of the Whirlpool website unless the posted privacy policy specifically says the privacy promises also apply to sites where the data is shared (neither of the authors has seen such a privacy policy with this type of statement). Does Arrayent have custodianship and management of consumer data? The data is based in its cloud, but its stance is that the device or appliance manufacturer is responsible for the user data it collects.

Here's what the Arrayent website says about data privacy for data that resides in its cloud: "If you are an end user of the Arrayent Cloud Service, please check with the applicable device manufacturer (or other Arrayent enterprise customer) regarding treatment of your information on and in connection with the Arrayent Cloud Service."*

This statement indicates that in the scenario described above, the data management responsibilities reside with Whirlpool. We do not know if the U.S. Federal Trade Commission or State Attorneys General offices would consider Arrayent's position to be congruent with their views of custodial responsibilities. Historically custodians of personal information, and information with privacy impacts, have

* At the time this book was written, this statement was extracted from the Arrayent privacy policy regarding the Arrayent Cloud Service at www.arrayent.com/privacy.

been accountable to varying degrees when security incidents and privacy breaches have occurred. We use this example to highlight today's realities about data in the connected home. We do not have any reason to believe that Whirlpool or Arrayent abuses or misuses consumer data. However, certain types of data—energy usage data—have special privacy safeguards in some states. Other data that may be used in conjunction with energy usage data may not enjoy the same safeguards, or may be governed by other policies, as is the case for financial data or health data.

Here's another example that blurs the line between energy usage data and other usage data. Smart phones and tablets are growing in popularity as the preferred device for home energy management. Some home goods manufacturers are installing Android or Apple operating systems into their appliances too. For instance, Google's Android operating system (OS) can be added to devices that range from rice cookers to refrigerators. The Android OS capability would offer convenience to consumers—that Android smart phone or tablet could notify you when a laundry cycle is complete or when it's time to take the cookies out of the oven. However, the OS also offers Google or appliance makers an opportunity to collect usage data. This data may or may not include energy usage data. This data will not be the revenue-grade usage data pulled from a meter that is used to calculate bills. This could be the appliance's own measurement of its electricity use, or this could be melded with Green Button data. One point is clear: at the time of this writing, this data did not enjoy the same protections imposed on electric utilities regarding energy usage data.

A new release of Android capabilities will allow proximity sensing so that your home lights could automatically turn on as you or your smart phone approach your dwelling. A smart tracking capability can be a great convenience. But there's probably some time-stamped data collected somewhere that creates a detailed mapping of personal movement inside a home. Apple has similar products and plans for more home/iOS connectivity. Its HomeKit allows iPhone control of appliances, door locks, and plugs.

Mobile devices and their operating systems offer portability, convenience, and ubiquity to consumers. We expect to see them used for status updates and more as home or business-based on-site generation, energy storage, and consumption management solutions are deployed.

Mobile devices have a very special role in data privacy, particularly with regard to capabilities such as location-based services (LBSs), geo-fencing, and smart tracking.

In summary, HEMSs, HANs, and smart appliances can help consumers intelligently manage energy use. Smart appliances can provide additional value, as noted, in the form of performance monitoring and troubleshooting diagnostics, and could save consumers money. However, the veritable explosion of sensors that can be embedded into appliances, and the communications capabilities that make them smart, creates new data. The addition of mobile devices and their operating systems creates even more data and the means to natively communicate it. The data provided by smart appliances may never be communicated with a regulated electric utility. But if it is, a regulatory agency may have provided guidance about utility practices for personal information and energy usage data. Consumers do need to pay close attention to privacy policies for the new devices installed in homes that have communications capabilities. Understanding the chain of data custody is critical to recognizing who has access to your data and what is being done with it.

6
Electric Vehicles, Charging Stations, and Privacy

On May 22, 2012, the U.S. White House issued* an Apps for Energy† data challenge, with one of the challenges focused on Apps for Vehicles in 2013.‡ Under the auspices of the Department of Energy, the challenge's objectives were to encourage development of applications that improve safety and fuel efficiency of vehicles using vehicle-generated open data. Data such as engine speed, distance, brake position, and headlights status are some examples of vehicle-generated data. In the past, this data was typically only available to auto technicians with specific diagnostic equipment.

Making this "open" data to vehicle owners means that they will be able to use this data and share it with authorized third parties or data managers. This data is called vehicle telematics.§ In some facets, this initiative to democratize data is similar to the Green Button initiative. It's another situation where existing data is now more readily available and accessible for its data owners, or it is new data being created because of improved sensor and communications technologies that can be leveraged to provide value to consumers and other organizations. Consumers can benefit from applications of this data into information that helps them drive safely or more cost effectively. Our discussion will focus on the implications of privacy at the intersection with the Smart Grid, which typically means public or private charging—with or without electric vehicle supply equipment (EVSE).

---

* See http://www.whitehouse.gov/blog/2012/05/22/unlocking-power-energy-data.

† See http://appsforenergy.challengepost.com/.

‡ See http://appsforvehicles.challenge.gov.

§ The privacy implications of vehicle telematics apply to traditional internal combustion engine vehicles as well as EVs.

There are three levels of charging associated with the delivery speed that can be deployed for EVs. Level 1 is the standard two-prong plug to handle 120 V. It takes the longest to fully charge an EV. Level 2 is the standard three-prong plug used for dryers and microwaves to handle 240 V. It is sometimes called AC fast charging, and is faster than a level 1 charge. Level 3 uses direct current (DC) for charging instead of alternating current (AC). DC charging delivers the fastest charging option of the three levels. However, AC is the wiring found in the vast majority of U.S. buildings today, although this may change over time.

If you charge directly from a standard two-prong wall outlet, an EV looks just like another appliance or device on the electrical grid. Energy usage data is treated exactly like any other device on the other side of a smart or traditional meter.

However, there are a number of reasons where EV owners will prefer to use specialized EVSE products for charging purposes. The majority of those reasons come down to the convenience of having an infrastructure of charging stations as EVs roam streets and highways. But there are trade-offs with privacy that we'll explore in this chapter.

At the time of this writing, the EV charging infrastructure was immature in comparison to the traditional internal combustion engine fueling infrastructure, which has had a century to work out the details. There are some parallels, and these serve to highlight similarities and differences. One similarity is the point of sale (POS) transaction. Gas tank and pump configurations can be privately owned, and are particularly common in rural areas and on farms. You won't have a POS transaction involving a credit or debit card with these stations since the owner buys gasoline in bulk and is billed on a periodic basis. Privately owned charging equipment that is associated with a meter is similar in operation. The meter functions as the POS device, long accustomed to a role as a utility cash register.

POS transactions at your corner gas station have more in common with public charging infrastructure options. There's a transaction that involves a credit or debit card—or a radio frequency identification (RFID)-enabled card that is read by the charging station and enables "authorization" to use the charging station. But while a corner gas station is generally owned by an oil company or a franchisee to that company, public charging stations can fit into several ownership options. These ownership options have impacts on the treatment of energy usage data as well as other data.

Publicly Owned Charging

Policies for EVs, and charging stations in particular, vary between states. Some states like California prohibit utilities from owning charging stations. In Texas, utilities can be more directly involved in setting up charging stations and networks. Some states don't allow an entity other than a utility to sell power. Therefore, if a charging station includes a financial transaction to pay for that EV charge, then the entity must be classified as a utility. It's a confusing patchwork of rules, and therefore consideration of privacy impacts has to be done on a state-by-state basis. As a more distributed energy resource (DER) is deployed across states and as transactive energy concepts translate into reality, we expect to see these rules change to remove obstacles to greater prosumer participation.

However, the current situation complicates the picture for privacy. In one state, a shopping center owner may install a charging station or two for customer use on a lease arrangement from a charging station network provider. The shopping center owner pays for the electricity to encourage shoppers to extend their time at the mall while recharging their EV or plug-in hybrid EV (PHEV). It also helps the shopping center avoid any issues with being confused with a utility.

In another state, a parking garage installs a number of charging stations and charges customers for the parking space to recharge their EVs and PHEVs. The electricity is free, but the EV driver uses a mobile app supplied by the parking garage to reserve an EV space via credit card.

Figuring out where the energy usage data goes in these two cases is fairly easy—it follows the meter that is associated with that charging station. Financial data follows the banking network that manages any POS transaction. But EV fueling creates new data, such as charging station locations and time spent obtaining the charge, as part of a consumer's charging history.

Another quick comparison and contrasting to traditional gas stations is instructive. Most people pay for gas by debit or credit card. Banks routinely note date, time, location, and total amount paid for gas. In some parts of the United States, you have to enter your zip code as a means to validate that you are the legitimate owner of the card used for payment. All this data is transmitted via secure networks. An EV charging station can perform very similar functions via very similar technologies and processes, but it may also identify the total time plugged in to the charging station, carbon credits or greenhouse gas savings, and alert you when your EV is completely recharged.

The data created and collected about driving and charging patterns of EVs is of tremendous value to governments and utilities. There are a number of good reasons for this interest. First, federal, state, and local governments can use this data as a gauge of consumer interest in EVs, their driving patterns, and the most popular charging locations. Such data helps them understand the impacts of policies and tax implications as more EVs share roads, but not the gas tax,* of fossil fuel-powered vehicles. Second, EV charging is equivalent to adding a new home's electricity burden on a local grid, so utilities are keenly interested in learning where EVs are plugging in to their grids. These charging locations may need prioritization for upgrades to support the increased electricity demand. In many of these cases, the interest is in aggregated data, not data that can be used to identify specific individuals. However, personal data is automatically involved in billing transactions.

ChargePoint®† is an example of a new public charging infrastructure business based on new technologies and delivering new business to business (B2B) and business to consumer (B2C) services. ChargePoint consists of software and networks to support public EVSE. It is targeted to:

- Companies that have EV fleets
- Companies that want to offer EV charging as a benefit for employees or customers
- Companies that want to become the service stations of the future
- Utilities that are authorized to offer charging stations
- EV drivers who want organized information about public charging stations, and charging reports about their use of ChargePoint-supported EVSE

---

* The federal gasoline tax funds highway projects.

† See http://www.chargepoint.com/

ChargePoint software gathers data from EV drivers at their charging stations about how their cars are used (number and distance of trips), number of charging events, number of kilowatt-hours used, and how this translates to greenhouse gas savings. The data has value to a number of stakeholders, as illustrated in the ChargePoint America example.

In June 2013 the company announced that it had successfully completed the ChargePoint America project,* a federal- and state-funded project to deploy 4,600 charging stations at single-family homes, multifamily housing, and commercial and public locations to support more than 2,000 EVs registered to participate. The purpose of the program, which ended in December 2013, was to gather data that was publicly available to researchers, municipal planners, and policy makers to help them learn more about EV charging patterns and avoided CO_2 emissions. EV drivers voluntarily participated in this program, and researchers reviewed the data results to create their summary of the project.

Whether part of the ChargePoint America program or not, the typical process that ChargePoint established is that EV drivers register with ChargePoint, which collects personal data (name, address, email address) as well as financial data (credit card† or other payment information) to accommodate those charging stations that bill for EV charges as well as pay for the ChargePoint cards. Because there are mobile apps that can provide many of the same capabilities available by the web, there's the possibility for collection of smart phone numbers and addresses for text and email alerts, or for collection of IP addresses for laptops and other types of mobile computers using the app. ChargePoint also interfaces with a couple of navigation solutions, so location-based data could also potentially be collected.

---

* See a summary of the project at http://www.plugandgonow.com/wp-content/uploads/2010/07/ChargePoint-America-Summary.pdf.

† Credit card data protection is governed by standards known as Payment Card Industry Data Security Standards (PCI-DSS) (https://www.pcisecuritystandards.org/). These standards establish the secure communications requirements of sensitive data, encryption of this data, and physical and cyber storage of sensitive data. Any organization accepting credit card payments must comply with, and be certified to, the PCI-DSS.

Now, let's reexamine the types of data that are collected by the type of ChargePoint user with an eye toward personal data.

- Companies that have EV fleets: Who is charging, time and duration of charge, location of charge. Greenhouse gas (GHG) credits and avoided gallons of gas by vehicle.
- Companies that want to offer EV charging as a benefit for employees or customers: Who is charging, time and duration of charge, location of charge. Behaviors based on different pricing structures—free versus fee based. Payment information for fee-based EVSE. GHG credits and avoided gallons of gas by vehicle.
- Companies that want to become the service stations of the future: Who is charging, time and duration of charge, location of charge. Payment information. Behaviors based on different pricing structures or offers tailored to different customer categories. GHG credits and avoided gallons of gas by vehicle.
- Utilities that are authorized to offer charging stations: Who is charging, time and duration of charge, location of charge. Behaviors based on different pricing structures or offers tailored to different tariffs or time of day. GHG credits and avoided gallons of gas by vehicle.
- EV drivers who want organized information about public charging stations, and charging reports about their use of ChargePoint-supported EVSE: Name, address, type of EV, credit card or other payment information, charging history (location, date, time), phone number, email address. Other data includes gallons of avoided gas and reductions in GHG emissions.

One important point: Retailers offer free charging to attract customers and have them linger for a couple of hours. ChargePoint and other similar businesses are set up for retailers to recognize who is reserving or connecting a charge at their EVSE. The retailer (or other retailers) can potentially send offers for discounts on products or services to the EV owners at those charging stations, to a mobile device, or possibly to the EV itself (e.g., the EV dashboard).

At the time this book was written, ChargePoint claims to have 65% of the commercial EVSE market. Other EVSE companies include CarCharging Group (which acquired Ecotality from bankruptcy) and Aerovironment. Their business models are similar in terms of how charging station markets are segmented—private versus public charging with subsegments of each (single family, multiunit residential, fleet, employer, etc.). When there's the possibility of a credit card payment, the implementation of the controls required by the Payment Card Industry Data Security Standards (PCI-DSS) helps to secure communications and handling of card and owner data. But the privacy policies for other EV driver data are very immature.

This gets to one of the most important points about EVs, the Smart Grid, and privacy. Charging stations blur existing privacy policy lines and the roles of data owner, data custodian, and data manager. Many EV drivers may assume that all charging stations adhere to the privacy policy in place for energy usage data enacted by their local utility. That may be true in some states, but the registered customer of the meter that is behind the charging station is usually considered to be the owner of the energy usage data produced by that meter. Charging stations that support point of sale (POS) transactions are governed by the privacy policy of the bank for financial data, and applicable industry regulations. Charging stations that support any form of electronic authorization without payment are generally governed by the posted privacy policy of the EVSE owner or sales vendor.

Prior to its bankruptcy and acquisition by CarCharging Group, Collaboratev, established by Ecotality and ChargePoint, was a new business entity to encourage interoperability between different EVSE networks for billing and station management. Think of it as a roaming agreement. Today, you can make mobile phone calls at your home location, and on the other side of the country. You get one bill, because there's a significant amount of work that's been done to negotiate agreements between different wireless carriers. Collaboratev aimed to let EV drivers plug in to any charging station, just as we can use almost any bank's ATM across the country. That's a great convenience, although there might be extra fees associated with charging at an EVSE that is outside of your network. While this arrangement was in limbo at the time of this writing, agreements like this will be inevitable to encourage the maximum convenience of charging locations for EV owners.

What are the protections for any personal data? The now defunct Collaboratev website offered this statement: "Driver information security is of utmost importance to us. Collaboratev will not have access to any personal or sensitive information other than your member number and network affiliation. The inclusion in the Collaboratev network will in no way compromise the personal or confidential information of any EV driver." That sounds promising, but there was an additional statement in its explanation of solution features: "Collect aggregated charge spot data and make it available to all industry stakeholders." EVSE owners are also promised the benefit of "improve profitability through monetization of charge spot data."

In our near future, if a major department store retailer offers free charging, the nearby national coffee chains may strike up deals to push offers for discounted beverages—advertising at the EVSE or pushing a text message to your smart phone. Just like Google collects web search data in exchange for providing its search services for free (along with a very nice business of selling advertising based on that search data), free charging in the future may come at the cost of collection of some personal data. From our perspective, there is no free lunch, and no free EV charging.

Private Charging

Experts note a trend about charging locations—most people charge their cars at home, plugging in to a wall outlet or EVSE installed in their garage or carport. As noted above, if you charge without using an EVSE, an EV or PHEV is just another electricity-consuming device on the electrical grid. The meter collects usage data (how much is consumed) and the utility reflects that information in billing statements.

Of the three types of charging that can be deployed in residential settings, the majority are configured for level 1 or level 2 charging using AC. An EV owner could theoretically plug his or her EV into an existing wall socket in the garage.* No EVSE installation is required. Utilities may view EVs as an appliance or device that gets special treatment in terms of pricing, which is determined by state-based regulatory decisions.† Because of the load a full charge can

* The amount of electricity drawn for a full EV charge is equivalent to an entire home, so an electrician should determine if existing electrical equipment (panels and wiring) can handle the additional electricity load.

† The authors make no recommendations about the pros and cons of regulations surrounding EV meter arrangements or charging station ownership, but point out that these regulations will have impacts on privacy.

require from the grid, utilities may also give EVs special treatment in terms of their short- and long-term distribution grid upgrade plans.

If there are no EV tariffs that encourage charging at off-peak hours through cheap electricity rates, then the EV is simply one additional power-consuming device. Plug in that EV to any available socket and charge. Utility bills will reflect the increased use of electricity. If a utility offers special EV tariffs, then there are two options. Option 1 is to install a separate meter and generate a second bill directed to the person identified with that meter. This option offers the flexibility for an EV owner and utility to agree to use a special electricity rate or tariff for the EV (typically with some restrictions on when charging can occur, which conforms to off-peak demand hours) and a separate tariff for all other home use. Option 2 is to install a submeter and generate one bill that has a line item for EV charging versus the rest of the household electricity use. This option is similar to option 1 from a billing flexibility perspective for both the utility and the EV owner.

In these scenarios, an EV owner is a utility customer with one or two meters, which would be addressed with the utility's typical billing processes. Data about EV charging activity that occurs at home is governed by the utility's existing privacy policies and practices, and any associated laws or regulations, for any appliance or device.

When a charging station is added into the equation, then the privacy questions harken back to the discussion on public charging. Understanding who owns the EVSE is important. Ownership of EVSE can become complicated. Depending on the state, investor-owned utilities (IOUs), municipal utilities, and rural cooperatives may own EVSE and have it installed at your home location for you. Homeowners may own EVSE. Owners of apartment buildings may purchase EVSE for tenant use. If the EVSE are registered with a network like Ecotality or ChargePoint or another service provider, then there is the potential for personal data about the users of the EVSE to be available to EVSE owners.

There's one other consideration regarding EVSE for private use. That concerns the equipment itself. Is it smart—meaning is it communications enabled? If it is, then there's a need to understand what data is transmitted, and who gets that data. The scenario could be as basic as a traditional direct load control device, similar to the equipment that is connected to a heating, ventilation, air conditioning (HVAC) unit or pool pump. It simply receives a signal from a utility to suspend operations until a later point in time in response to peak demand conditions. This would be most likely used when there is a single meter for all devices—EVSE plus all the typical electrical loads within a dwelling.

If the EVSE is on its own meter or a submeter, it could be enabled to respond to price signals sent by the utility to the meter, which then uses ZigBee, HomePlug, or another communications mode to the EVSE. This scenario would most likely play out in dynamic pricing.

As previously explored in Chapter 4, personally identifiable information is not transmitted by the smart meters in use at the time of this writing. Therefore, EVSE that is connected to smart meters is sending consumption information at established intervals of consumption reads (e.g., once per hour, once every 15 minutes, etc.) and might be receiving pricing information, if the local utility supports that arrangement.

Utility-Supplied Network Charging

Austin Energy serves as an example of a utility that offers an EV charging program within its territory. The utility has offers for rebates for its customers to purchase and install level 2 EVSE. It also offers a subscription-based program for unlimited charging at a network of EVSE within the boundaries of the city of Austin. The utility contracts with ChargePoint America to run this charging network. The state of Texas makes it clear that the customer is the owner for smart meter data. Is that equally true of EV data that is generated in EV programs like the one offered by Austin Energy? It's difficult to discern from the utility's website. The lines of demarcation between data owner, custodian, and manager are not well defined.

Table 6.1 shows the status, as of 2014, of state decisions regarding EV charging and state regulation. It answers a basic question: Do states exempt electric charging from existing regulation?

Other Privacy Implications with EVs

Our discussion has focused on EV electricity usage for billing purposes and charging station data collection. There are other types of data that may become more important to a variety of stakeholders over time, for instance, the federal excise tax on gasoline funds road projects across

Table 6.1 State Utilities Laws and Electric Vehicle Charging Stations

STATE	EXEMPT	NOTES
Alaska	No	
Arizona	No	
Arkansas	No	
California	Yes	
Colorado	Yes	
Connecticut	No	
Delaware	No	PSC has chosen not to exercise its authority.
Florida	Yes	
Georgia	No	
Hawaii	Yes	
Idaho	No	
Illinois	Yes	
Indiana	No	
Iowa	No	
Kansas	No	
Kentucky	No	
Louisiana	No	
Maine	No	
Maryland	Yes	
Massachusetts	No	
Michigan	No	
Minnesota	Yes	
Mississippi	No	
Missouri	No	
Montana	No	
Nebraska	No	
Nevada	No	
New Hampshire	No	
New Jersey	No	
New Mexico	No	
New York	No	Open for public comment.
North Carolina	No	
North Dakota	No	
Ohio	No	
Oklahoma	No	
Oregon	Yes	
Pennsylvania	No	
Rhode Island	No	
South Carolina	No	
South Dakota	No	

(continued)

Table 6.1 State Utilities Laws and Electric Vehicle Charging Stations (continued)

STATE	EXEMPT	NOTES
Tennessee	No	
Texas	No	
Utah	No	
Vermont	No	
Virginia	Yes	
Washington	Yes	
West Virginia	No	
Wisconsin	No	
Wyoming	No	
District of Columbia	Yes	

Source: Kendrick Vonderschmitt, Council of State Governments, October 9, 2013, http://knowledge center.csg.org/kc/content/state-utilities-law-and-electric-vehicle-charging-stations.

the nation. EVs don't pay this tax, but still enjoy use of the roads. Governments may wish to learn about total EV miles driven and location of those miles to figure out new road infrastructure funding mechanisms that fairly allocate costs across all road users.

States that have low carbon fuel standards (LCFSs) or clean fuel standards (CFSs) would benefit from data on the miles that EVs drive to calculate miles avoided in CO_2-spewing vehicles or supply data for other petroleum displacement programs. For instance, LCFSs are a key component of California Assembly Bill 32 (AB32), the state's signature clean energy and climate law. This type of data could create credits that accrue to individual EV owners, fleet owners, or other agencies. These two examples elegantly illustrate the monetization of data. Accurate collection of data can lead to money in the form of tax revenues, air quality credits for cap and trade purposes, or other programs that reward desired behaviors. Although there's been speculation that this information should be gathered from meters, it seems an easier collection mechanism is vehicle telematics. Cars already have odometers, and EVs and gas-powered cars, like smart phones, can have location-based sensing.

Telematics

Vehicle telematics certainly apply to all cars, not just EVs, but because EVs are new, their manufacturers are eager to collect data about driving habits and charging times as basic market research into what consumers want and do. For instance, MyFord Mobile* is a smart phone app that connects drivers with their EVs. App users can check the status of charging activities, and find charging stations. A wireless service subscription is included with each Ford EV. Ford is now converging telematics with the connected home realm—it is in a partnership with Whirlpool, SunPower, Nest Labs, and Eaton. The initiative is called MyEnergiLifestyle and combines data from renewable energy generation with EV charging data and appliance use data to inform residential prosumers about intelligent energy management.†

General Motors has cracked open its OnStar communications platform to apps that link Volt charging to home energy management systems (HEMSs) and utilities. Its OnStar RemoteLink‡ mobile app lets users of traditional gas guzzlers or EVs lock or unlock their car doors from any distance or remotely start their vehicles, among other capabilities. It also collects mobile and vehicle location data when it is active. Volt owners also have the ability to connect to social media applications like Facebook or Twitter to let them share information about their driving history, energy efficiency, and charging details (which creates other types of privacy risks). GM hosts a website for Volt owners called MyVolt.com to "access an unprecedented level of real-time data along with remote vehicle commands and critical vehicle diagnostics."§ Much of this data has nothing to do with the Smart Grid, but we highlight it here to emphasize that much of this data is new or newly available, and may have associated privacy risks. It no longer exists in containerized settings like car service diagnostics equipment. Event data recorders (EDRs) can now transmit data to a manufacturer, which is what enables OnStar's collision detection service to automatically inform about accidents to expedite emergency responses.

---

* MyFord Mobile site: https://phev.myfordmobile.com/content/mfm/en_us/site/login.html.

† http://www.sustainablebrands.com/news_and_views/info_tech/jennifer-elks/ford-utilizing-analytics-big-data-guide-sustainability-innova.

‡ GM MyLink site: https://play.google.com/store/apps/details?id=com.gm.onstar.mobile.mylink&hl=en.

§ https://secure.myvolt.com/web/portal/home;jsessionid=541BBE50549F6E342002870FA5FC0F86.

Privacy policies are an interesting facet of vehicle telematics. For instance, the GM privacy policy governs its websites, but not OnStar, and not mobile apps. Mobile apps—both GM and third party—are governed by separate privacy policies, and GM is explicit in its guidance*: "GM is not responsible for the collection or use of information by 3rd Party Applications. We recommend that you carefully review the privacy statement of each 3rd Party Application prior to downloading or using them." We couldn't agree more.

* GM privacy statement; see mobile applications section: http://www.gm.com/privacy/.

7

Mitigating Privacy Risks

Basic Risk Mitigation Strategies

Once privacy risks have been identified, organizations must determine the best way to mitigate them. Before jumping right into mitigation, it is important to first understand the four basic categories of risk mitigation.

- **Risk avoidance:** Risk avoidance consists of the actions taken to avoid as much exposure to the risk as possible. Risk avoidance is usually the most expensive of all risk mitigation options because organizations can never eliminate 100%, even though some will go to great lengths trying to do so. Many organizations have outsourced processing, collection, or other types of access to personal information and energy usage and consumption data thinking that will eliminate (thus avoiding) their risks. However, as explained in Chapter 2, the organization that collected personal information and energy usage and consumption data will continue to have some obligations and liability for it, even if the data is sent to another contracted entity.
- **Risk limitation:** Risk limitation is the most common risk management strategy used by businesses. Risk mitigation limits an organization's exposure by taking actions to help protect against the risk, and reduce the possibility of the risk being exploited to a level deemed acceptable by the appropriate business leaders. An example of limiting the risk of data loss for energy consumption data would be making regular backups of the data. The more frequently the backups are created, the less data that is possible to be lost by a hardware failure. An example of mitigating a privacy breach involving customer energy usage data that is stored on a smart meter would be to encrypt the data using a strong encryption algorithm.

- **Risk transference:** Risk transference involves transferring the risks to a third party. For example, it is becoming common for organizations to purchase cyber security insurance to transfer the cost of information security incidents and privacy breaches to an insurance company. While this will address the monetary losses involved with any exploitation of the associated data risk, the organization must still have appropriate safeguards, controls, and privacy protections in place for legitimate insurers to pay for any incidents that occur.
- **Risk acceptance:** Risk acceptance is the opposite of risk avoidance. Risk acceptance does not reduce risks, but it is still considered a valid strategy. Risk acceptance is actually a common choice whenever the cost of other risk mitigation strategies, such as avoidance or limitation, outweighs the estimated cost of the risk impact itself. If a risk does not have a high possibility of happening, many organizations will simply accept the risk.

Smart Grid Privacy Risks

In general, privacy risks within the Smart Grid fall into one of two broad categories:

- Type I: Personal information and energy data not previously readily obtainable.
- Type II: Methods and technologies for obtaining (or manipulating) personal information and energy data that did not previously exist.

Energy Usage Data Privacy Risks*

Throughout this book many different types of privacy risks within the Smart Grid have been described at a high level. Appendix A provides a table documenting the different categories of data that will be found

* This section is an updated version of the corresponding section of NISTIR 7628 Rev. 1: Guidelines for Smart Grid Cybersecurity: Volume 2–Privacy and the Smart Grid; September 2014; http://nvlpubs.nist.gov/nistpubs/ir/2014/NIST.IR.7628r1.pdf; that was originally created in 2010 by the NIST Smart Grid CSWG Privacy Group that Rebecca Herold has led since mid-2009, and in which Christine Hertzog managed the use cases reviews for 3 years.

within the Smart Grid, and that can be obtained from smart devices, along with the likelihood that the specific types of data found within each category will have privacy implications. Also shown are the various types of audiences and groups that may have an interest, legitimate or not, to get access to each type of data. Table 7.1 provides a summary of the primary privacy risks considered at the time of this writing.

A detailed sense of activities within a house or building can be derived from equipment electricity signatures, individual appliance usage data, time patterns of usage, and other data. Especially when collected and analyzed over a period of time, this information can provide a basis for potentially determining occupant activities and lifestyle. For example, a forecast may be made about:

- The number of individuals at a premise
- When the location is unoccupied
- Sleep schedules
- Work schedules
- Other personal routines that involve usage of the building's electricity grid*

While technology that communicates directly with appliances and other energy consumption elements and devices already exists, increased energy usage data may create broader incentives for its use and provide easier access by interested parties.† Appliances so equipped may deliver granular energy consumption data to their data owners, data custodians, and data managers, as well as to outside parties. The increased collection of and access to granular energy usage data will create new uses for this data. Some examples include:

- Residential demand response (DR) systems
- Marketing
- Insurance actuarial tables
- Law enforcement

* It is important to emphasize that the activities that can be determined, or that are inferred, must be attached to the electric grid. There have been some outrageous claims regarding activities, such as using a traditional battery-powered electric toothbrush, flashlights, or vibrators can be determined by smart meters; this is simply not true and not possible. Smart meters and customer-owned home energy management systems and apps cannot determine the usage of objects that are not even drawing electricity from the grid.

† See Appendix A.

Table 7.1 Potential Privacy Impacts that Arise from the Collection and Use of Smart Grid Data

TYPE OF DATA	PRIVACY-RELATED INFORMATION POTENTIALLY REVEALED BY THIS TYPE OF DATA	PARTIES POTENTIALLY COLLECTING OR USING THIS TYPE OF DATA	TYPE OF POTENTIAL USE[a]	SPECIFIC POTENTIAL USES OF THIS TYPE OF DATA
Captures detailed energy usage at a location, whether in real time or on a delayed basis	**Personal behavior patterns and activities inside the home:** Behavioral patterns, habits, and activities taking place inside the home by monitoring electricity usage patterns and appliance use, including activities like sleeping, eating, showering, and watching TV Patterns over time to determine number of people in the household, work schedule, sleeping habits, vacation, health, affluence, or other lifestyle details and habits When specific appliances are being used in a home, or when industrial equipment is in use, via granular energy data and appliance energy consumption profiles	Utilities	Primary	Load monitoring and forecasting; demand response; efficiency analysis and monitoring; billing
		Consumer direct services[b] and other types of entities obtaining data directly from energy consumers		Efficiency analysis and monitoring; demand response; public or limited disclosure to promote conservation; to access and control home appliances and energy controls, raise energy awareness, etc. (e.g., posting energy usage to social media)
		Insurance companies	Secondary	Determine premiums (e.g., specific behavior patterns, like erratic sleep, that could indicate health problems)
		Marketers		Profile for targeted advertisements; to sell personal information for revenue generation
	Real-time surveillance information: Via real-time energy use data, determine if anyone is home, what they are doing, and where they are located in the home	Law enforcement		Identify suspicious or illegal activity; investigations; real-time surveillance to determine if residents are present and determine current activities inside the home (e.g., marijuana greenhouses)
		Civil litigation		Determine when someone is at home or the estimated number of people present

		Landlord/lessor		Use tenants' energy profiles to verify lease compliance
		Private investigators		Investigations; monitoring for specific events; provide evidence for divorce proceedings or various types of lawsuits
		The press		Public interest in the activities of famous individuals;[c] use for political campaigns
		Creditors		Determine behavior that seems to indicate creditworthiness or changes in credit risk.[d]
		Criminals and other unauthorized users	Illicit	Identify the best times for a burglary; determine if residents are present; identify assets that might be present; commit fraud; use for identity theft; sell to other criminals; disrupt service; corporate espionage—determine confidential processes or proprietary data; to commit political or social protests
Identifies location/ recharge information for plug-in electric vehicles (PEVs) or other location-aware appliances	**Determine location information:** Historical PEV data, which can be used to determine range of use since last recharge Location of active PEV charging activities, which can be used to determine the location of driver	Utilities	Primary	Bill energy consumption to owner of the PEV; distributed energy resource management; emergency response
		Insurance companies	Secondary	Determine premiums based on driving habits and recharge location
		Marketers		Profile and send targeted marketing communications based on driving habits and PEV condition

(continued)

Table 7.1 Potential Privacy Impacts that Arise from the Collection and Use of Smart Grid Data (continued)

TYPE OF DATA	PRIVACY-RELATED INFORMATION POTENTIALLY REVEALED BY THIS TYPE OF DATA	PARTIES POTENTIALLY COLLECTING OR USING THIS TYPE OF DATA	TYPE OF POTENTIAL USE[a]	SPECIFIC POTENTIAL USES OF THIS TYPE OF DATA
		Private investigators/law enforcement agencies		Investigations; locating or creating tracking histories for persons of interest; gain evidence to dispute a legal accusation
		Civil litigation		Determine when someone was home or at a different location
		PEV lessor		Verify a lessee's compliance regarding the mileage, car speed, etc., of a lease agreement
Identifies individual meters or consumer-owned equipment and capabilities	**Identify household appliances:** Identifying information (such as a MAC address); directly reported usage information provided by smart appliances Data revealed from compromised smart meter, HAN, or other appliance	Utilities	Primary	Load monitoring and forecasting; efficiency analysis and monitoring; reliability; demand response; distributed energy resource management; emergency response
		Consumer direct services and other types of entities obtaining data directly from energy consumers		Efficiency analysis and monitoring; broadcasting appliance use to social media; smart appliance remote control via smart phone apps

		Insurance companies	Secondary	Make claim adjustments (e.g., determine if claimant actually owned appliances that were claimed to have been destroyed by house fire); determine or modify premiums based upon the presence of appliances that might indicate increased risk; identify activities that might change risk profiles
		Marketers		Profile for targeted advertisements based upon owned and unowned appliances or activities indicated by appliance use
		Law enforcement		Substantiate energy usage that may indicate illegal activity; identify activities on premises
		Civil litigation		Identify property; identify activities on premises
		Criminals and other unauthorized users	Illicit	Identify what assets may be present to target for theft; disrupt operation of appliances or electric service; introduce a virus or other attack to collect personal information or disrupt service; compromise smart meters to steal energy; hack to obtain data files.[e]

[a] Primary uses of Smart Grid data are those used to provide direct services to customers that are directly based on those data, including energy generation services or load monitoring services. Secondary uses of data are uses that apply Smart Grid data to other business purposes, such as insurance adjustment or marketing, or to nonbusiness purposes, such as government investigations or civil litigation. Illicit uses of data are uses that are never authorized and are often criminal.

[b] Edge services include businesses providing services based directly upon electrical usage but not providing services related to the actual generation, transportation, or distribution of electricity. Some examples of edge services would include OPOWER, GE Energy Management, Green Button services, vendors with energy management apps and tools, smart appliance vendors, and consulting services based upon electricity usage, just to name a few.

(continued)

Table 7.1 Potential Privacy Impacts that Arise from the Collection and Use of Smart Grid Data (continued)

[c] For example, there were numerous news stories about the amount of electricity used by Al Gore's Tennessee home. See, e.g., Gore's High Energy-Use Home Target of Critical Report, Fox News, February 28, 2007, http://www.foxnews.com/story/0,2933,254908,00.html.

[d] Sudden changes in when residents are home could indicate the loss of a job. Erratic sleep patterns could indicate possible stress and increased likelihood of job loss. See, e.g., Charles Duhigg, What Does Your Credit-Card Company Know about You? *New York Times Magazine*, May 17, 2009, p. MM40, http://www.nytimes.com/2009/05/17/magazine/17credit-t.html.

[e] See Matthew Carpenter et al., *Advanced Metering Infrastructure Attack Methodology*, January 5, 2009, pp. 55–56, http://inguardians.com/pubs/AMI_Attack_Methodology.pdf (discussing how attackers could manipulate the data reported to utilities); Robert Lemos, Hacking the Smart Grid, *Technology Review*, April 5, 2010, http://www.technologyreview.com/printer_friendly_article.aspx?id=24977&channel=energy&section=.

Source: This is a table updated by the authors that was originally created in 2010 by the NIST Smart Grid CSWG Privacy Group that Rebecca Herold has led since mid-2009, and in which Christine Hertzog managed the use cases reviews for 3 years. The original table is available in NISTIR 7628 Rev. 1: Guidelines for Smart Grid Cybersecurity: Volume 2–Privacy and the Smart Grid; September 2014; http://nvlpubs.nist.gov/nistpubs/ir/2014/NIST.IR.7628r1.pdf.

Many of these new uses will be innovative and provide individual and consumer benefits, some will impact privacy, and many will do both.

Such data might be used in ways that raise privacy concerns. Some examples include:

- Granular energy usage data may allow numerous assumptions about the health of a dwelling's resident in which some insurance companies, employers, newspapers (when regarding public figures), civil litigants, and others could be interested.
- Most directly, specific medical devices may be uniquely identified through serial numbers or MAC addresses,[*] or may have unique electrical signatures; either could indicate that the resident suffers from a particular disease or condition that requires the device.[†]
- More generally, inferences might be used to determine behavioral and health patterns and risk. For example, the amount of time the computer or television is on could be compared to the amount of time the treadmill is used.[‡]
- Electricity use could also reveal how much the resident sleeps and whether he gets up in the middle of the night.[§]

---

[*] A media access control address (MAC address) is a unique identifier assigned to network interfaces to allow for communications on the physical network segment. MAC addresses are used as network addresses for most IEEE 802 network technologies. MAC addresses are typically established by the manufacturer of a network interface controller (NIC) and are programmed within its hardware, such as the card's read-only memory or some other firmware mechanism.

[†] Susan Lyon and John Roche, Smart Grid News, Smart Grid Privacy Tips Part 2: Anticipate the Unanticipated, February 9, 2010, http://www.SmartGridnews.com/artman/publish/Business_Policy_Regulation_News/Smart-Grid-Privacy-Tips-Part-2-Anticipate-the-Unanticipated-1873.html.

[‡] Elias Quinn mentions an Alabama tax provision that requires obese state employees to pay for health insurance unless they work to reduce their body mass index. Elias Quinn, Privacy and the New Energy Infrastructure (draft), February 2009, p. 31, http://papers.ssrn.com/sol3/papers.cfm?abstract_id=1370731. He suggests that Smart Grid data could be used to see how often a treadmill was being used in the home.

[§] Ann Cavoukian, Jules Polonetsky, and Christopher Wolf, Privacy by Design, SmartPrivacy for the Smart Grid: Embedding Privacy into the Design of Electricity Conservation, November 2009, http://www.ipc.on.ca/images/Resources/pbd-smart-priv-Smart Grid.pdf (describing the types of information that could be gleaned from combining personal information with granular energy consumption data).

- Similarly, appliance usage data could indicate how often meals are cooked with the microwave, the stove, or not cooked at all, as well as implying the frequency of meals.*

Energy Production Data Privacy Risks

More consumers are becoming energy prosumers and pumping electricity into the Smart Grid that is generated from their distributed energy resources (DERs). This book's authors live in states that are leaders in prosumer energy generations. Rebecca lives in Iowa, which is number 1 in the nation in wind energy production.† Rebecca is acquainted with many who have wind generators on their land. Iowa landowners with wind turbines on their land receive more than $16 million annually in lease payments.‡ Christine lives in California, which just passed SB871, which provides substantial incentives to photovoltaic (PV) solar system owners, such as full residential tariff credit for their excess daytime power and a 30% investment tax credit for buying a capital asset that generates long-term tax-free income in the form of avoided utility bills.§ California leads the United States in cumulative solar energy production and capacity.¶ There are privacy risks that are also related to prosumer energy production data. Some of the data that is involved in these risks includes:

- Name and address of the prosumer
- Amount of energy produced
- Amount of energy used by the prosumer on-site
- Payments made for the energy sold back to the utility
- Log of electricity generation history

---

* Ibid., p. 11.

† During 2012, Iowa produced a national record of almost 25% of all the electricity generated in the state from wind turbines. Iowa is back to first in the nation in terms of the percentage of total generation from wind energy. Iowa was also the first state in the nation to exceed 20% of total generation coming from wind energy. Iowa's installed wind generators can produce enough power to provide electricity to over 1,500,000 average-sized homes. http://www.iowawindenergy.org/whywind.php (accessed June 20, 2014).

‡ http://www.iowawindenergy.org/whywind.php (accessed June 20, 2014).

§ Published June 27, 2014, http://www.breitbart.com/Breitbart-California/2014/06/27/Solar-Power-is-not-Green-it-s-Filthy.

¶ http://www.seia.org/research-resources/solar-industry-data (accessed June 29, 2014).

Not only are utilities interested in this data (and they have a primary purpose by logic of maintaining grid stability as well as financial settlements), but also many other entities would likely want to know this information—all creating privacy concerns. Some of these entities include:

- Neighbors of the prosumers
- Insurance companies
- Government agencies
- Law enforcement
- Smart Grid component vendors
- Marketing agencies
- Ex-partners and ex-spouses
- Criminals
- Politicians

Identifying Risks

The most effective way to identify specific privacy risks, such as those described in Table 7.1, is by doing a privacy impact assessment (PIA).* A PIA† is a structured and repeatable type of analysis of how information relating to or about individuals, or groups of individuals, is handled. A report similar to an audit report is generated to describe the types of privacy risks discovered based upon each privacy category, to document the findings, and then to provide recommendations for mitigating the privacy risk findings. Common goals of a PIA include:

1. Determining if the information handling and use within the identified scope complies with legal, regulatory, and policy requirements regarding privacy
2. Determining the risks and effects of collecting, maintaining, and disseminating information in identifiable, or clear text, form in an electronic information system or groups of systems

* For more information about PIAs, along with PIA tools, see http://www.privacyprofessor.org.

† This section is updated text originally from Rebecca Herold, *The Privacy Management Toolkit*, Houston: Information Shield, January 2006.

3. Examining and evaluating the protections and alternative processes for handling information to mitigate the identified potential privacy risks

There are many times when a PIA can be beneficial and should be conducted by utilities, vendors of products or services, energy services providers (ESPs), and any other entities that may handle energy usage data. Here are some of the most important times to conduct a PIA:

1. Conduct an initial PIA before making the decision to deploy a Smart Grid service, tool, or participate in the Smart Grid.
2. Conduct a PIA following significant organizational, systems, applications, or legal changes.
3. Conduct a PIA following privacy breaches and information security incidents involving personal information.
4. Conduct a PIA as an alternative, or in addition, to an independent audit.
5. Conduct a PIA on the designs of any new Smart Grid product or service.
6. Conduct a PIA when mergers or acquisitions occur.
7. Conduct a PIA on divestiture plans prior to initiating the divestiture.

Privacy Risk Mitigation Methods

Once an organization identifies privacy risks, appropriate risk mitigation actions need to be determined. Here are some of the most effective methods to mitigate privacy risks within the Smart Grid.

1. Adopt existing and recognized privacy principles and frameworks to guide your organization's decisions involving personal information or energy data of all kinds.

   When creating or updating a privacy management program, organizations should start with existing, comprehensive, well-vetted, and widely accepted privacy standards or principles. The following are some of the most commonly used privacy standards and policies:

   a. **OECD Privacy Framework.** On September 23, 1980, the Organization for Economic Cooperation and

Development (OECD), whose membership consists of 34 countries, reached a consensus on issues related to the protection of privacy to promote the free flow of information across country borders and to prevent legal issues related to the protection of privacy from creating obstacles to the development of their economic and social relations. These are reflected in the eight OECD Privacy Guidelines, which were most recently updated at the time this book was written in 2013.*

b. **American Institute of Certified Public Accountants (AICPA)/Canadian Institute of Chartered Accountants (CICA) Generally Accepted Privacy Principles (GAPPs).** Most commonly known as the AICPA/CICA GAPPs, these privacy tools include a universal framework for CPAs to conduct risk assessments and provide criteria to protect the privacy of personal information. The AICPA/CICA GAPPs' Security for Privacy Principles have been mapped to ISO/IEC 27002.†

c. **APEC Privacy Framework.** Published in 2005, this framework establishes and promotes an approach to protecting privacy when sharing information throughout Asia Pacific Economic Cooperation (APEC) member countries, with a goal of removing barriers to the free flow of information.‡

d. **European Union (EU) Privacy Framework.** The European Commission has proposed reforms to existing 1995 data protection rules that include a single set of rules on data protection that include a policy communication, a regulation setting out a general EU framework for data protection, and a directive to protect personal data processed for judicial activities.§

---

* See full OECD Guidelines on the Protection of Privacy and Transborder Flows of Personal Data, http://www.oecd.org/sti/ieconomy/privacy.htm.

† See more at http://www.aicpa.org/INTERESTAREAS/INFORMATIONTECHNOLOGY/RESOURCES/PRIVACY/Pages/default.aspx.

‡ See more at http://www.apec.org/Groups/Committee-on-Trade-and-Investment/~/media/Files/Groups/ECSG/05_ecsg_privacyframewk.ashx.

§ See http://ec.europa.eu/justice/data-protection/index_en.htm.

e. **Fair Information Practice Principles (FIPPs).** The FIPPs are a set of principles based upon the tenets of the U.S. Privacy Act of 1974. Several slightly different versions are used by various U.S. federal agencies, including the Department of Homeland Security, the Federal Trade Commission, and the Department of Commerce. For the Department of Homeland Security (DHS), the FIPPs are transparency, individual participation, purpose specification, data minimization, use limitation, data quality and integrity, security, and accountability and auditing. For the Federal Trade Commission (FTC), they are notice/awareness, choice/consent, access/participation, integrity/security, and enforcement/redress.

f. **ISO/IEC 15944-8 Information Technology. Business Operational View.** Identification of privacy protection requirements as external constraints on business transactions. Modeling business transactions using scenarios and scenario components is done by specifying the applicable constraints on the data content using explicitly stated rules. External constraints apply to most business transactions. This part of ISO/IEC 15944 describes the business semantic descriptive techniques needed to support privacy protection requirements when modeling business transactions using the external constraints of jurisdictional domains. It was published in April 2012.

g. **ISO/IEC 27002: Information Technology—Security Techniques—Code of Practice for Information Security Management. Section 15.** The International Organization for Standardization (ISO) and the International Electrotechnical Commission (IEC) jointly issued this international standard, last updated and published in December 2005. It is part of a growing family of ISO/IEC information security management systems (ISMSs) standards. It is the security compliance standard. ISO/IEC 27002 provides a security framework. Section 15 covers compliance, including legal requirements; security policies and standards and technical compliance; and information systems audit considerations. It is part of a growing family of ISO/IEC ISMSs standards.

h. **ISO/IEC 29100: Information Technology—Security Techniques—Privacy Framework.** This international standard published in December 2011 provides a privacy framework that specifies a common privacy terminology; defines the actors and their roles in processing personal information; describes privacy safeguarding considerations; and provides references to known privacy principles for information technology.

i. **Privacy by Design (PbD).** This is a privacy framework by Ann Cavoukian, PhD, information and privacy commissioner of Ontario. PbD promotes the proactive incorporation of privacy as the default and data protections embedded throughout the entire life cycle of systems and technologies. The seven foundational principles of PbD were published in August 2009.*

2. Identify and use privacy standards and guidelines from authoritative organizations to support privacy efforts.

Many different organizations have created privacy standards and guidelines to support the privacy principles and frameworks. The following is a good representation of some of the groups that have established a wide variety of privacy-related standards and guidelines on various topics that entities in the Smart Grid can use to help mitigate their privacy risks.

a. In 2011, the North American Energy Standards Board (NAESB) created a Data Privacy Task Force to develop model business practices for third-party access to consumer Smart Grid data. The task force's goal was to develop model business practices based on existing reports and laws.† At the time of this writing, NAESB had published the following nonbinding privacy standards for the energy industry:

i. NAESB REQ.22, Third Party Access to Smart Meter-Based Information. Per NAESB, the "document

* See more at http://privacybydesign.ca/.

† See information about the NAESB Data Privacy Task Force activities at http://www.naesb.org/news.asp.

establishes voluntary Model Business Practices for Third Party access to Smart Meter-based information. These business practices are intended only to serve as flexible guidelines rather than requirements, with the onus on regulatory authorities or similar bodies to establish the actual requirements."[*] NAESB based the privacy recommendations within this standard largely upon the recommendations provided within NISTIR 7628 Rev. 1.[†] After completing the draft of REQ.22, the NIST Smart Grid CSWG Privacy Group also provided recommendations for how it could add privacy protection improvements to the standard.[‡] NAESB subsequently made updates to the original version of the standard.[§]

ii. NAESB REQ.21, Energy Services Provider Interface.[¶] Per NAESB, the "purpose of the NAESB Energy Services Provider Interface (ESPI) standard (REQ.21) is to create a standardized process and interface for the exchange of a retail customer's energy usage information between their designated data custodian (i.e., distribution company) and an authorized third party service provider." REQ.21 includes some recommendations for mitigating the associated privacy risks.

b. On December 16, 2010, the U.S. Department of Commerce National Telecommunications and Information Administration (NTIA) published "Commercial Data Privacy and Innovation in the Internet Economy: A Dynamic Policy Framework."[**] Because many consider the Smart Grid to be a new type of telecommunications net-

---

* See the background and accompanying information NAESB provided about the standard at http://members.sgip.org/apps/group_public/download.php/2883/NAESB%20REQ%2022%20Voting%20Package.pdf.

† See http://nvlpubs.nist.gov/nistpubs/ir/2014/NIST.IR.7628v1.pdf

‡ See https://www.naesb.org/pdf4/r12008.doc.

§ See naesb.org/pdf4/naesb_bulletin_vol5_issue3.pdf.

¶ See the text at http://www.naesb.org/ESPI_standards.asp.

** See it at https://www.smartgrid.gov/news/doe_addresses_privacy_data_enabled_smart_grid_technologies_convenes_multistakeholder_process.

work, utilities and other Smart Grid participants are using this for their privacy program implementation.

c. On January 31, 2012, the U.S. Department of Energy, Office of Electricity Delivery and Energy Reliability (DOE OE) hosted the Smart Grid Privacy Workshop to facilitate a dialog among key industry stakeholders. In response to workshop findings and in support of the privacy blueprint, DOE OE and the Federal Smart Grid Task Force are facilitating a multistakeholder process to develop a voluntary code of conduct (VCC) for utilities and third parties providing consumer energy use services that addresses privacy related to data enabled by Smart Grid technologies. The following work groups were created to develop a set of privacy standards to support this effort:
   - Mission Statement Work Group
   - Notice/Awareness Work Group
   - Choice/Consent Work Group
   - Access/Participation Work Group
   - Integrity/Security Work Group
   - Management/Redress Work Group
   - Integration Work Group
   - Implementation Work Group

   At the time of this writing a wide collection of draft and final privacy principles had been created.*
d. In October 2009 the Home-to-Grid Domain Expert Working Group (H2G DEWG) at NIST published the "Privacy of Consumer Information and Devices in the Electric Power Industry."† The paper outlined:
   - The importance of providing consumers ownership of their associated energy usage data
   - Recommended industry privacy policies

* Rebecca Herold also participates in some of these groups. See all the content created by the work groups at https://www.smartgrid.gov/news/doe_addresses_privacy_data_enabled_smart_grid_technologies_convenes_multistakeholder_process.

† This document was written by Rik Drummond and edited by Rebecca Herold and Dr. Ken Wacks. Also participating in the development of this document were Dr. Matthew Schneider of Emerson Electric and Larry Silverman of GridPlex, Inc. See it at http://collaborate.nist.gov/twiki-sggrid/pub/SmartGrid/H2G/Priv-V3.pdf.

   - Privacy risks of inappropriate energy usage data use

e. In December 2012, the State and Local Energy Efficiency Action Network published "A Regulator's Privacy Guide to Third-Party Data Access for Energy Efficiency: Customer Information and Behavior Working Group."* This document contains a summary of privacy legal requirements throughout the energy industry, as well as in other industries. It also includes a long list of references to a wide variety of privacy standards.

3. Document and implement organizational privacy policies, procedures, and assigned responsibilities.

   Organizations within the Smart Grid sector will mitigate privacy risks by developing documented privacy policies† to define the consumer and premises information, how the information will be safeguarded, how that information should be retained, how information can and cannot be shared with third parties, and how information will be secured against breach. The policies should be supported by documented procedures that are written to support the business environment. Providing education to employees is critical to the success of the policies and procedures. All employees should be provided regular privacy training,‡ which should include clear explanation of each employee's responsibilities for complying with the privacy policies. Ongoing awareness communications should be provided to make sure employees are reminded of the privacy policies requirements, their personal responsibilities for privacy, and the privacy procedures that are applicable to them.

   Similarly, Smart Grid services consumers and customers should be provided with a privacy notice that clearly and

* Prepared by M. Dworkin, K. Johnson, D. Kreis, C. Rosser, and J. Voegele, Vermont Law School; S. Weissman, UC Berkeley; and M. Billingsley and C. Goldman, Lawrence Berkeley National Laboratory. See http://www1.eere.energy.gov/seeaction/pdfs/cib_regulator_privacy_guide.pdf.

† For privacy policies templates specific to utilities and other Smart Grid entities, see http://www.privacyprofessor.org.

‡ For guidance on privacy training and awareness programs, see Rebecca Herold, Managing an Information Security and Privacy Awareness and Training Program, Boca Raton: Auerbach, 2010, http://www.crcpress.com/product/isbn/9781439815458.

succinctly describes the information the organization is collecting and how that information will be used, shared, and secured. The consumers and customers should also be told the procedures they need to follow to gain access to their own applicable information, and their options for submitting requests to correct information, as well as to delete information that is no longer valid, or no longer needed to support the service provided by the organization.

4. Utilize privacy use cases to identify where to include privacy protections and data safeguards.

   Develop privacy use cases that track data flows containing personal information, energy usage data, energy consumption data, or energy production data to address and mitigate common privacy risks that exist for business processes within an organization or between organizations. Privacy use cases help IT and network architects, functional process owners, and engineers build or specify privacy protections into their products, processes, and operations to mitigate privacy risks.

   A privacy use case is a description of data flows within a specific scenario or scope that will help entities to rigorously track data flows and the privacy implications of collecting and using data, and will help organizations to address and mitigate the associated privacy risks within common technical design and business practices. Privacy use cases reflect the electricity value chain and the impacts that Smart Grid technologies, new policies, new markets, and new consumer interactions will have on the privacy of customers and consumers within the Smart Grid. The privacy use cases can serve as a valuable tool for all types of Smart Grid entities, including utilities; energy service companies (ESCOs); vendors of products and services that may include collection, storage, or communication of personal data; and policy makers, to better understand the implications of Smart Grid technology changes to existing processes and procedures.

   When the general privacy concerns have been identified, the entities within each part of the Smart Grid sector can then look at their associated business processes and technical components to determine the privacy concerns that exist within their scope of use and participation. Privacy use cases may be utilized to represent generalizations of specific scenarios that require interoperability between systems and participants in support of business processes and workflow. Through structured and repeatable analysis, business use cases can be elaborated upon as interoperability/technical privacy use cases to be implemented by the associated entities. The resulting details will allow those responsible for creating, implementing, and managing the controls that impact privacy to do so more effectively and consistently.

Table 7.2 is one of the 44 privacy use cases within NISTIR 7628 Rev. 1.* This provides an example of a privacy use case format that can be used by Smart Grid entities to establish their own Smart Grid privacy use cases for their own specific services and products they are creating for Smart Grid use. Developers of Smart Grid applications, systems, and operational processes can employ a more comprehensive set of privacy use cases to create architectures that build in privacy protections to mitigate identified privacy risks.

5. Use data aggregation, de-identification, and other similar techniques, where appropriate and effective, to protect privacy.

Throughout hundreds of Smart Grid meetings the authors have attended over the years, one of the most common methods touted to protect privacy is to use aggregated data so that individual energy consumers and prosumers and their associated activities and personal information are not able to be revealed. However, there are real concerns with how well aggregation and de-identification methods work, and the lack

* The privacy use cases in NISTIR 7628 Rev. 1 were created by a subteam of the NIST Smart Grid CSWG Privacy Group. The subteam was led by Christine Hertzog and the team included Rebecca Herold, Tanya Brewer (NIST), Sarah Cortes (Inman Technologies), and Brandon Robinson (Balch & Bingham). Marianne Swanson, who was the senior advisor, Information Systems Security, Information Technology Laboratory, and leader of the NIST CSWG groups at the time, was also a strong supporter of the efforts of the subteam to create the privacy use cases. The subteam created the privacy use cases by expanding the collection of CSWG use cases to cover all Smart Grid value chain participants, in addition to utilities (regulated or not) that will offer Smart Grid-related products and services. See the full set of 44 privacy use cases in Appendix E of NISTIR 7628 Rev. 1; see http://nvlpubs.nist.gov/nistpubs/ir/2014/NIST.IR.7628r1.pdf.

Table 7.2 Example Privacy Use Case

Category: AMI **Scenario:** Meter sends information	Privacy use case 1	
CATEGORY DESCRIPTION Advanced metering infrastructure (AMI) systems consist of the hardware, software, and associated system and data management applications that create a communications network between end systems at customer premises (including meters, gateways, and other equipment) and diverse business and operational systems of utilities and third parties. AMI systems provide the technology to allow the exchange of information between customer end systems and those other utility and third-party systems. In order to protect this critical infrastructure, end-to-end security must be provided across the AMI systems, encompassing the customer end systems as well as the utility and third-party systems that are interfaced to the AMI systems.		
SCENARIO DESCRIPTION A meter sends automated energy usage information to the utility (e.g., meter read (usage data)). The automated send of energy usage information is initiated by the meter and is sent to the advanced metering infrastructure (AMI) head end system (HES). The head end system message flows to the meter reading and control (MRC). The MRC evaluates the message. The MRC archives the automated energy usage information and forwards the information to the meter data management systems (MDMSs). • Meter configuration information • Periodic meter reading • On-demand meter reading Net metering for distributed energy resources (DERs) and plug-in electric vehicle (PEV)		
SMART GRID CHARACTERISTICS • Enables active participation by consumers • Enables new products, services, and markets • Optimizes asset utilization and operates efficiently	CYBER SECURITY OBJECTIVES/REQUIREMENTS • Confidentiality (privacy) of customer metering data over the AMI system, metering database, and billing database to avoid serious breaches of privacy and potential legal repercussions • Integrity of meter data is important, but the impact of incorrect data is not large • Availability of meter data is not critical in real time	POTENTIAL STAKEHOLDER ISSUES • Customer data privacy and security • Third party or party acting as an agent of the utility has access to energy usage information for market or consumer services • Third party or party acting on behalf of the utility has reliable data • Customer data access • Reliable data for billing

(continued)

Table 7.2 Example Privacy Use Case (continued)

1.1	DATA PRIVACY RECOMMENDATIONS Any individually negotiated purchase agreement that contains or is associated with personally identifiable customer data should be subject to the same privacy and security applications as personally identifiable data.		
1.2	Meter read data should be evaluated to determine if they should be protected data regardless of type of service or tariff or scheduled meter read frequency, and the same policy notice can apply. Similarly, the same choice and consent information can be used across all scenarios noted above, with the caveat that if any contracted agents are involved, the individual has been notified and consented to the contracted agent's access to the data identified as necessary for that activity. This notice may happen within the initial privacy notice given at account setup.		
1.3	Customer access to data in real time or near real time, particularly for net metering/feed-in tariff (FiT) data, is important for many customers to optimize performance of assets that generate or store electricity. This access should be limited to the consumer associated with the meter, the utility for operational and billing purposes or its authorized agent, and consumer-authorized third parties. (The OECD principle for access indicates that individuals should have access to data associated with them.)		
1.4	Meter reading is an ongoing activity, so it is important that utilities create a monitoring and enforcement process that ensures compliance on a continuous basis.		
1.5	Utility-authorized agents or third parties may be given access to meter reading data for various customer peer performance/comparison purposes. These agents or third parties should also conform and comply with utility privacy policies, and customers should consent to the disclosure of their information to these agents or third parties.		
	AICPA PRINCIPLE	APPLIES: X	NOTES
1.6	Management principle	X	An individual, team, or department should be assigned responsibility for ensuring policies and procedures exist that cover the situations involved within this use case scenario.
1.7	Notice principle	X	Should be provided for all meter reading, regular consumption, and net metering scenarios.

1.8	Choice and consent principle	X	Ensures that when customers sign up for service that this choice and consent requirement is met.
1.9	Collection principle	X	Over time, data collection may change as new applications, technologies, or correlations of data are made available. Utility policy should indicate that collection purposes may change over time, and that utilities will notify customers of any proposed changes that may impact collection in order to secure an updated choice and consent.
1.10	Use and retention principle	X	Retention may be impacted by time frames to record and compensate for net metering scenarios. Data retention may also be impacted by local, state, or federal laws/regulations/requirements outside of utility operational needs.
1.11	Access principle	X	Access to the meter usage data, and any associated data that could reveal personal data, should be limited to only those who need such access to perform their job activities.
1.12	Disclosure to third parties principle	X	Utility net metering payments to customers may be considered revenue or income, and thus subject to tax laws, or garnishments for child support, legal claims, etc. Requests may come from law enforcement agencies or other entities that make requests for information from utilities. Some of the legal implications may not require implicit or explicit consent.
1.13	Security for privacy principle	X	Safeguards should be applied as appropriate to mitigate associated risks to an acceptable level.[a] (For more discussion on security particulars, please see NISTIR 7628 Volume 3 Revision 1 on high-level security requirements.)
1.14	Quality principle	X	Controls should be established to ensure meter usage is as accurate as necessary for the purposes for which they are being collected.
1.15	Monitoring and enforcement principle	X	This should not be just a once and done audit on a yearly basis since meter reading is an ongoing activity. Utilities should create a practice of regular compliance monitoring on a rolling basis to completely cover the customer records on a several times a year frequency.

of control over each aggregated or de-identified data set once it has been created. Here are just a couple of the problems:

a. For one de-identification risk example, it may not be possible to reidentify individuals from a single de-identified data set. However, if other data is combined with a de-identified data set, use of a variety of different types of algorithms may be used to achieve reidentification. Reidentification refers to the ability to use methodologies to determine specific individuals that were removed from de-identified data sets.
b. As an example of an aggregation risk example, disaggregation refers to a set of statistical approaches for extracting end use or appliance-level data from an aggregated energy signal from a meter or other specialized device.* Disaggregation technologies can be used on energy usage data to analyze the frequency and durations for use of the studied appliances. See Figures 7.1 and 7.2 for examples of the details disaggregation can reveal.

The possibility of disaggregation of anonymized data and reidentification is not just theory; it has been demonstrated multiple times in recent years.† The interest in disaggregation continues to increase, as demonstrated in 2013 when Belkin Energy had a disaggregation competition to advance

* For a discussion of disaggregation, see *Energy Policy*, 52, 213–234, 2013, Special Section: Transition Pathways to a Low Carbon Economy, http://www.sciencedirect.com/science/article/pii/S0301421512007446.

† As described in Klaus Kursawe, *How to Have the Cake and Eat It, Too: Protecting Privacy and Energy Efficiency in the Smart Grid*, Institute for Computing and Information Science, Radboud University, Nijmegen, The Netherlands:

That this kind of re-identification is possible has been shown in past studies, e.g., on Netflix move preference data [NaSh08]. In all those cases, data that was anonymised (such as movie preferences, or anonymised health data) could be de-anonymised with a surprising efficiency. It is therefore no longer possible to cleanly separate between personal identifiable data and harmless data, as each additional data item makes identification a little bit easier. Due to the wealth of data that can be derived in smart grid readings, there is a clear indication that the approach of simply separating identifiable and anonymous data is a good start, but will quickly reach its limits.

As a more concrete example, grid data may reveal that a person always stays up late when a particular TV show is on, which in return may give some demographic data. It also can be linked with some semi-public data (e.g., people who 'like' this show on social networks) to assist in the de-anonymisation. Additional data mining may give information about my occupation, holiday schedule, religious preference, etc, which all narrow down the anonymity.

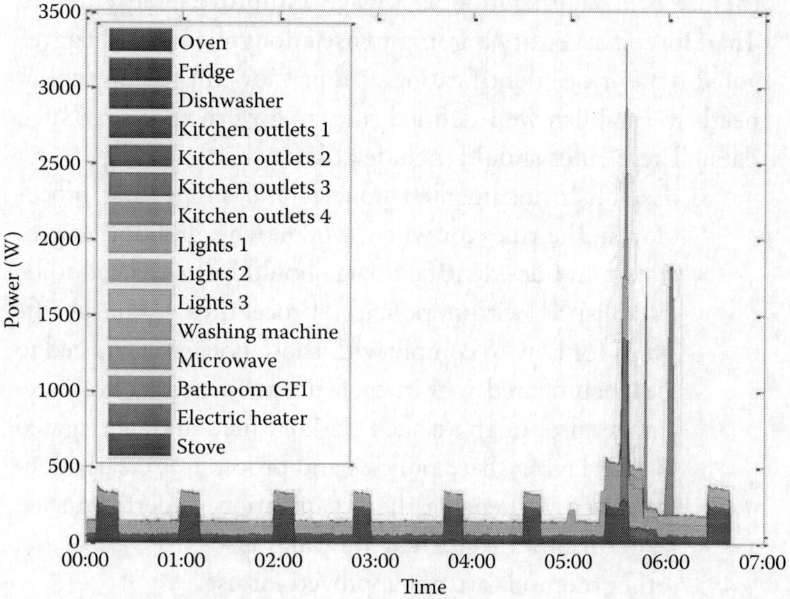

Figure 7.1 Examples of the details disaggregation can reveal. (From O. Parson et al., Non-Intrusive Load Monitoring Using Prior Models of General Appliance Types, presented at 1st International Workshop on Non-Intrusive Load Monitoring, Pittsburgh, PA, 2012.)

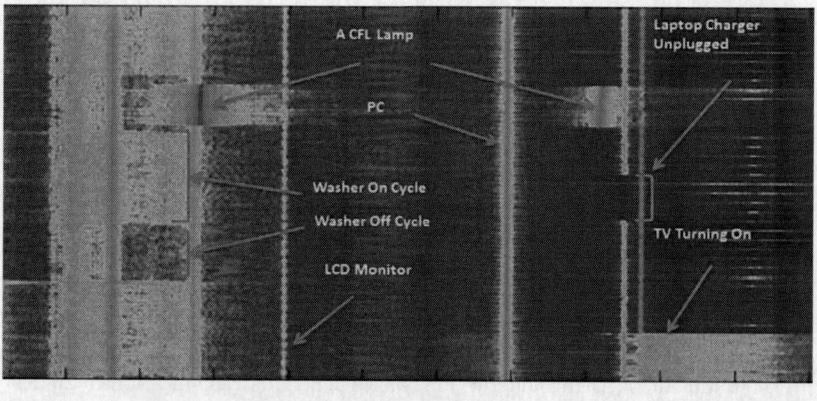

Figure 7.2 Examples of the details disaggregation can reveal. (From Sidhant Gupta et al., ElectriSense: Single-Point Sensing Using EMI for Electrical Event Detection and Classification in the Home Best Paper Award, November 2012, http://homes.cs.washington.edu/~sidhant/research.html. See accompanying video at https://www.youtube.com/watch?v=dcPI1Cp0VZI.)

the use of disaggregation as a way to improve energy usage.* Therefore, if an entity is going to use anonymization of aggregated data or de-identification as a privacy mitigation tool, it needs to establish well-defined rules to govern the use of such data.† These rules should include at least the following:

i. Establish documented policies and supporting procedures. The rules for when, where, why, and how aggregated and de-identified data should be used need to be established within policies. Procedures with specific steps for how to comply with those policies also need to be documented within each department that wants to create, use, or share such de-identified and aggregated data. Having these policies and procedures clearly documented will enable the organization to perform such activities in a consistent way, and also make clear that other methods are not approved for use.

ii. Use an aggregation protocol that has been demonstrated to be effective for preserving privacy. Too many ineffective de-identification and aggregation methods are used by organizations, using simplistic methods that provide little to no privacy protections. For example, throughout her work with many energy industry organizations over the past decade, one of the authors (Rebecca Herold) found that many organizations simply removed the name or address from a data set and called it de-identified. Two examples of proven effective aggregation methods include the Diffie–Hellman-based private aggregation (DiPA) protocol and the low-overhead private aggregation (LoPA) protocol.‡

---

* See https://www.kaggle.com/c/belkin-energy-disaggregation-competition.

† For in-depth discussion of the need for de-identified data controls, see Daniel C. Barth-Jones, The 'Re-Identification' of Governor William Weld's Medical Information: A Critical Re-Examination of Health Data Identification Risks and Privacy Protections, Then and Now, June 4, 2012, http://ssrn.com/abstract=2076397 or http://dx.doi.org/10.2139/ssrn.2076397.

‡ See a good explanation of these protocols within Klaus Kursawe, *How to Have the Cake and Eat It, Too: Protecting Privacy and Energy Efficiency in the Smart Grid*, Institute for Computing and Information Science, Radboud University, Nijmegen, The Netherlands.

iii. Establish data minimization requirements for de-identified and aggregated data. Besides removing the more obvious personal information items, all other items that are not necessary for the purposes for which the aggregated data is being used should also be removed. The less data that remains, but still supports the de-identification and aggregation purposes, the less privacy risk there will be.

iv. Do not combine aggregated or de-identified data sets with other data sets that contain the types of data that have been removed, or new types of data that were not in the original data set. This applies to other aggregated and de-identified data sets. Whenever additional types of data items are introduced to an aggregated or de-identified data set, this will pollute the integrity of the data set and increase the risk that those additional items may have allowed for reidentification or disaggregation. Clearly documented policies and procedures need to be in place for this issue.

v. Require any employee, contractor, or other third party that wants to include new data elements (which might add quasi-identifiers and thus increase reidentification risks) with de-identified or aggregated data to provide legitimate validation that the data remain de-identified or aggregated following the introduction of the new data elements.

vi. Prohibit attempts to reidentify or disaggregate data if statisticians with expertise in reidentification and disaggregation indicate a valid risk exists that such activities could reveal individuals and their relatives, family, or household members. As indicated earlier, many organizations are actively are using such disaggregation methods, so it is important for the privacy, information security, and legal offices to discuss the needs for such actions and balance the approved activities with privacy risk mitigation actions.

vii. Specify that de-identification status no longer applies if, at any time, the data contains data elements that can now be used to identify an individual in some manner.

viii. Formally document within policies and procedures a requirement for data recipients and users of statistically de-identified and aggregated data to always comply with any time limits, data use restrictions, qualifications, or conditions established within the statistical de-identification determination associated with the data.

ix. Establish policies and procedures to require others to protect the data to prevent unauthorized access. Require that those holding and using de-identified and aggregated data implement and maintain appropriate data security and privacy policies, procedures, and associated physical, technical, and administrative safeguards as appropriate to ensure the data is accessed and used only by personnel or parties who have agreed to these same restrictions and conditions. Also require that the data will remain de-identified and aggregated, and that reidentification and disaggregation attempts are prohibited. It is important to note that extensive safeguards and associated security controls may not be necessary for data that has statistically been determined to have a low probability of reidentification. However, for data sets with mid to high likelihood, safeguards and security controls need to ensure risks of reidentification and disaggregation attempts are controlled and kept acceptably low.

x. Require those transferring de-identified or aggregated data to third parties to enter into data use agreements and contracts that require the data recipients to also comply with the previously described actions and requirements. This will enable the important chain of custody* data stewardship principle to be maintained for the accompanying de-identified or aggregated data throughout its uses.

---

* See Chapter 4 for more information on the chain of custody concept.

6. Build privacy controls into smart meters and other smart devices.

   Use the results of research and the privacy use cases to build privacy controls into smart meters and other smart devices. Some effective controls to consider include*:

   a. Encrypt the meter data in storage locations and while being transmitted through networks.
   b. Provide the associated smart meter, or other type of smart device, and consumer the ability to control the levels of aggregation and de-identification within the smart device, to the level that still allows for the utility or smart device supplier to be able to obtain the necessary business value.
   c. Collect the minimum amount possible of personal information from the individuals using smart meters and smart devices without lessening the range and quality of services provided.
   d. Retain data within the smart device for only the amount of time necessary to provide the associated service.
   e. Provide methods for consumers to have choices and control over how the associated data from smart devices is used and shared.
   f. Securely dispose of personal information and energy data when they are no longer needed for the purpose for which they were originally collected.
   g. Obtain consent whenever possible prior to collecting personal information and energy data.
   h. Implement data integrity methods and tools.
   i. Implement technical logs to record each entity or individual that has accessed personal information and energy data.

   For more details about security safeguards to use, see NISTIR 7628 Volume 1 Revision 1 and NISTIR 7628 Volume 3 Revision 1.

* For a detailed paper discussing how to build some of these privacy controls into smart meters, in addition to others, see Future of Privacy Forum and Dr. Ann Cavoukian, SmartPrivacy for the Smart Grid: Embedding Privacy into the Design of Electricity Conservation, Information and Privacy Commissioner, Ontario, Canada, November 2009, http://www.ipc.on.ca/images/Resources/pbd-smartpriv-smartgrid.pdf.

7. Obtain cyber security and breach insurance.

It is becoming common, and indeed a basic expected business practice, to obtain cyber security and breach insurance in many industries, such as the financial and retail sectors. It is also a good idea for entities within the Smart Grid sector to obtain cyber security and breach insurance given the many risks that are involved within this vast new converged grid and network.* Such insurance will be a way to transfer some of the liability risk to another entity in the event of a security incident or privacy breach; it does not replace the need to implement a comprehensive information security and privacy program.

Of paramount importance is getting valuable insurance, and not simply purchasing the first cyber insurance that may pop up in an online search. Look for insurance that covers the following:

a. Privacy breaches and the associated costs. Look for policies that provide discounts for implementing a comprehensive privacy program (as described in this book).
b. Information security incidents and associated costs, including the downtime and any associated financial losses.
c. Cost of lawyers and related court costs in the event of lawsuits.
d. Fines and penalties applied by regulatory oversight agencies, if not expressly forbidden by any applicable laws or regulations.
e. Insurance that assigns a value to both tangible and intangible assets, such as customer information and energy data.
f. Physical damage to the network components, including smart meters and smart appliances, as applicable. Many cyber security insurance policies don't cover physical damage, so it is important to be sure and check on this. Many cyber security policies also exclude physical

* For a full discussion of the need for cyber security insurance, including considerations for utilities and others within the Smart Grid, see Cybersecurity Insurance Workshop Readout Report, National Protection and Programs Directorate, U.S. Department of Homeland Security, November 2012, https://www.dhs.gov/sites/default/files/publications/cybersecurity-insurance-read-out-report.pdf.

damage from supervisory control and data acquisition (SCADA) system attacks.

g. Incidents and breaches that are caused by insiders (employees and contracted entities).
h. Reputational risk provisions that protect corporate boards of directors are built in to many cyber security insurance policies. These are designed to reward companies that adopt information security and privacy policies, standards, practices, and controls that restore their operations (and reputations) quickly.
i. Provisions for guaranteed service and backup operations, as available and possible.

It is to be expected that the more these coverages include, the higher the premium will be. Each entity needs to determine the risks that apply to it, and then choose coverage to mitigate the possible costs of those risks, if they would be exploited, that it wants to transfer to the insurer.

8. Include privacy provisions within vendor contracts.

As mentioned within the de-identification and aggregation controls, other individuals and entities that are given access to the data must be contractually bound to protect that data. A high-level listing of requirements to include in outsourced vendor contracts when personal information or energy data is shared with them, or if they have access to it any way, follows*:

a. **Privacy notices.** Require contractors and other third parties to provide a privacy notice to energy customers prior to sharing personal information or energy data with another party, and also when a significant change in organizational structure, such as merger, bankruptcy, or outsourcing, occurs.
b. **Customer authorization for disclosures.** Require contractors and other third parties to seek customer authorization prior to disclosing personal information or energy

* See the full details for each of these requirements within NISTIR 7628 Rev. 1 at http://nvlpubs.nist.gov/nistpubs/ir/2014/NIST.IR.7628r1.pdf. Also see NAESB REQ.22 http://www.naesb.org/retail_request.asp.

data to other parties unless the service for which the data disclosure is necessary has been previously authorized by the customer.

c. **Data disclosure and minimization.** Require contractors and other third parties to not collect more personal information and energy data than is required to fulfill the agreed upon service, and to obtain a separate authorization before personal information or energy data is used in a different manner.
d. **Customer education and awareness.** Require contractors and other third parties to educate their employees, and customers as appropriate, about their privacy protection policies and practices, including the steps the contractor or other type of third party is taking to protect privacy.
e. **Data quality.** Require contractors and other third parties to implement processes and technologies, as necessary, to ensure data is kept as accurate and complete as possible.
f. **Data security.** Require contractors and other third parties to have clearly documented security policies and supporting procedures that are periodically reviewed and updated as necessary.
g. **Privacy impact assessment.** Require contractors and other third parties to perform periodic privacy impact assessments (PIAs) in accordance with the recommendations earlier in this chapter.
h. **Data retention and disposal.** Require contractors and other third parties to have clearly documented policies and procedures establishing how long data will be retained, as well as when and how personal information and energy data will be disposed of. This should be detailed in the privacy notice given to the customer.
i. **Data breaches.** Require contractors and other third parties to be aware of and comply with any laws or requirements governing data breaches. This applies not just to the third party, but also to its contracted agents.
j. **Employee training.** Require contractors and other third parties to provide employees and their contracted agents

security and privacy training regularly so they know how to protect customer personal information and energy data.

k. **Audits.** Require contractors and other third parties to have independent third-party audits of security and privacy practices performed, and also to provide the organization a copy of their documented information security and privacy policies, and any other supporting documentation, upon request.

9. Comply with privacy laws and regulations.

Be sure to know and comply with all your applicable data protection laws,* regulations, and industry standards. And don't forget to ensure you will also comply with all your contracts that include requirements for protecting personal information and energy data.

* In the United States, a good source of information about state-level Smart Grid laws and rules is http://www.ncsl.org/research/energy/smart-grid-state-action-update.aspx.

8

How to Take Charge of Your Privacy

Roles and Responsibilities

It is important to consider the primary roles that exist for the associated privacy responsibilities for energy usage and production data and who has control over that data. There are terms used in the privacy profession* for those that have responsibilities for protecting privacy. There are sometimes different terms used to describe data or data relationships within the energy industry. In order to have those in the privacy professions better understand the terminologies used within the energy professions, and vice versa, it is instructive to relate the privacy roles to the data owner/custodian/manager roles identified in Chapter 2. This will also help the professionals from different areas of expertise to communicate with each other more successfully. Therefore, within this chapter we are going to take a departure from our other chapters and use both the roles and responsibilities terms from the privacy profession and the Smart Grid sector to help establish a better understanding and linkage between the two sets of terms.

* The privacy responsibility categories/terms used in this chapter are the ones used not only by privacy professionals throughout the world, but also by those who are certified for various categories of privacy expertise by the International Association of Privacy Professionals (IAPP), effectively validating and promoting the use of these terms by privacy professionals and experts throughout the world. One of the authors, Rebecca Herold, holds three of the certifications, CIPT, CIPP/US, and CIPM, and teaches the corresponding certification classes for the IAPP. For more information about the IAPP, see http://www.privacyassociation.org.

- **Data subject.*** In the privacy profession, the data subject is considered to be a person who can be identified, directly or indirectly, by reference to an identification number or to one or more factors specific to his or her physical, physiological, mental, economic, cultural, or social identity, or by the characteristics of the person's activities.

  When considering privacy within the Smart Grid, the data subject is the individual about whom energy usage or production data applies and is processed, along with any associated personal information items, such as name, address, account number, and so on. As discussed in Chapter 2, the energy consumer or prosumer, or as it relates to privacy terms, the data subject, is legally considered to be the data owner in increasing numbers of states, as well as in some countries outside of the United States. This chapter will look at the ways in which the data owner, which we will recognize here as the data subject, can exercise control of his or her associated data, and the responsibilities he or she has for protecting his or her own privacy.
- **Data controller.**† In the privacy profession, this is the organization or individual that collected (or in some situations created, such as when a doctor creates the vital signs for a patient with tools used during the provision of care) the personal information from the data subject. The data controller has the obligation to decide how and why information about data subjects will be processed within the bounds of legal requirements and existing privacy risks, and has the responsibility to appropriately safeguard the data throughout the time that he or she is a custodian of the data.

  In the Smart Grid sector, the data controller is the data custodian, and is generally one of two types of entities:

* This is the definition provided during IAPP training for the CIPP Foundations course, and within the CIPP Foundations Textbook. It closely aligns with the description provided for the EU Data Protection Directive at http://ico.org.uk/for_organisations/data_protection/the_guide/key_definitions. The OECD Privacy Framework also use these terms; see http://www.oecd.org/sti/ieconomy/oecd_privacy_framework.pdf.

† Ibid.

1. The utility that collects from the consumers' or prosumers' energy usage data from the smart meter and the energy production data from the energy production devices
2. The third parties that directly collect data from energy consumers or prosumers that is not used by or has any oversight from a utility. These would be organizations such as energy service providers (ESPs), smart appliance vendors, and energy app creators.

As discussed in Chapter 2, the data custodian, or data controller, is responsible for establishing the controls to ensure the secure transmission, handling, and storage of energy data and the associated personal information of the consumers. This chapter will look at the ways in which the data custodian or data controller can implement privacy protections and security controls for the energy data and associated personal information that he or she has collected, and for which he or she is responsible.

- **Data processor.**[*] In the privacy profession this is an organization or individual that processes data on behalf of the data controller. The employees of data controllers with access to the data are considered to be data processors. The outsourced entities hired by the data controllers to do any type of storage, processing, or transmission, or have access of any kind to the data, are also considered to be data processors.

In the Smart Grid sector, the data processor is typically referenced as the data manager. The following types of entities are data managers in handling energy data and associated personal information:

1. Utility employees with access to energy data or the associated personal information. As indicated in Chapter 2, data custodians can be data managers. To be more specific, the employees of the data custodians are the data managers (data processors) because they are the ones within the data

[*] Ibid.

custodian's (data controller's) enterprise with direct access[*] to the energy data or personal information.

2. Contracted workers with direct access to the energy data or personal information are also the data managers (data processors) of the data custodians (data controllers).
3. The employees of third parties that directly collect data from energy consumers that is not used by or has any oversight from a utility are data managers (data processors) of the third-party data custodian (data controller).

Data managers/data processors are responsible for knowing, understanding, and complying with the data custodian's (data controller's) internal information security and privacy policies to protect energy data and personal information.

- **Data protection authority.** In the privacy profession, this is the term used to indicate the supervisory entity chartered to enforce privacy or data protection laws and regulations. Some countries have one centralized data protection authority (DPA) to oversee compliance for all the country's data protection laws and regulations. As a few examples:
    - The UK has the Information Commissioner's Office (ICO).[†]
    - Canada has the Privacy Commissioner.[‡]
    - Germany has the Federal Data Protection Commissioner.[§]
    - Hong Kong has the Office of the Privacy Commissioner.[¶]

    In contrast, the United States does not have a single centralized DPA. There are multiple groups, sometimes determined by industry consensus or through legislation, that function as a DPA for a specified scope of responsibility. Some of these include:

---

* If an individual or entity has access of any kind to energy usage data or personal information to fulfill his or her job responsibilities or a contractual requirement, this is considered to be direct access. Direct access would include viewing energy data or personal information on a computer screen, handling hard copy documents that contain energy data or personal information, maintaining, manipulating, and storing data in cloud-based services, or any other way in which the individual can see or access data as an integral part of his or her job responsibilities and activities.

† See http://ico.org.uk/.

‡ See https://www.priv.gc.ca.

§ Seehttps://www.ldi.nrw.de/LDI_EnglishCorner/mainmenu_DataProtection/Inhalt2/authorities/authorities.php.

¶ See http://www.pcpd.org.hk/.

- Federal Trade Commission (FTC)
- State Attorneys General offices
- Federal financial regulators
- Payment Card Industry Data Security Standards (PCI-DSS)

When considering privacy within the Smart Grid, state public utility commissions (PUCs), the Department of Commerce (DOC), and a wide range of other regulatory agencies and energy industry standards groups can be considered DPAs. It is important to point out that the FTC also has DPA authority over utilities and other Smart Grid entities with regard to the posted privacy notices and the corporate privacy policies of those entities.

Table 8.1 maps the relationships between the Smart Grid sector terms and the privacy profession's terms.

Privacy Possibilities and Responsibilities for the Data Subject

Energy consumers and prosumers, as data subjects/data owners, can proactively take a variety of actions to protect their own privacy by safeguarding their own energy usage and production data and personal information that they provide to Smart Grid entities. Additionally, there are actions they can take to ensure the utilities and third parties to whom they provide their energy data and personal information have appropriate safeguards and policies in place to protect their privacy.

Table 8.1 Relationship Map for Privacy Terms and Smart Grid Terms

PRIVACY PROFESSION		SMART GRID SECTOR
Data subject	Is the same as	Data owner
Data protection authority	Is the same as	Energy or privacy rule-making authority
Data controller	Is the same as	Data custodian
Data processor	Is the same as	Data manager

Table 8.2 Recommended Information for a Data Custodian's Privacy Notice[a]

- The purpose for which energy usage and production data and personal information are being collected
- A high-level description of the security controls that have been implemented
- The ways in which data is kept accurate
- The ways in which the data is used
- How data subjects can make choices about how their data is used and shared
- Individual access to corresponding data, and rights to make corrections to the data
- How notifications will be made when the privacy policy changes
- Contact information for questions about the privacy policy

[a] These are based upon the OECD Privacy Framework; see http://www.oecd.org/sti/ieconomy/oecd_privacy_framework.pdf. These principles are the basis of many other privacy standards and frameworks.

Here are a few of the actions energy consumers and prosumers should consider taking to help protect their privacy:

1. Read the privacy notices* posted on the websites and in the contracts provided by the data custodians (e.g., utilities, energy service providers (ESPs)—traditional or new entrants such as broadband or mobile carriers, smart appliance vendors, and mobile app-based energy management services).
2. Before a data custodian collects your energy data or personal information, ask him or her for a copy of his or her privacy notice if he or she does not have one posted. Make sure it describes how the custodian secures the data and information he or she collects, and the rights data subjects have over their data. If the data custodian does not have one, that is a red flag. See Table 8.2 for content recommendations for a good privacy notice.
3. If you do not understand some of the information within the notices or contracts, or if some of the information concerns you, contact the data custodian and ask for clarification. If energy data or personal information is collected by a utility, the utility is the custodian, but if the data is not collected by a utility, then the custodian is the entity that collected the data.

* Some organizations call privacy notices, which describe the privacy promises made to the public and to customers, their privacy policies. However, in the information security and privacy professions, the term policy is used to refer to the business's rules that employees must follow.

4. If the terms described within the posted privacy notice are too invasive,* and you have not received a satisfactory explanation from the data custodian, find another data custodian, if possible. If not possible, contact the data custodian's privacy officer. If the data custodian takes privacy seriously, he or she will have a privacy officer, or at least some position that has been assigned to address privacy issues. If he or she does not have a privacy officer or someone with privacy responsibilities, that is a red flag in and of itself.
5. If you call or send a message to a utility or third-party customer service agent with a privacy question or concern, and he or she cannot provide an answer or he or she avoids answering your question directly, that is a red flag. You should then get in touch with the privacy officer or identified privacy contact.
6. Understand the chain of custody for energy data to identify the organizations (data custodian and associated data processors) that have access to your energy data and personal information and their roles.
7. Know the DPAs that establish the privacy protections for your energy usage and production data and personal information, and how to get in touch with them if you have any concerns about the privacy protections for your data.
8. Ensure the data custodian has a documented information security and privacy breach plan in place.
9. Determine the recourse process to follow if you suspect or know your privacy has been compromised.
10. Occasionally do an online search to see if the data custodian has had a privacy breach, or any type of information security incident or privacy breach.†

---

* For example, if the notice contains a blanket statement that they may share any data collected from you with any others for any reason they determine to be appropriate, that would be a statement that is overly broad that you would want to obtain clarification about.

† At the time of this writing, 51 U.S. states and territories had laws requiring businesses to disclose data breaches to affected data owners or subjects. See the list at http://www.ncsl.org/research/telecommunications-and-information-technology/security-breach-notification-laws.aspx.

Why take the time and trouble of doing these actions? Because you cannot expect the data custodians that collect your energy data and personal information to always have all the safeguards in place necessary to lessen privacy risks.

Bottom line: With so much data being generated and shared, it is important for consumers to not just assume the data custodians that collect their energy data and personal information are appropriately protecting their privacy and effectively safeguarding their data.*

Data Subject Privacy Use Case Example

Privacy use cases† are valuable to use to break down specific scenarios involving access to energy usage and production data and personal information. The data custodians and data processors that obtain and access your energy data and personal information rely on privacy use cases to identify where risks exist and document the best controls to mitigate the identified risks.

As an example, let's consider the privacy issues involved with using electric vehicles (EVs). Consumers can use a privacy use case to help determine the privacy issues that they should be aware of for situations where their energy data and personal information are involved. Table 8.3 shows one of the EV privacy use cases from NISTIR 7628 Rev. 1,‡ updated by the authors to reflect how a consumer privacy use case can be created by a data custodian and provided to consumers as an awareness-raising document, in addition to the privacy notice.

---

* For more advice and tools to help consumers to protect their privacy and effectively secure their energy usage and production data personal information, see Rebecca's site: http://www.privacyprofessor.org.

† As described within NISTIR 7628 Rev. 1: "A Privacy Use Case is a method of looking at data flows that will help entities within the Smart Grid to rigorously track data flows and the privacy implications of collecting and using data, and will help organizations to address and mitigate the associated privacy risks within common technical design and business practices. Use cases can help Smart Grid architects and engineers build privacy protections into the Smart Grid." See http://nvlpubs.nist.gov/nistpubs/ir/2014/NIST.IR.7628r1.pdf.

‡ See all 44 Smart Grid privacy uses in NISTIR 7628 Rev. 1; http://nvlpubs.nist.gov/nistpubs/ir/2014/NIST.IR.7628r1.pdf.

Table 8.3 Privacy Use Case for Consumer Use

Category: Demand response Privacy use case 12

Scenario: Mobile plug-in electric vehicle (PEV) functions

CATEGORY DESCRIPTION

Demand response is a general capability that could be implemented in many different ways. The primary focus is to provide prosumers with pricing information for current or future time periods so they may respond by modifying their demand. This may entail just decreasing load or may involve shifting load by increasing demand during lower-priced time periods so that they can decrease demand during higher-priced time periods. The pricing periods may be real time based or tariff based, while the prices may also be operationally based or fixed, or some combination. Real-time pricing inherently requires computer-based responses, while the fixed time-of-use pricing may be manually handled once the prosumer is aware of the time periods and the pricing.

SCENARIO DESCRIPTION

- In addition to prosumers with PEVs participating in their home-based demand response functions, they will have additional requirements for managing the charging and discharging of their mobile PEVs in other locations:
  - Prosumer connects PEV at another home
  - Prosumer connects PEV outside home territory
  - Prosumer connects PEV at public location

POTENTIAL DATA OWNER/DATA SUBJECT PRIVACY ISSUES

- Privacy and security controls for the PEV energy usage data and personal information about the PEV owner/operator
- Retail electric supplier (utility or charging service providers (CSPs)) access to the energy usage data and personal information about the PEV owner/operator
- Unauthorized access to the energy usage data and personal information about the PEV owner/operator by those in the vicinity of the retail electric supplier charging station
- Retail electric supplier (nonutility) access to the energy usage data and personal information about the PEV owner/operator that the utility possesses
- Security and privacy controls for the energy usage data and personal information about the PEV owner/operator under the control of the retail electric supplier (utility or CSP)
- Prosumer access to, and ability to correct, their corresponding energy usage data and personal information about the PEV owner/operator

DATA PRIVACY RECOMMENDATIONS FOCUSED ON THE DATA OWNER/DATA SUBJECT

This use case presumes a single residential (one owner/car) situation. (There are other scenarios as well, but for simplicity's sake we limit our discussion to one scenario per use case.) There are three possible grid interfaces considered here:

  - Basic 120 or 240 V plug for electricity downloads connected to a dumb or smart meter
  - A meter that is capable of running backwards for download and upload of electricity (net metering)
  - Charging stations that can charge/discharge electricity to and from the grid

1. From the perspective of the prosumer, utilities are involved in the first two interfaces in terms of owning the meter at the time this book was written, but the third scenario may involve third parties that own the meters connected to charging stations and interact directly with prosumers without utility intervention. It is important for prosumers to understand the chain of custody in scenario C.

(continued)

Table 8.3 Privacy Use Case for Consumer Use (continued)

2. Look for privacy notices from the utilities and third parties such as CSPs that clearly delineate all responsibilities and collection processes and uses for energy usage data and personal information.
3. When utilities are the data custodian, look for statements in their privacy notices that describe when there are situations where EV energy consumption data (or other data) could be handled by third parties like CSPs, and if these third parties must comply with utility privacy policies.
4. Utilities and CSPs may have personal data such as name, credit card/debit card, phone number, and address for billing for any roaming charge programs that they manage. Look for descriptions of security safeguards in privacy notices or contracts, which should include information about monitoring and security responsibilities by data custodians.
5. Prosumers may have an electronic payment arrangement, so the utility or CSP would also have sensitive financial data and perhaps authorized access to deposit funds in cases of payments to prosumers for participation in demand response (DR) programs or other smart charging situations. For instance, California investor-owned utilities (IOUs) are not allowed to provide charging stations, so all charging stations will be owned by third-party CSPs, energy service providers, property owners, municipal entities, or businesses. However, these utilities may still have smart charging agreements in place with specific cars or charging stations and will require this information. Appropriate security controls need to be in place here. Prosumers should also carefully examine statements about if any data is sold to other parties and who those parties are.
6. For charging or discharging that occurs away from the consumer's home address, but is billed back to a utility account, utilities will need to determine what nonhome address location information is necessary to collect for billing/payment purposes, and what should be displayed on paper or electronic bills. There should be the minimum necessary information about charge time, date, and location on electric bills provided to the utility.
7. CSPs or other contracted agents who act as utility agents may have access to personal data for billing purposes. The utility should provide clear, simple identification of all entities involved, or provide a formal statement to document the data chain of custody that may be in place based on their relationships with the utility, authorized third parties, and CSPs.
8. Note: The collection of location information creates special privacy concerns regarding EVs. It creates special safety and security concerns as well. This is pertinent for charging information that occurs at the consumer's home, not just away from home. This is because EV charging at home could establish vehicle location for a given date and time if the EV is plugged in and actively charging or discharging.

Information Security Controls to Support Privacy Protection

Table 8.4 lists some of the types of information security controls the data controllers and data processors should be using to effectively secure energy data and personal information. If data subjects have concerns after asking the questions previously listed, they can ask their data controller about these information security controls as well. There are also situations where the data subject should be implementing his or her own information security controls within his or her own home or property where electricity service is provided to help protect his or her privacy, particularly when he or she is sharing energy usage

Table 8.4 Effective Information Security Controls

INFORMATION SECURITY CONTROLS	CAN BE USED BY DATA CONTROLLERS AND DATA PROCESSORS?	CAN BE APPLIED BY DATA SUBJECTS FOR THE SYSTEMS AND ACTIONS UNDER THEIR CONTROL?
TECHNICAL INFORMATION SECURITY CONTROLS The following are just some of the technical security controls that can be used. In the 25+ years one author (Rebecca) has been an information security and privacy practitioner and professor, she has found these to be the necessary technical controls for organizations, throughout all industries, as well as individuals on their personal computing systems.[a]		
• Password protection: Use strong passwords. Use passwords to log in to computing devices as well as to access networks and communications networks.	Yes	Yes
• Network security controls: Use firewalls, intrusion prevention systems (IPSs), intrusion detection systems (IDSs), and log monitoring.	Yes	Yes, if the third-party solutions support them
• Encryption: Use for data in storage as well as for data in transit (passing through the public and privacy networks).	Yes	Yes, if the third-party solutions support them
• Wireless data security controls: When wireless networks are used, ensure the transmissions are encrypted, and that strong passwords are used. Avoid public networks that do not use encryption.	Yes	Yes, if the third-party solutions support them, and if within the data subject's own network
• Antimalware software and systems: Use comprehensive antimalware software and systems to protect against viruses, Trojan horses, key loggers, and other types of malicious code.	Yes	Yes
ADMINISTRATIVE AND BEHAVIORAL INFORMATION SECURITY CONTROLS The following are some of the administrative security controls that can be used, and have been found by Rebecca to be the most important and effective for generally all organizations and individuals.[b]		
• Security and privacy responsibility: Assign a role to have primary responsibility for information security and privacy throughout the organization, as well as include privacy responsibilities to specific positions.	Yes	Not applicable

(continued)

Table 8.4 Effective Information Security Controls (continued)

INFORMATION SECURITY CONTROLS	CAN BE USED BY DATA CONTROLLERS AND DATA PROCESSORS?	CAN BE APPLIED BY DATA SUBJECTS FOR THE SYSTEMS AND ACTIONS UNDER THEIR CONTROL?
• Privacy impact assessment (PIAs) and risk assessments (RAs): Perform PIAs and RAs to identify where risks exist throughout the organization. Use the results to determine actions to appropriately mitigate the risks.	Yes	Generally not applicable
• Privacy and information security policies and procedures: Establish documented information security and privacy policies and supporting procedures to appropriately mitigate risks, as well as to meet existing legal requirements.	Yes	Data subjects should review the data controller's privacy notice to ensure he or she has established internal policies for the data managers to follow
• Provide regular training, with attendance required, as well as provide ongoing awareness communications: Ensure all data processors understand and comply with privacy policies.	Yes	Data subjects need to stay aware of new privacy threats; they will usually need to do this on their own; some data controllers are also providing this type of awareness information to their customers, so this is a possibility as well
• Enforce compliance: Enforce compliance with internal privacy policies and supporting procedures. Ensure sanctions are defined and applied appropriately and consistently for noncompliance with information security and privacy policies.	Yes	Data subjects should understand how they can raise privacy concerns that could warn of potential noncompliance
• Audits: Perform regular privacy and information security audits.	Yes	Review data controller privacy notices to ensure audits are conducted

(continued)

Table 8.4 Effective Information Security Controls (continued)

INFORMATION SECURITY CONTROLS	CAN BE USED BY DATA CONTROLLERS AND DATA PROCESSORS?	CAN BE APPLIED BY DATA SUBJECTS FOR THE SYSTEMS AND ACTIONS UNDER THEIR CONTROL?
PHYSICAL INFORMATION SECURITY POSSIBILITIES The following are some of the physical security controls that can be used, and have been found to be effective for generally all types of organizations.[c]		
• Protect against loss and theft: Establish controls to help prevent loss and theft of computing and digital storage devices and hard copy information. Use device tracking tools. Implement remote data wipe tools. Encrypt data on mobile storage devices to protect them in the event the devices are lost or stolen.	Yes	Yes
• Disposal controls: Establish controls to help prevent disposal of readable or otherwise accessible data on digital storage devices and hard copy.	Yes	Yes
• Don't post sensitive information: Do not write down passwords and post in work areas, or anywhere else for that matter. Do not leave confidential information on whiteboards or in meeting areas. Do not include sensitive information within photos or videos.[d]	Yes	Yes
• Establish effective physical security perimeters: Install walls, card-controlled entry gates, manned reception desks, fences, door locks, etc., as appropriate to mitigate risks around facilities that contain information and information processing facilities.	Yes	Yes
• Entry controls: Secure areas should be protected by appropriate entry controls to ensure that only authorized personnel are allowed access.	Yes	Yes
• Protect against external and environmental threats: Install physical protection to data storage and collection devices against damage from fire, flood, earthquake, explosion, civil unrest, and other forms of natural or man-made disasters.	Yes	Yes
• Secure work areas: Implement physical protection and guidelines for working in secure areas. This includes when working in the field, within vehicles used for servicing, within home offices, etc.	Yes	Yes

(continued)

Table 8.4 Effective Information Security Controls (continued)

INFORMATION SECURITY CONTROLS	CAN BE USED BY DATA CONTROLLERS AND DATA PROCESSORS?	CAN BE APPLIED BY DATA SUBJECTS FOR THE SYSTEMS AND ACTIONS UNDER THEIR CONTROL?
• Environmental protections: Protect data collection, transmission, and processing equipment from environmental threats and hazards.	Yes	Yes

[a] More detailed descriptions of technical security controls can be found in ISO/IEC 27002:2013; see http://www.iso.org/iso/home/store/catalogue_tc/catalogue_detail.htm?csnumber=54533. NIST also has good resources available in multiple publications in the Computer Security Resource Center: http://csrc.nist.gov/.)

[b] Ibid.

[c] Ibid.

[d] This happens much too often. For example, see https://twitter.com/GarethDEdwards/status/197403763152138240/photo/1.

data and personal information directly with data processors such as third parties, or with data controllers that offer energy management services without any involvement of utilities. Such instances are indicated within the table.

Privacy Responsibilities for the Data Controller/Data Custodian and the Data Processor/Data Manager*

Data custodians, as well as their data processors, need to have all the appropriate security and privacy controls implemented that are listed in the "Privacy Possibilities and Responsibilities for the Data Subject" section, as necessary to reduce their privacy risks to an acceptable level. This means you should first perform a privacy impact assessment (PIA) to determine your risks.†

Table 8.5 shows the same privacy use case as in Table 8.3, which showed the data subject point of view for the privacy issues involved with using plug-in electric vehicles (PEVs). Table 8.5 is the same

* There may be scenarios where the data controller has a different use case than the use case the data processor should use. However, for the purposes of illustrating privacy use cases here, we've combined the two since they would both have the same responsibilities for this particular privacy use case.

† An example PIA report is in NISTIR 7628 Rev. 1; see http://nvlpubs.nist.gov/nistpubs/ir/2014/NIST.IR.7628r1.pdf. For tools and additional information on how to do PIAs, see http://hipaaprivacy.org/product/privacy-impact-assessment-training.

Table 8.5 Privacy Use Case for Data Custodian Use

Category: Demand response Privacy use case 12

Scenario: Mobile plug-in electric vehicle functions

CATEGORY DESCRIPTION

Demand response is a general capability that could be implemented in many different ways. The primary focus is to provide prosumers with pricing information for current or future time periods so they may respond by modifying their demand. This may entail just decreasing load or may involve shifting load by increasing demand during lower-priced time periods so that they can decrease demand during higher-priced time periods. The pricing periods may be real time based or tariff based, while the prices may also be operationally based or fixed, or some combination. Real-time pricing inherently requires computer-based responses, while the fixed time-of-use pricing may be manually handled once the prosumer is aware of the time periods and the pricing.

SCENARIO DESCRIPTION

In addition to customers with PEVs participating in their home-based demand response functions, prosumers will have additional requirements for managing the charging and discharging of their mobile PEVs in other locations:

- Prosumer connects PEV at another home
- Prosumer connects PEV outside home territory
- Prosumer connects PEV at public location

SMART GRID CHARACTERISTICS	CYBER SECURITY OBJECTIVES/REQUIREMENTS	POTENTIAL STAKEHOLDER ISSUES
• Enables active participation by prosumers • Accommodates all generation and storage options • Enables new products, services, and markets	• Integrity is not critical, since feed-in tariff pricing is fixed for long periods and is generally not transmitted electronically • Availability is not an issue • Confidentiality is not an issue, except with respect to meter reading	• Prosumer data privacy and security • Retail electric supplier access • Prosumer data access

12.1 DATA PRIVACY RECOMMENDATIONS

This use case presumes residential (one owner/car) situations, but DR may also be used with EV fleets that are common to governmental entities and other businesses. These recommendations address residential situations only. There are three possible grid interfaces considered here: basic 120 or 240 V plug for electricity downloads connected to a dumb or smart meter; a meter that is capable of running backwards for download and upload of electricity (net metering); and charging stations that can charge/discharge electricity to and from the grid. From the perspective of the prosumer relationship, utilities are involved in the first two interfaces in terms of owning the meter, but the third scenario may involve third parties that intermediate the utility-consumer relationship with ownership of charging stations. This would be similar to the situation in which old pay telephones were owned by a number of different vendors, not just the phone company. Consumers may not always be aware of

(continued)

Table 8.5 Privacy Use Case for Data Custodian Use (continued)

	the ownership of the charging point and may assume that the privacy policies and practices the utility adopts apply in all scenarios. Utilities may wish to add a statement in their general privacy policies that serves to educate prosumers that there are select situations where EV energy consumption data (or other data) could be handled by third parties that are not required to abide by utility privacy policies.		
12.2	Roaming models for AC charge billing purposes are developing around the world. DC or fast charging appears to follow the familiar gas station analogy of credit/debit/cash payments, although these charging stations may be installed for private use too. Credit cards or mobile phones will be the common payment mechanism for roaming charging, and may entirely bypass utilities as data custodians—other than the supply of electricity to the meter connected to the charging station equipment. However, here are some other scenarios to consider: Utilities may have personal prosumer data such as name, credit card/debit card, phone number, and address for billing for any roaming charge programs that they manage. In addition, customers may have opted for an electronic payment arrangement, so the utility would also have sensitive financial data and perhaps authorized access to deposit funds in cases of payments to consumers. For instance, California IOUs are not allowed to provide charging stations, so all charging stations will be owned by third-party energy service providers, property owners, municipal entities, or businesses. However, these utilities may still have smart charging agreements in place with specific cars or charging stations and will require this information. The AICPA security safeguard principle has specific application here. For charging or discharging that occurs away from the prosumer's home address but is billed back to a utility account, utilities will need to determine what nonhome address location information is necessary to collect for billing/payment purposes, and what should be displayed on paper or electronic bills. Consider the amount of identification that appears on a bank statement if a consumer uses an ATM, or the level of detail on credit card statements for gas purchases to develop policies. Consider the minimum necessary information about charge time, date, and location on electric bills. The AICPA purpose specification and accountability principles apply here. Charging service providers (CSPs) or other contracted agents who act as utility agents may have access to personal data for billing purposes. Prosumers may not be aware of all the entities involved when they plug in to a charging station. The utility should consider clear, simple identification of all entities or some formal statement of the data management principle to help educate consumers as to the "data chain" that may be in place based on their relationships with utility, authorized contracted agents, and CSPs. The notice principle applies here. Note: The collection of location information creates special privacy concerns regarding EVs. It creates special safety and security concerns as well. This is pertinent for charging information that occurs at the consumer's home, not just away from home. This is because EV charging at home could establish vehicle location for a given date and time if the EV is plugged in and actively charging or discharging.		
	AICPA PRINCIPLE	APPLIES: X	NOTES
12.3	Management principle	X	This use case covers mobile or roaming charge/discharge. At home, charging/discharging information related to

(continued)

Table 8.5 Privacy Use Case for Data Custodian Use (continued)

	AICPA PRINCIPLE	APPLIES: X	NOTES
			PEVs provides motoring range and habit information that can endanger a person's safety and freedom. This requires special privacy protection. When using a third-party charging station, there is a need to determine how all principles apply, and how consumers are educated is important. It may not be appropriate for a utility to address this issue, but it could still be a smart grid issue. Consumers will appreciate education from a trusted source to understand what personal data may be collected, used, and retained by various entities in mobile charging scenarios. Utilities will need to determine and assign responsibility for how EVs are incorporated into DR programs, and then develop appropriate privacy policies regarding any personal data that would accompany the reporting, billing, and management of these DR programs.
12.4	Notice principle	X	Notice may be challenging when it is a charging station owned by a third party as discussed in 12.1. Special efforts must be required of third parties through the contracts between the third parties, utility-authorized contracted agents, and utilities. Utilities should ensure that authorized contracted agents adhere to the privacy policies and practices enacted by the utility to protect personal information and energy consumption data. For unrelated third parties, utilities lack immediate or ongoing opportunities to inform consumers that different privacy policies may be in effect. Utilities may wish to add a statement to their general privacy policies that addresses EV charging devices that are "in their control" or "out of their control," and the consumers must be made aware of the risk of disclosure of this information.
12.5	Choice and consent principle	X	There may be choices available at the charging stations/points. If not, then the charging station should clearly indicate the data being collected, how they will be used, shared, and retained, and then obtain consent to use the data as a consequence of charging at that location.
12.6	Collection principle	X	This principle applies for any entity that is delivering power or maintaining a financial transaction. Only the data necessary for the customer to obtain the electricity charge, and then for the charging company to be financially reimbursed, should be collected.

(continued)

Table 8.5 Privacy Use Case for Data Custodian Use (continued)

	AICPA PRINCIPLE	APPLIES: X	NOTES
12.7	Use and retention principle	X	Data collected from PEV charging stations should be used only for the purposes of supporting the associated payments, and then irreversibly deleted after they are no longer needed for business purposes. If data is intended for planning, balancing, or operational purposes, the utility should adopt privacy-enhancing technologies and practice to anonymize this data and de-identify it.
12.8	Access principle	X	Since charging stations may be owned by a number of entities, it may be difficult for individuals to know who to contact to gain access to their personal data. PEV charging stations need to ensure customers can get access to their associated PEV charging data, and access to this data within related businesses should be limited to only those with a business need to know.
12.9	Disclosure to third parties principle	X	Since charging stations may be owned by a number of entities, it may be challenging to obtain implicit or explicit consent before sharing data. Even if consent is not feasible, consumers should be told the ways in which the data **is** used.
12.10	Security for privacy principle	X	Applies with special regard to any financial transactions. Applies with special regard to location-based information. All personal data collected and created during these activities must be appropriately safeguarded to ensure unauthorized access to the data does not occur, to preserve integrity of the data, and to allow for appropriate availability.
12.11	Quality principle	X	PEV charging data must be accurate, and controls need to be incorporated to ensure this.
12.12	Monitoring and enforcement principle	X	Develop and maintain audit policies to ensure that procedures are consistently applied with regard to personal data.

privacy use case, but now with the focus on data custodians. Data custodians and data processors can use privacy use cases to help determine the privacy risks and then identify the most appropriate controls to mitigate the risks. The privacy use cases within NISTIR 7628 Rev. 1 use the American Institute of Certified Public Accountants

(AICPA) Generally Accepted Privacy Principles (GAPPs).* These are commonly used by auditors, and so make a practical tool to also use for privacy use cases.

Other Helpful Privacy and Information Security Resources

This chapter provides an excellent foundation for resources with privacy responsibilities to identify privacy and information security risks, and a description of some of the controls to implement to mitigate those risks. Here are some additional resources, in addition to the other resources listed in the footnotes throughout the book, that the authors recommend to energy data custodians, data processors, data subjects, and DPAs to protect privacy.

From the authors:

- Christine Hertzog's Smart Grid blog posts: http://www.smartgridlibrary.com/home-2/blog/
- SGL Partners consulting services: http://www.smartgridlibrary.com/consulting-services/
- Rebecca Herold's blog posts: http://www.privacyguidance.com/blog
- Rebecca Herold's Smart Grid privacy and information security tools and services: http://hipaaprivacy.org/product-category/energy-smart-grid-privacy/

From government and industry:

- National Institute of Standards and Technology (NIST): http://www.nist.gov/smartgrid/
- Federal government initiatives: https://www.smartgrid.gov/federal_initiatives/featured_initiatives
- Department of Energy: http://energy.gov/oe/services/technology-development/smart-grid
- National Conference of State Legislatures (NCSL): http://www.ncsl.org/research/energy/smart-grid-state-action-update.aspx

* See http://www.aicpa.org/INTERESTAREAS/INFORMATIONTECHNOLOGY/RESOURCES/PRIVACY/GENERALLYACCEPTEDPRIVACYPRINCIPLES/Pages/default.aspx.

From other sources:

- Electronic Privacy Information Center (EPIC): http://epic.org/privacy/smartgrid/smartgrid.html
- Organization for the Advancement of Structured Information Standards (OASIS): https://www.oasis-open.org/committees/tc_cat.php?cat=smartgrid

9

Transactive Energy

We introduced the term *transactive energy*[*] as the future evolution of the Smart Grid in Chapter 2. Transactive energy is an evolving concept, as initial pilots are testing the capacities of existing technologies, policies, processes, and business models.[†] The Department of Energy, Pacific Northwest National Lab, and utilities including Bonneville Power Administration and Portland General Electric are participating in a pilot discussed later in this chapter.

Transactive energy proponents envision an organized marketplace where prosumers can buy or sell electricity with confidence that transactions are managed through enforceable rules that apply to all. This marketplace is managed in coordination with utility grid operations to ensure a safe and reliable supply of power for consumers. But the concept of transactive energy also encourages grid resiliency—the ability to recover from man-made and natural disruptions—and reduces some of the grid fragility that we currently experience. Technologies such as renewables coupled with energy storage, inexpensive sensors coupled with wireless networks, and analytics coupled with cost-effective data storage can support distributed energy resources (generation, demand response, energy efficiency, and storage) with highly distributed intelligence. All this helps grid managers operate with enhanced situational awareness, and that increases grid resiliency.

Transactive energy requires a convergence of technologies, policies, and financial drivers in an active prosumer market—where prosumers are buildings, electric vehicles (EVs), microgrids, or distributed

[*] From the *Smart Grid Dictionary*, 6th edition: "Transactive energy is a business model that enables market participation for distributed energy resources (DER) supplying negawatts or kilowatts to an interconnected grid to support the delivery of safe, clean, resilient, reliable and cost-effective electricity."

[†] An early pilot or demonstration is occurring in the U.S. Pacific Northwest. The Pacific Northwest Smart Grid Demonstration Project publishes an annual report with the latest details at it website: http://www.pnwsmartgrid.org.

energy resources (DERs) assets like solar panels, wind generators, or energy storage. In other words, the current market that exists at the wholesale electricity level for large-scale energy transactions will be mirrored at the distribution grid for smaller-scale transactions. Transactive energy democratizes the currently closed electricity market. However, this market will have to be much more flexible, robust, and scalable to support millions of participants instead of hundreds to thousands of participants. It is a challenge, but Wall Street has managed stock markets with participation by large funds as well as individual investors.

We'll briefly examine the three main drivers before exploring the privacy considerations in the evolution from today's grid to a Smart Grid that includes transactive energy.

Technology

The Smart Grid technologies of remote monitoring and control, advanced analytics, and robust communications networks enable the transition to transactive energy at every point in the value chain from generation to consumption and prosumption. The growth of competitive, cost-effective solutions for co-generation, energy storage, and microgrids will accelerate partial to full self-sufficiency on the part of critical infrastructure (i.e., first responder command centers and stations) at state, city, and county levels. Such initiatives are already under way in some states spurred by the experiences of Superstorm Sandy.* However, private enterprise, particularly commercial entities that place a high valuation on "uptime" of grids, can't tolerate the service disruptions that cost the American economy billions of dollars annually, as noted in Chapter 2. Businesses will invest in DERs and include sales of excess energy back to the grid in their return on investment (ROI) calculations. This practice already occurs when businesses consider the value of payments offered by utilities or energy services providers (ESPs) for demand response (DR) participation.

Many buildings may already participate in utility or third-party DR programs and voluntarily reduce electricity (or gas) consumption

* One example is the state of Connecticut. For more information, see http://www.governor.ct.gov/malloy/cwp/view.asp?A=4010&Q=528770.

during peak times of demand. Transactive markets envision the expansion of DR programs through automated demand response (ADR) technologies. We'll discuss an initiative called OpenADR later in this chapter.

Some large commercial buildings already deploy various building automation systems* (BASs) and energy management systems† (EMSs). These systems remotely monitor and control HVAC, lighting, and other significant usages of electricity in buildings and may collect and conduct data analysis to identify potential reductions in energy use. The most sophisticated EMS solutions engage in continuous commissioning‡ through data accumulated from heating, ventilation, air conditioning (HVAC) sensors, occupant activities, and other sources, like weather reports.

EMS and ADR technologies help infuse buildings with much more intelligence—also known as smart buildings. These technologies help position buildings as participants in transactive energy. For example, buildings can now automatically respond to price signals or utility grid management requests to alter consumption for specific time durations. Transactive energy extends this functionality to kilowatt production or generation, so that buildings can automatically respond to grid requests for energy.

---

* From the *Smart Grid Dictionary*: "Software and hardware deployed in buildings to automatically manage refrigeration, HVAC, lighting and other building energy usage on a continuous basis. These control systems are the integrating components to fans, pumps, heating/cooling equipment, dampers, mixing boxes, and thermostats. Monitoring and optimizing temperature, pressure, humidity, and flow rates are key functions of modern building control systems. Many are designed to operate a single system, like refrigeration or HVAC. Sometimes known as EMCS (Energy Management and Control Systems) or Energy Management Systems (EMS), these systems integrate more control functions such as lighting as well as HVAC."

† From the *Smart Grid Dictionary*: "These control systems integrate HVAC, lighting, and other high-energy uses to effectively manage commercial and multifamily building energy consumption. The objective is to deliver optimal occupant comfort while minimizing energy use. Also known as EMCS (Energy Management and Control Systems)."

‡ From the *Smart Grid Dictionary*: "A combination of processes, hardware, and software to ensure that buildings are operating at peak energy efficiency to reduce overall energy costs and carbon emissions and optimize performance of building HVAC gear."

Buildings can also become "hardened" nodes in the grid—meaning they can provide some or all of their own energy as more renewable generation, co-generation, and energy storage options are introduced to the market. It's a small but growing trend to use Smart Grid technologies for generation of kilowatts and not just negawatts.

Microgrids

One of the most disruptive technologies in terms of altering today's power grids will be microgrids. A microgrid is a small power system that integrates self-contained generation, distribution, sensors, energy storage, and energy management software with a seamless and synchronized connection to a utility power system, and can operate independently as an island from that system. Generation includes renewable energy sources and the ability to sell back excess capacity to a utility. On-site microgrid management software includes controls for the power generation, utility connect/disconnect, distribution, and energy storage equipment along with building energy management applications for commercial and industrial (C&I) or home use.*

Microgrids reduce the reliance on a utility to deliver electricity. Industry research firms are optimistic about microgrid market potential, with market projections that include $6 billion in 2020 or $17 billion by 2017. In the United States, microgrids can provide energy surety for their owners.† Even when the surrounding grid is experiencing an outage, a microgrid can provide at least a percentage of power for the most important uses within its boundaries. For example, a college campus that operates a microgrid may prioritize occupied dormitories and critical research facilities over unoccupied classroom buildings to receive power from a microgrid when utility-supplied power is disrupted. Today, operational and safety standards require that any microgrid connected (or grid-tied) to the utility grid has to shut down if the larger grid experiences an outage. There

---

* From the *Smart Grid Dictionary*, 6th edition.

† In developing economies, microgrids hold significant promise to eliminate energy poverty that afflicts over 1 billion humans, according to the International Energy Agency (IEA).

are standards bodies working to change this without compromising worker safety, which is of paramount concern for everyone.

Microgrids will be attractive first to critical infrastructure and large commercial customers with the highest utility bills to seek to reduce their operating costs and gain more control over their energy surety. Over time, as more cost effective solutions are available, smaller commercial customers and even residential customers will adopt microgrid technologies for some or all of their electricity. Smart Grid technologies are evolutionary drivers enabling transitions to transactive energy. Leveraging these technologies will help build grid resiliency and open the electricity market participation by prosumers.

Regulatory Policy

Regulatory policy is a revolutionary driver for transactive energy. The increase in severe storms, ranging from Superstorm Sandy to the polar vortex, is the causative factor for legislative actions and regulatory policies that encourage utilities to invest in grid resiliency with deployments of DERs and microgrids. This is one of the anticipated outcomes of the previously referenced "Reforming the Energy Vision" report from the New York Public Service Commission and the California Public Utilities Commission's energy storage mandates to its regulated investor-owned utilities (IOUs).

Historically, regulated utilities were encouraged to build reliable grids with the expectations of downtime. The real costs of outages were not factored in to regulatory decisions, but that practice has lost its luster and more utility commissions now encourage grid designs and deployments that build resiliency. However, there's growing acknowledgment that utilities cannot create more resilient grids on their own. The Interstate Renewable Energy Council (IREC) published a white paper that should be read by every utility regulator and state legislator interested in grid modernization involving DER deployments. "The Integrated Distribution Planning Concept Paper"* offers practical suggestions that help build the foundation for transactive energy by leveraging private investments.

* Available at http://www.irecusa.org/2013/05/new-proactive-planning-strategy-proposed-for-distributed-generation/.

IREC focuses on regulatory policy innovations to enable deployment and interconnection of clean energy like solar in the distribution grid. Interconnection from the distribution grid perspective refers to the utility processes that ensure that interconnection of DERs like solar occur in a timely manner with safe, reliable, and high-quality electricity flow. It's sorely needed. Grid-connected solar photovoltaic capacity jumped 4,000% from 2005 to 2012, according to IREC research. That's a good indicator that DER deployments won't wait for state or local policies when and where investors and owners can make favorable business cases now.

Interconnection requests might require utility upgrades of grid equipment. Utility planners have to consider the local circuit design and the type, size, and location of the DER asset on that circuit. Since distribution grids were designed for a one-way power flow from generators to consumers, not the new Smart Grid value chain that includes prosumers enabled to supplement/substitute/sell power, there's a good chance that some grid investment is required.

The paper described interconnection processes in California, Hawaii, Massachusetts, and PEPCO, a utility with a footprint in New Jersey, Delaware, and Maryland. These entities have demonstrated leadership in regulatory policies to address the explosive growth of DER interconnection requests. Creative policies identified in the paper include development of new utility plans that incorporate DERs into grid modernization initiatives. California's policy requires utilities to consider how generation assets in the distribution grid can "defer transformer and transmission line upgrades, extend equipment maintenance intervals, reduce electrical line, losses, and improve distribution system reliability, all with cost savings to utilities." This policy statement is significant because it determines that assets that are not owned by a utility can have *a quantifiable value to the utility*, and therefore helps create the policy foundation for a transactive energy market.

The paper's approach, called integrated distribution planning (IDP), determines the status (particularly capacity) of the existing distribution equipment and identifies potential upgrades that may be needed to accommodate anticipated distributed generation (DG) growth in a five-step process. With adoption of the policies and practices as promulgated in IREC's paper, utilities can identify distribution grid points where independently owned DER assets can engineer resiliency into the local grid or defer expensive capacity upgrades. Potential DER asset owners—commercial and residential—could be financially motivated to take on these types of projects with reduced risks because utilities could think about these assets in newly useful ways.

These regulatory policies are significant and new, making policy a revolutionary driver in building an electricity value chain based on transactive energy concepts.

Finance

There is growing innovation in the types of financial tools available for utility and nonutility investments in generation, creating new *sources of capital* that bring down the costs of funding. It's a complicated topic because financing mechanisms for residential purposes are sometimes quite different than commercial or utility-scale funding options. On top of that, financing tools and considerations may differ for generation of kilowatts (such as solar production) versus generation of negawatts (like energy efficiency projects).

Finance drivers are often closely intertwined with policy drivers, and those synergies are quite apparent here. We'll start at the federal level and work down to local initiatives, and then briefly discuss private enterprise activity in innovative financial mechanisms that have ramifications for the Smart Grid and transactive energy.

A master limited partnership (MLP) is a publicly traded partnership for an energy asset. First launched in 1981, today's MLPs are traded on public stock exchanges, offering individual as well as institutional investors the necessary structures to buy and sell shares in gas/oil/coal extraction and pipeline projects. In 2008, Congress expanded the definitions of MLP projects to include ethanol, biodiesel, and other alternative fuels projects. There are two primary benefits of MLPs. First, they operate on a pass-through tax structure,* which lowers the cost of capital. Second, they allow companies to build and operate energy-producing assets and offer a sufficient rate of return that is appealing to investors.

* A pass-through means that the MLP does not pay tax, just the shareholders (typically called unit holders).

In 2012, traditional MLPs attracted $23 billion for projects, for a total of about $325 billion in market capital. Imagine what a similar pool of money could do for investments in clean generation from solar, wind, and geothermal as well as energy storage. This amount of capital dwarfs the $4 billion spent on the Smart Grid in the American Recovery and Reinvestment Act (ARRA) or Stimulus Fund of 2009. Were a similar pool of capital available for renewable energy and energy storage projects, it would give investors opportunities to be green with their money and make a steady income return on their investments. MLPs could be a game changer for utilities and corporations seeking sources of capital for large-scale renewables and energy storage projects. There's a proposed bipartisan U.S. Senate bill* to extend MLP structures to renewables and energy storage, but as this book was written, it faces an uncertain future.

Residential and commercial property assessed clean energy (PACE) programs are another promising strategy to finance DER projects. To date, 28 states and Washington, D.C., have approved PACE programs for residential use. Two states, California and Colorado, have approved commercial PACE programs. These programs rely on bonds whose proceeds are used by borrowers (building owners) to fund renewable or energy efficiency projects. PACE loans remove the substantial up-front costs of projects and enable owners to save on energy costs and create local jobs during the deployment phases of those projects. By some industry estimates, the market for commercial PACE projects could exceed $180 billion.

There are other interesting state initiatives to encourage investment in DER assets. Voter initiatives like California's Proposition 39, enacted in 2013, closed a corporate tax loophole and mandated that 50% of the newly recovered tax revenues for the next 5 years ($500 million/year) be spent on renewable and energy efficiency projects in California public schools. The California Energy Commission calculates that the state's schools (excluding colleges and universities) spend $132 in energy costs per student each year. That's an annual bill of $700 million. A projected average of 30% savings for energy efficiency

* The Master Limited Partnerships Parity Act (S. 795) introduced by Sen. Chris Coons. For more information, see http://www.bna.com/expanding-master-limited-n17179876658/.

initiatives alone would result in $240 million per year that could go to textbooks and teacher salaries.

Green Bank initiatives are another innovative funding mechanism for grid modernization. New York is the third state to launch a Green Bank to fund clean energy projects. Seeded with $210 million to start, it intends to attract enough private capital to fund $1 billion in projects. The Green Bank addresses significant barriers for development and deployment of clean energy and DER projects. These are the lack of funding for cost-effective loans and for loan loss reserves, and the lack of securitization for such projects. Investment criteria will be aligned with the state's Public Service Commission's clean energy and system resiliency program goals. While the state of Connecticut gets the distinction for having the first Green Bank, New York has the largest fund to date.*

At the private enterprise level, one of the most intriguing financial innovations uses crowd-sourced funds to encourage retail investors to participate in renewable energy-generation projects—not just large institutional investors. As the Smart Grid enables consumers of electricity to become producers of electricity (prosumers), the Internet democratizes the investment marketplace—much as transactive energy democratizes the electricity marketplace.

One of these services is offered by a company called Mosaic.† The company finds and qualifies solar projects and connects investors to them. Investment minimums are $25, opening the market to motivated investors eager to join renewable energy markets. Residents of New York and California can participate by virtue of their location. People in other states must be accredited investors. Every solar project is fully subscribed—some in as little as 24 hours. It is an innovative approach that addresses a significant unmet need for investors who wish to participate in DER deployments but lack opportunities. Some of those reasons include tenants who cannot put solar on the rooftops of their rental homes or apartments, and their landlords who derive no financial benefits from deploying such systems on their rental

* Hawaii is the third Green Bank state, and California is organizing a similar initiative. New Jersey has proposed creation of an Energy Resilience Bank, which also relies on deployment of DERs.

† https://joinmosaic.com.

properties. It will be interesting to see if this same program can be applied to energy storage projects in the future.

From a landlord's perspective, real estate values are often higher for green buildings with Leadership in Energy and Environmental Design (LEED) recognition. Tenants are willing to pay a premium for the status of living or working in energy-efficient and carbon-reduced buildings. In the future, buildings that are grid hardened or energy self-sufficient may also command premium prices because they preserve comfort and safety of occupants regardless of utility grid status. It is a compelling new variable in value propositions for property owners as they seek competitive differentiators from other rental properties. It is also a sign of the times about how financial motivations can serve as drivers for DER investments, and create more participants in transactive energy markets.

These innovative financing mechanisms drive grid transformation investments along the entire value chain, from generation to consumption. In the process, we increase grid resiliency through distributed renewables generation, reduce our carbon footprints, and allocate profits and cost savings into local economies. Financial innovations also open up energy markets for prosumers and small investors. As a Smart Grid driver, finance is revolutionary and can accelerate investments in DERs and microgrids, help democratize the market, and deliver a broader range of Smart Grid benefits to a wider pool of participants.

As noted earlier, these transactive energy drivers portend significant changes from today's electricity markets, which are only available to qualified suppliers able to trade in large quantities (megawatts and negawatts) of electricity. The U.S. stock market offers some good analogies. The large institutional traders like pension funds would be the equivalent of qualified suppliers of electricity, buying or selling huge blocks of stock. Prosumers at the distribution grid level would be the equivalent of individuals managing their 401(k) stock portfolios and buying or selling electricity at preferred price points.

So what does this chapter have to do with privacy? Most of our discussion about privacy has so far focused on energy usage data. Transactive energy expands the discussion to *energy production data*. Transactive energy means new varieties of data coming from many market participants and sector players, with data velocities that rival those of existing stock markets. It will also mean new volumes of data that will present challenges for existing utility communications networks. And finally, the need for absolute confidence in the data to accurately settle, buy, and sell transactions based on dynamic pricing will put an emphasis on data veracity.

The transactive energy market will evolve over time, and we'll examine the initial steps with commentary on the energy production data that is created. Let's first define energy production data and its value. Energy production data is data that identifies the flow of electricity for a device that generates or discharges electricity.* Energy production data describes how much energy is produced by a generation device so it can be used for operational or financial purposes. If it's a smart device (and most of them are), it will have communication capabilities and could be enabled for remote monitoring and control. Various stakeholders will have different interests in this data, and we group them into four categories: prosumers, governments, utilities, and vendors.

Prosumers are the owners of DER assets. They can be individuals or businesses. Prosumers will want data that details the performance of their assets. This data would help answer questions such as:

- How much electricity is the asset producing?
- Is the device operating at optimal levels?
- How much electricity is used on-site versus sold back to the grid?
- What is the price of electricity at buy/sell transaction points?
- How much money has been saved, offset, or earned?

Obviously, there is other data that is combined with energy production data to answer these questions. As noted before, the accurate measurement of the electricity sold back to the grid would come from a utility-supplied meter—the ultimate cash register for buying and selling. Pricing data would not reside in a generation device, but an energy management system that controls it would most likely have programmed instructions regarding the price points for buy and sell transactions. Prosumers may not want others to know how much energy they are producing from their solar panels or wind generators, or how much electricity their EV sells back to the grid. The bottom line is that financial information is sensitive information, and therefore establishing privacy controls for this data is important.

* From the *Smart Grid Dictionary*, 6th edition.

Governments range from local to federal entities and regulatory agencies. They may want to track overall production from DER assets and microgrids to measure the success of policies that encourage these investments to build grid resiliency. Given that this is a new area with many research interests and more questions than answers, we could see similar pilot programs like the ChargeAmerica project, with volunteers who consent to provide energy production data. Governments would be interested in data that answered the same questions prosumers would have, but at an aggregated scale. This data could be anonymized to protect asset owner privacy. From another perspective, there may also be interest in identifying electricity production that seems oversized to site needs.

Utilities need energy production data to appropriately plan for ongoing or backstop load requirements for interconnected DERs and microgrids. By virtue of their meter ownership, they already have an established "primary purpose" right to energy usage data for billing and operational purposes. Without a doubt, they would want the same arrangement for energy production data. In a transactive energy scenario, they may manage DER assets on behalf of the asset owners (private individuals or businesses) and would need all performance data, along with remote monitoring and control capabilities of those DER assets. This data would be necessary to provide safe grid operations and accurate settlement reports (think of stock sales and purchases).

Utility treatment of energy production data should be governed by the same privacy policies in place for energy usage data, but special consideration needs to be given to situations where third parties are involved. The scenarios previously discussed for Green Button data—in which some vendors are covered entities and bound by utility policies, while others are not—would need to be documented in use cases to fully understand the chain of data custody.

Vendors have a number of interests in energy production data. For example, if solar panel vendors and installers have access to energy production data for the solar panels on your roof, perhaps they could determine if your selected product produced the solar efficiency claimed by a competitor. They could certainly use production data to spot trends in performance degradation and pitch their upgrade or maintenance services. Interesting distinctions arise around the relationship that an ESP or product vendor has with the asset owner—presumably the owner of the energy production data. This is similar to the distinctions made between third parties that are covered entities or have some affiliation with the utility or with the asset owner and those that do not have a relationship. A comprehensive portfolio of use cases can fully detail the data ownership and resulting privacy risk mitigation strategies.

Now that we've described energy production data and some of its potential values, let's explore the evolutionary transition to transactive energy and the role of energy production data. Net metering isn't often thought of in transactive energy terms, but it is an illuminating first evolutionary step.

Net metering is the capability for residential and commercial and industrial (C&I) customers to generate electricity and sell back excess power to the utility.* Net metering uses either a single, bidirectional electric meter or two meters to separately measure production and consumption electricity flows at a prosumer's location. Net metering is currently implemented on a state-by-state basis with significant variation between states and utilities. Some net metering setups use smart meters; others rely on traditional electromechanical meters. Net metering has experienced significant growth in the United States, as tracked by the Energy Information Administration in Figure 9.1.

Note: The chart counts the number of net metering customers and does not indicate the generator size or amount of generation. Nonresidential includes the commercial and industrial sectors;

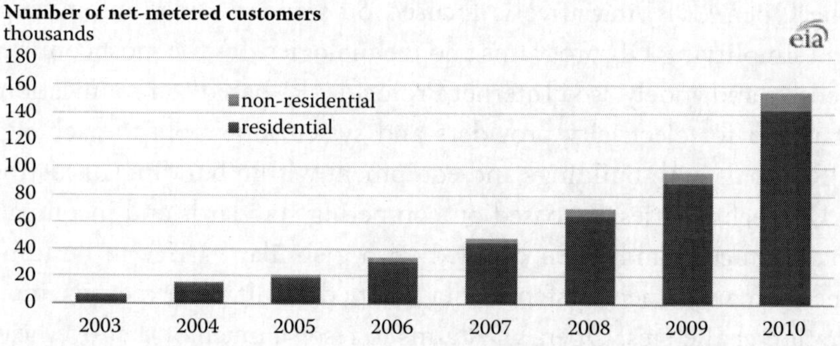

Figure 9.1 Growth of net metering in the USA. (Courtesy of the U.S. Energy Information Administration, Electric Power Annual.)

* Ibid.

net-metered generators in these sectors are typically larger than residential generators.

Net metering essentially is self-generation structured in organized transactions with a utility. Pricing is fixed by utility tariffs, so unlike a true transactive energy market, there's no dynamism in prices. It does serve as the first step to transactive energy, since many utilities have long-term plans to switch from fixed pricing to time of use pricing or dynamic pricing. In today's net metering scenarios, the utility still owns the meters, and all the existing meter data privacy guidelines apply to the energy production data. Could this change in transactive energy? Possibly. We see similarities to the scenario for energy usage data. If the state or utility policy holds that the prosumer owns his or her meter data, then production data should be handled just like usage data. If the status of ownership of meter data is not well defined, or if the position is the utility owns the data, that would trigger real concerns about the privacy of energy production data. From a future transactive energy perspective, if an ESP is aggregating power generated from a number of locations and selling it back to utilities (much like they do with DR aggregation today), then the situation is even more complicated. It will be important to consider the entire data chain of custody through use cases to develop appropriate privacy policies and practices.

OpenADR

The OpenADR* initiative is focused on standardizing, automating, and simplifying DR programs and technologies. It's the most comprehensive and widely used Internet Protocol (IP)-based communications standard for electricity providers and system operators to exchange DR signals with buildings and equipment within buildings. Existing ADR technologies are based on competing standards and incompatible protocols, and when coupled with a similar variety in building energy management systems, they create difficult and expensive integration challenges. OpenADR aims to resolve much of that overhead complexity, and thus accelerate the participation rates of buildings into DR programs and negawatt production. OpenADR is the *de facto*

* For more information, visit http://www.openadr.org.

standard for the state of California's building code,* which mandates that all new buildings must support a standards-based DR signal.

As described before, for building owners and managers, participation delivers payments for reductions in electricity use or lower rates throughout the year—nice impacts to their operating costs. The OpenADR Alliance is currently piloting an offer of LEED credits for participation in ADR, which means that buildings will receive sustainability recognition too. That reinforces the premium value that property owners can charge to tenants in buildings participating in ADR. However, the alliance has a very ambitious goal—to be the "last mile" of transactive energy. In fact, there is a profile held in reserve (2.0c) that will have features supportive of the transactive energy model.

From a privacy perspective, there are important distinctions to note between commercial buildings and residential buildings, which can be subcategorized into multifamily and single-family dwellings. There is an incredible amount of energy usage data that is created, transmitted, and analyzed to manage commercial buildings. In the future, this data would include energy production data regarding measured electricity from devices, performance alarms and status updates for those devices, as well as financial transaction data such as buy and sell details. This data may have significant value in delivering detailed knowledge of building operations, but it may not reveal any useful personal information since the meter may be assigned to a corporation rather than an individual.

For residential scenarios, energy production data would have the same sensitivities as energy usage data, or the data produced in net metering scenarios. However, with the exception of multifamily residential properties, many residential OpenADR participants may have a relationship with an ESP who serves as an intermediary to the local utility. Multifamily residential properties may have a similar arrangement, or be large enough to have a facilities manager who coordinates directly with a utility.

Going Forward

The Pacific Northwest Smart Grid Demonstration Project† is a multiyear initiative that is now testing transactive controls as key

* Title 24 of the California Energy Code went into effect January 1, 2014.

† For more detailed descriptions of the pilot, go to http://www.pnwsmartgrid.org.

components to transactive energy markets. The project defines transactive control as a distributed system that uses signals communicating the current and expected state of the grid, so that electricity users and energy resources can adapt to time-granular changes in grid supply and demand. DER assets such as solar panels, smart appliances, energy storage units, plug-in hybrid electric vehicles (PHEVs), and backup generators are participating in this demonstration. The project is collecting data from 60,000 metered customers who have a variety of voluntary participation options through the 11 utilities throughout five states, shown in Figure 9.2, that are also part of the demonstration.

These customers cover residential and C&I categories, and are engaged in programs through the utilities that make up this pilot. Participation for the most part consists of negawatt production, although two utilities installed solar panels for distributed generation with volunteers from their customer base, and one utility had a commercial enterprise with an existing solar installation share its energy production data. There is no single overarching privacy policy that covers all participants of this pilot, although this simply reflects the fragmented nature of our electricity sector as well as our privacy legislation. Given the research mission of this pilot, data

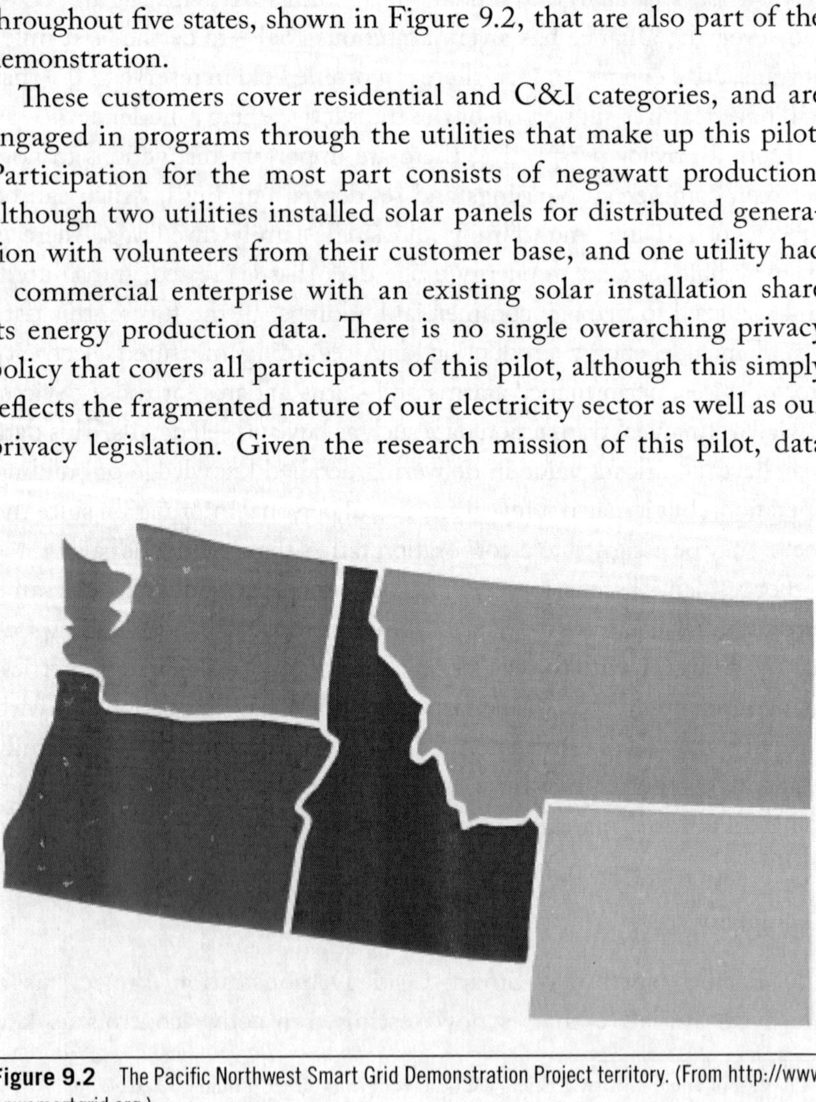

Figure 9.2 The Pacific Northwest Smart Grid Demonstration Project territory. (From http://www.pnwsmartgrid.org.)

collection is extremely important to gain knowledge and insights to apply to future transactive energy operations and market models. All pilot participants' privacy needs must be carefully documented to ensure that the appropriate policies and procedures are in place to protect privacy.

Transactive energy creates new data—energy production data. In many scenarios, its treatment should not vary from the privacy protections for energy usage data. However, if energy usage data has weak privacy protections, the expansion into energy production data offers an excellent opportunity to update and enhance privacy protections for all data. Development of scenarios or use cases that reflect the coming transactive energy changes and identify the data chain of custody can help prepare regulators and legislators, utilities, vendors, and consumer agencies to ensure that the proper privacy protections are in place.

10

Addressing Common Privacy Claims

There are many individuals and groups that are taking bits of truth with regard to Smart Grid privacy risks and blowing them up into unsubstantiated, and often completely fictional, claims to spread fear, uncertainty, and doubt (FUD). Such alarmists are found quickly via an Internet search. Many are using scare tactics to encourage individuals to remove smart meters themselves from their homes, a very physically dangerous thing to do!

Here are some facts, pointing out what is possible and what is not, to address some of the most common unsubstantiated claims made by groups or individuals with regard to Smart Grid privacy.

Claim 1: Data from smart meters goes directly to government agencies through the Smart Grid transmission lines.

No, in the United States, data from smart meters does not go directly to government agencies. Smart meter data goes to the utilities that use them for billing purposes. If a government agency wants smart meter data, it must bring a subpoena or other appropriate documentation to the utility, and list the specific types of data it needs (e.g., from a specific address for a specific range of time). The utility will then give it only the specified data, as required by law and energy standards. This process has been in place for decades, and is not becoming less strenuous because of smart meters.

There may be some types of smart meters that homeowners have connected directly to their home area networks (HANs) or home energy management systems (HEMSs). In this case, it would be possible for the homeowner to purposefully and knowingly send his or her energy usage data to others. And, if he or she did not set up his or her HAN or HEMS securely, he or she may leave it vulnerable for unauthorized access. However, those situations are under the control of the residents, are not made from the smart meter, and are not something the utility can control.

Claim 2: The utilities share all smart meter data with third parties, including mail houses, debt collectors, and data processing analysts.

No, in the United States the utilities are not sharing energy usage data with third parties without consumer consent with two exceptions:

1. Data may be shared with a company under contract to a utility to provide a service necessary to the delivery of electricity, such as meter repairs.
2. Data may be shared if there is a state-level legal reason to do so. For instance, a public utility commission may order data to be shared for energy efficiency studies.

Most U.S. utilities are regulated at the state level, by public utilities commissions or public service commissions. These state regulations govern when, why, and with whom data may be shared. There are typically fines for breaking these regulations. These regulations have been in place for decades, and are not becoming more lenient because of smart meters.

Municipal utilities and rural electric member cooperatives (coops) answer to their city governments or utility boards and their electricity customers serving as owners and voters. These categories of utilities are governed by existing state and local privacy laws and often follow the policy lead of the regulated, investor-owned utilities (IOUs). In some states, the commissions that regulate IOUs also have jurisdiction over municipals and cooperatives.

At the time of this writing, outside the United States, there was a wide range of protections, and often no protections, governing energy usage data. Possibly the most guidance and rules have been established within the European Union.*

* See more about EU Smart Grid rules and recommendations at http://ec.europa.eu/energy/gas_electricity/smartgrids/smartgrids_en.htm.

Claim 3: Smart meters are not optional. The U.S. government is forcing them on the public to spy on them!

The U.S. government does not govern the use of smart meters, or any other hardware components used at the energy consumers' residence, to provision the delivery of energy services. Requirements for consumer hardware necessary for energy delivery services are governed at the state level. Many states have begun offering an opt-out capability with regard to smart meters. However, this opt-out option often comes with an extra fee to cover the additional work of reading an analog meter. This also means a customer would not gain any benefits of a smart meter, such as faster repair times following a service disruption.

Claim 4: The utilities and U.S. government will now be able to control every appliance within each consumer's home, shutting off energy supply without warning.

U.S. regulations* do not allow utilities to modify the working of any appliance or electronics within a customer's home without first gaining customer approval. Also, an energy-consuming device has to be correctly enabled, usually by setting a special device on appliances or electronics, in order to be controlled by a utility. This function, commonly known as demand response, has been around for many years. Regulations are not becoming less stringent because of smart meters.

Related to this, it is important for energy consumers to be aware of the access they are providing directly to third parties as a result of using smart appliances, HANs, and HEMSs. Energy consumers must perform their own due diligence to ensure these third parties have appropriate privacy protections and security controls implemented.

Claim 5: Utilities will be able to use smart meters to know your in-home activities based upon detailed energy usage, down to the appliance level.

* See the primary U.S. federal regulations governing utilities at http://energy.gov/NODE/11611.

Using nonintrusive appliance load monitoring (NALM) techniques,* interval energy usage at different time periods can be used to infer individual appliances' portions of energy usage by comparison to libraries of known patterns matched to individual appliances. However, studies have shown that individual appliance inference or patterns of appliance usage are not truly possible unless the usage data is gathered more frequently than every 15 minutes. Many utilities in the United States are only gathering usage data once per hour or less frequently.† It is important to keep in mind that such analysis has already been shown to be possible with an analog meter‡ as well, so this capability is not new with smart meters.

Disaggregation technologies§ can provide this level of detail, but require consumer consent and active participation in order to develop it.

Claim 6: Smart meters transmit personal information.

In the United States, at the time of this writing, no traditional personal information (e.g., name, address, phone number, etc.) was being transmitted by smart meters. There is a unique code associated with each smart meter to ensure billing accuracy that is part of the ANSI C12.19 standards for meter data that is sent with the energy usage data transmission.

---

* From NISTIR 7628 Rev. 1: "Using nonintrusive appliance load monitoring (NALM) techniques, interval energy usage at different time periods can be used to infer individual appliances' portions of energy usage by comparison to libraries of known patterns matched to individual appliances. NALM techniques have many beneficial uses for managing energy usage and demand, including pinpointing loads for purposes of load balancing or increasing energy efficiency. However, such detailed information about appliance use has the potential to indicate whether a building is occupied or vacant, show residency patterns over time, and potentially reflect intimate details of people's lives and activities inside their homes."

† Per information gathered from utilities during NIST Smart Grid CSWG Working Group research, which occurred between July 2009 and the publication of this book. Also per a representative from the Utility Analytics Institute.

‡ This is demonstrated in the famous research study by Elias Leake Quinn, Smart Metering and Privacy: Existing Law and Competing Policies, Spring 2009, p. 3, http://www.dora.state.co.us/puc/DocketsDecisions/DocketFilings/09I-593EG/09I-593EG_Spring2009Report-Smart GridPrivacy.pdf. Note: A hob heater is a top-of-stove cooking surface.

§ Discussed in Chapters 5 and 7 of this book.

This unique identifier for the smart meter does not explicitly indicate name, address, or other traditional types of personal information. It is important to establish safeguards for those smart meter codes used for billing to ensure they cannot be accessed by others who are not authorized.

Claim 7: Smart meters can tell when people are at home or when the home is empty, so burglars will have an easy time finding targets.

The answer depends upon the security controls implemented within the smart meter. This claim is most likely correct if, for example, everyone is away from a home and if a burglar had access to this smart meter information. The ability for bad guys to have access to smart meter data is determined by the security and encryption of data at the meter, during transmissions, and in utility networks and computer systems. Utilities do need to ensure that they exercise appropriate security precautions.

When considering the actions that energy customers take related to this, it is important to point out that energy customers using HANs and HEMSs need to also have the appropriate security controls established to keep such burglars, or any others for that matter, from being able to access this data to determine whether or not the home is empty.

And, outside of the Smart Grid, everyone must ensure they do not communicate on online social media sites or other places when they are away from their homes. Growing numbers of burglars are finding targets by reading Facebook pages.*

Claim 8: Smart meters can determine how you spend your time.

This is a true statement about your use of electrically run devices if the smart meter is used with technology that

* Many news stories over the years support this. For example, see Most Burglars Using Facebook and Twitter to Target Victims, Survey Suggests, http://www.telegraph.co.uk/technology/news/8789538/Most-burglars-using-Facebook-and-Twitter-to-target-victims-survey-suggests.html and Going on Summer Vacation? Don't Tip Off Criminals on Social Media, http://blogs.findlaw.com/blotter/2014/06/going-on-summer-vacation-dont-tip-off-criminals-on-social-media.html.

disaggregates* electricity signatures, or if the data is subsequently obtained and analyzed with a disaggregation method. However, without disaggregation, a meter transmission on an hourly basis would not be able to distinguish any difference in kWh consumed plus the other measurements, like voltage and current, that would be able to provide a clear picture of how time was being spent within the home.

Claim 9: Smart meters can be used to identify medical equipment and give insurance companies information that affects your premiums.

This is possible only if the electricity usage data is disaggregated and unique signatures of electricity used by devices and appliances are identified, and if the data is subsequently provided to insurance companies. At the time of this writing, within the United States, and possibly in other countries as well, there are no laws, regulations, or agreements giving any other entity beyond the utility and its contracted third parties access to smart meter data.

This points to the need for any entity with legitimate and authorized access to or possession of the data to have strong security controls to protect the energy usage data, in addition to having defined organizational privacy policies governing the use and sharing of the data.

It is important to note that other methods exist for insurance companies to suss this out, such as buying your credit card history to examine purchases of medical services, or buying search history data from Google.

* See the Chapters 5 and 7 for more thorough discussions of disaggregation technologies and associated risks.

11

Beyond the Smart Grid: The Monetization of Data

The Smart Grid sector made and continues to make significant investments in machine-to-machine (M2M) communications and applications that rely on sensors to collect data from connected devices. Depending on sensor functionalities, data collection can include:

- Measurements of flow: Voltage, current, phase angle, watts produced or used.
- Performance: Parameters like temperature, vibration, or pressure.
- Date and time stamps.
- Geographic information: Latitude and longitude.
- Identification/authentication of user.

Smart Grid technologies create greater volumes of data and new sources of data—almost exclusively structured data* since it is obtained from devices like smart meters or other sensored machines and components. But the electricity sector is not the only sector to confront challenges and opportunities with this new data. The transformations that are occurring now in the electricity sector are also causing disruptions in other sectors, such as transportation and the growth of vehicle telematics,† as well as healthcare medical devices and the adoption of personal monitoring devices.‡ Data has significant promise to change

* Structured data is data that is organized according to a consistent standard. Much of it is generated by devices in the form of events (such as a change in a temperature measurement or a detection of motion), but it also includes data input by humans, such as name, address, gender, age, etc.

† Telematics is the equivalent of Smart Grid technologies embedded in a car—it includes sensors, communications technologies, and onboard and remote analytics applications, and it can improve operational performance as well as human interactions with a vehicle.

‡ Google's plans for tracking health data: http://spectrum.ieee.org/tech-talk/biomedical/devices/google-fit-wants-to-rule-all-your-wearable-health-fitness-devices.

how we do business, how we conduct our lives, and how we see the world. It is important to remember, though, that with more data and more capabilities to make such changes also come more privacy risks that must be addressed and appropriately mitigated.

The Internet of Things (IOT) includes the Smart Grid plus a growing array of M2M applications that leverage sophisticated sensors. The newest buzzword, the Internet of Everything (IOE), converges human interactions with device networks. The IOE correlates machine-generated data with human-generated data for action and insights.

Sensor Proliferation

A quick digression is needed about sensors, because sensors have been around for a long time, but now are rapidly proliferating in both traditional and innovative new applications. Sensors require power to operate, and in many cases, these sensors require batteries for power. Batteries expire, making it impractical to consider replacing power supplies in mass quantities of sensors on a periodic basis. Technology advances on many fronts, ranging from materials science discoveries to continued improvements in microprocessors, and has led to a veritable explosion of much more flexible sensors that require much less power to function, or now have embedded capabilities to produce their own power.[*] For instance, it is now not only technically but also practically feasible to deploy sensors for applications that would benefit from remote monitoring capabilities. For instance, a solution called Waspmote[†] can be deployed in forests for early fire detection. Researchers in South Korea announced the development of a prototype sensor the size of a postage stamp that detects goose bumps on skin to monitor physical and emotional responses in humans.[‡] Sensors will continue to proliferate in every imaginable business sector and generate new varieties of data.

---

[*] Energy harvesting advances are announced with some regularity, eliminating the need for batteries in many sensors, and thus dramatically increasing the possibilities for what can be monitored. See http://electronicdesign.com/power/energy-harvesting-and-wireless-sensor-networks-drive-industrial-applications and http://newsoffice.mit.edu/2010/energy-harvesting for some examples.

[†] http://www.libelium.com/products/waspmote/.

[‡] http://spectrum.ieee.org/tech-talk/biomedical/diagnostics/goose-bump-detector-senses-your-skin-crawling.

Social media participation and electronic production and consumption of content are increasing too—and creating daily terabytes and petabytes[*] and more of unstructured data. Sensors create big data.

The ability to digest this big data as its variety, volume, velocity, and veracity grow presents significant challenges. Data analytics, leveraging impressive computing power, is the main tool to make sense of all this data. Data analytics has a sense of time and function. Analytics can be descriptive, predictive, or prescriptive. Descriptive is by far the most common. The energy management systems described earlier typically use descriptive analytics to provide a summary of what happened or what is happening, usually directed to a smart phone or computer. A car's dashboard reflects descriptive data analytics as well as some predictive analytics, such as messages regarding maintenance. At the time of this writing, utilities were in the early stages of deploying more sophisticated analytics for predictive purposes, particularly to model anticipated electricity demand or the condition of grid components to determine best repair or replacement times.[†] Predictive analytics combines historical and real-time data from any number of sources to forecast the probabilities of an outcome, such as a malfunctioning transformer. For many retailers, predictive analytics create suggestions for purchases to shoppers visiting their websites.[‡] Prescriptive analytics is the latest evolution of data analytics, and it narrows down multiple probabilities to one action, which may be automatically enacted. Google's self-driving or autonomous car[§] is an example of an application that relies on prescriptive analytics.

[*] A Terabyte is 1000 Gigabytes, a Petabyte is 1000 Terabytes, using the simpler designation that identifies a Kilobyte as 1000 bytes. For the purists out there, it's 1024 Gigabytes to a Terabyte and 1024 Terabytes to a Petabyte. The successive designations are Exa, Zetta, Yotta, and Bronto. Bronto! Dinosaurs are extinct, but they still live on.

[†] Traditional utility practice was to run to failure or when the equipment failed, but the advent of sensors for remote monitoring and control enables a transition to more proactive grid management.

[‡] For example, see Amazon Knows What You Want Before You Buy It, January 27, 2014, http://www.predictiveanalyticsworld.com/patimes/amazon-knows-what-you-want-before-you-buy-it/.

[§] For example, see A Self-Driving Car Will Create 1 Gigabyte of Data per Second: New Big Data Opportunity? July 22, 2013, http://www.predictiveanalyticsworld.com/patimes/a-self-driving-car-will-create-1-gigabyte-of-data-per-second-new-big-data-opportunity/.

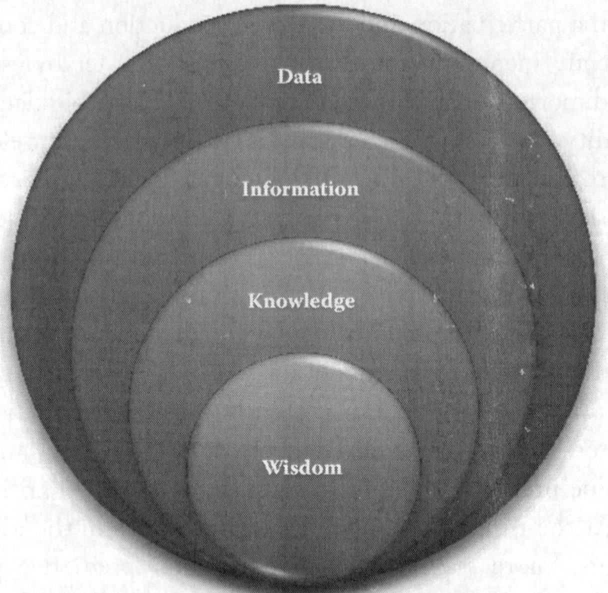

Figure 11.1 The value of data.

Applications of advanced analytics are the value multiplier for data—big or otherwise. The ads that you see on the side of a search engine screen are based on your search history plus demographic data and countless other variables from multiple data brokers melded together to detect patterns and predict your probabilities of interest in products and services. Figure 11.1 illustrates the foundational value of data, and how analytics begets information, information coupled with human insights produces knowledge, and knowledge coupled with thoughtful human experience leads to wisdom. (This is not to say that if you have a lot of data you are wise.)

There are important privacy questions regarding the treatment of all these new sources of data, but there are also very serious questions about the monetary value of data. Monetization of the data can create privacy issues.

For instance, an appliance manufacturer may be interested in collecting data about how many times the cold water wash setting is used versus a hot water wash setting for a smart clothes washer. That data has value if it aids a diagnosis of a performance issue like a failing rubber gasket. It would reduce downtime and inconvenience for the owner of that asset, while the manufacturer would enjoy improved productivity on the part of its service resources and have evidence of malfunctioning components. The benefits of this data are shared between the appliance owner and manufacturer or service center. Similarly, if your refrigerator could alert you to a water leak or pending failure that would defrost all the contents in the freezer, getting an urgent text message on your smart phone would be timely actionable information. Maybe the refrigerator would automatically schedule a repair request with your designated maintenance center. You might be willing to pay extra for that data and service.

But advertisers want this data too, and as we already know, they are willing to pay handsomely for it.[*] They might send mobile ads promoting a replacement refrigerator or telemarket repair services. Is this really valuable for consumers? Maybe, maybe not. Did the refrigerator owner derive any financial benefit from the sales of the data created by his or her refrigerator that was collected by the manufacturer and sold by the said manufacturer to the advertiser? There is no universal "the consumer owns his or her data" statement applicable to this data in the United States. To date we are unaware of this type of statement anywhere in the world.

CVS pharmacy, a nationwide retailer, created a program where shoppers can opt in to receive a loyalty card. Their ExtraCare program has 70 million active members.[†] In exchange for some personal information like name, contact details, gender, age, and household data, this company rewards cardholders with discounts on purchases that are not available to noncardholders buying the same items. Of course, loyalty cards track purchase details for future use and create more personalized experiences[‡] in the form of targeted offers and coupons. However, consumers can choose to share their purchase data in exchange for price reductions—an exchange of value for this voluntary sharing of data.

In some cases, lawmakers have legislated privacy protections for data. For instance, health data has federal-level privacy protections

---

[*] Ninety-five percent of Google's revenue is attributed to advertising as reported here: https://investor.google.com/financial/tables.html.

[†] From article on CVS loyalty program at http://www.colloquy.com/article_view.asp?xd=11417.

[‡] Ibid.

defined in the Health Insurance Portability and Accountability Act (HIPAA). The same is true for financial data via the Gramm–Leach–Bliley federal law. Energy usage, consumption, and production data has some laws and regulations at the state level, but they are not consistently protected in the same fashion across all 50 states. Vehicle telematics did not have any existing federal protections when this book was written.

Wearable technology data is in an ambiguous situation with debates about the agencies responsible for privacy protection of the associated health data. Under HIPAA, if that health data is collected on behalf of a healthcare covered entity (healthcare provider, healthcare insurer, or healthcare clearinghouse) and used for treatment, payment, or operations, then that data would be subject to HIPAA requirements. However, if that data is collected and used on one of the growing types of personal health information data vaults, then the Federal Trade Commission (FTC) would generally have oversight of it under the HITECH Act. In yet a third scenario, if the data being generated is being collected and used solely by the individual with the device, or being shared with or sent to a cloud service or social media site that does not meet the definition of a health vault, then there is much argument about whether or not that data is protected by any existing law or regulation. Laws and regulations generally lag new technology, leaving the individuals using those technologies, and the technology manufacturers, with no clear guidance about what they must do to protect or use new varieties of data.

Vehicle telematics serves as an interesting example of how new data is monetized and can be used for shared benefit or not. The quid pro quo structure that exists with card loyalty programs seems to be the basis for the initial auto insurance industry's introduction of usage-based insurance* (UBI) programs. The first programs† had only been operating for a couple of years at the time this book was written, so we suspend any judgments until we have more data. The initial results and feedback from consumers may be encouraging, since insurance

* Usage-based insurance leverages in-vehicle or mobile apps to collect driving data to determine insurance premiums. In the United States, existing programs are opt-in and offer discounts for participation.

† Progressive, State Farm Insurance, and American Family are three insurance companies with forms of UBI.

companies are now bundling additional services to increase the incentives, as well as increase their revenue streams beyond insurance payments. These services include roadside assistance and vehicle diagnostic reports. These arrangements provide value back to the consumer for the data that they agree to share on a voluntary or opt-in basis. However, other stakeholders* are focused on the value that vehicle telematics provides to car manufacturers and their original equipment manufacturers (OEMs). Reading between the lines, it seems that while auto insurance companies recognize the importance of socializing the value of data with the vehicle data creators (drivers as owners or operators), other stakeholders believe they have a right to the data whether or not the driver of the vehicle consents to share it.

What does your structured and unstructured data reveal about you? Much more than you may realize, and chances are you are not sharing in the monetization of most of that data. The Smart Grid has received lots of attention, but as our chapter illuminates, there are other business sectors that may have as many or more privacy concerns, as well as more issues about who owns the data and what entities have the right to access or sell it. What are the privacy and security responsibilities assigned to all this new data being generated? What are the penalties for misuse or abuse of data that results in a loss of privacy? There are more questions than answers. We're overdue for a serious discussion of how we want to treat the growth of new types of data as we continue to transition to the Smart Grid and other sectors also transform to the IOT and the IOE. One encouraging sign is that the leading newspaper for Silicon Valley, home to Google and Facebook, published an editorial calling for a Bill of Rights on data and personal information.† The White House published a Consumer Privacy Bill of Rights in February 2012,‡ so perhaps the consciousness is raised on the value of data in the IOT and the IOE.

What should be the future for all the data generated? We look forward to continuing that conversation with you.

---

* Telematics Update, September 2013 and October 2013 issues: http://analysis.telematicsupdate.com/infotainment/telematics-and-value-big-data-part-i and http://analysis.telematicsupdate.com/infotainment/telematics-and-value-big-data-part-ii.

† Editorial in reaction to Facebook's 2012 psychological experiment on almost 700,000 users, *San Jose Mercury News,* July 3, 2014.

‡ See http://www.whitehouse.gov/sites/default/files/privacy-final.pdf.

Appendix A
Smart Grid Categories and Associated Privacy Risks

This spreadsheet was created in 2010 by a subteam, led by Rebecca Herold, of the National Institute of Standards and Technology (NIST) Smart Grid Cyber Security Working Group (CSWG) Privacy Group.*

* See the NIST Smart Grid CSWG Privacy Group work from that time period at http://collaborate.nist.gov/twiki-sggrid/bin/view/SmartGrid/CSCTGPrivacy.

Note: See purpose of matrix and definitions by scrolling to the bottom.

Legend: X = likely privacy risks, P = possible privacy risks, — = no anticipated privacy risks, Ph = physical privacy risks, Ad = administrative privacy risks, Te = technical privacy risks, PD = privacy-impacting data is involved.

ENTITIES WITH INTERESTS IN SMART GRID DATA

SMART GRID CATEGORIES WITH POTENTIAL PRIVACY ISSUES	CONSUMERS (EXPANDING UPON VERSION 1 OF NISTIR 7628)				COMMERCIAL/ INSTITUTIONAL (APARTMENTS, HOSPITALS, DORMITORIES, ETC.)				COMMERCIAL/ NONINSTITUTIONAL (OFFICE BUILDINGS, RETAIL STORES, DATA CENTERS, CAR RENTALS, ETC.)				INDUSTRIAL (STEEL MILLS, AUTO ASSEMBLY PLANTS, ETC.)				THIRD PARTIES (RESEARCHERS, VENDORS, SERVICE PROVIDERS, REGULATORS, MARKETERS, ETC., WHO ARE *NOT* UNDER THE SAME LEGAL AND CONTRACTUAL OBLIGATIONS AS THE UTILITIES)				UTILITIES				CONTRACTED AGENTS (ENTITIES THAT UTILITIES HAVE CONTRACTED TO DO WORK ON THEIR BEHALF AND MUST ABIDE BY THE SAME LEGAL AND CONTRACTUAL OBLIGATIONS AS THE UTILITY)				LAW ENFORCEMENT AND INVESTIGATIONS			
	Ph	Ad	Te	PD	Ph	Ad	Te	PD	Ph	Ad	Te	PD	Ph	Ad	Te	PD	Ph	Ad	Te	PD	Ph	Ad	Te	PD	Ph	Ad	Te	PD	Ph	Ad	Te	PD
SMART METERS																																
Energy usage	X	X	X	X	X	X	X	X	—	P	P	P	—	P	P	P	X	X	X	X	X	X	X	X	X	X	X	X	—	—	X	X
Pricing data	X	X	X	X	X	X	X	X	—	P	P	P	—	P	P	P	X	X	X	X	X	X	X	X	X	X	X	X	—	—	X	X
Smart device data	X	X	X	X	X	X	X	X	—	P	P	P	—	P	P	P	X	X	X	X	X	X	X	X	X	X	X	X	—	—	X	X
PEVs																																
Private charging station	X	X	X	X	X	X	X	X	—	P	P	P	—	P	P	P	X	X	X	X	X	X	X	X	X	X	X	X	—	X	X	X
Energy usage	X	X	X	X	X	X	X	X	—	P	P	P	—	P	P	P	X	X	X	X	X	X	X	X	X	X	X	X	—	X	X	X
Pricing data	X	X	X	X	X	X	X	X	—	P	P	P	—	P	P	P	X	X	X	X	X	X	X	X	X	X	X	X	—	X	X	X
PEV—related data	X	X	X	X	X	X	X	X	—	P	P	P	—	P	P	P	X	X	X	X	X	X	X	X	X	X	X	X	—	X	X	X

Public charging station	P	P	P	P	P	P	—	P	—	P	P	P	—	P	P	P	X	X	X	X	X	X	X	X	X	X	X	X	—	X	X	X
PEV—related data	P	P	P	P	P	P	—	P	—	P	P	P	—	P	P	P	X	X	X	X	X	X	X	X	X	X	X	X	—	X	X	X
Servicing	X	X	X	X	P	P	P	P	—	P	P	P	—	P	P	P	X	X	X	X	X	X	X	X	X	X	X	X	—	X	X	X
OTHER TYPES OF PRIVATELY OWNED MOBILE DEVICES OR REMOTE APPLICATIONS THAT CONNECT TO THE SMART GRID																																
Mobile devices: smart phones and laptops, apps, etc.	X	X	X	X	X	X	X	X	—	X	X	X	—	—	—	—	—	X	X	X	—	P	P	P	—	P	P	P	X	X	X	X
Servicing for mobile devices	X	X	X	X	X	X	X	X	X	X	X	X	—	—	—	—	X	X	X	X	—	P	P	P	—	P	P	P	X	X	X	X
HOME AREA NETWORK (AKA HAN, METER TO UTILITY)																																
HAN WITH EMS																																
Energy production	X	X	X	X	—	—	—	—	—	—	—	—	—	—	—	—	X	X	X	X	P	X	X	X	P	X	X	X	P	P	P	P
Energy use	X	X	X	X	P	X	P	X	—	—	—	—	—	—	—	—	X	X	X	X	X	X	X	X	X	X	X	X	X	X	X	X
HAN WITHOUT EMS																																
Energy production	P	P	P	P	—	—	—	—	—	—	—	—	—	—	—	—	P	P	P	P	P	X	X	X	P	X	X	X	P	P	P	P
Energy use	P	X	X	X	P	X	P	X	—	—	—	—	—	—	—	—	P	X	X	X	X	X	X	X	X	X	X	X	P	X	X	X
Smart appliances/end points	P	X	X	X	P	X	X	X	—	—	—	—	—	—	—	—	P	X	X	X	P	X	X	X	P	X	X	X	P	X	X	X
BUSINESS AREA NETWORK (BAN)																																
Business area network (BAN), i.e., sensitive devices	—	—	—	—	—	—	—	—	—	—	—	—	—	—	—	—	—	—	—	—	—	—	—	—	—	—	—	—	—	—	—	—
FIELD AREA NETWORK (FAN)																																
Field area network (aka FAN, meter to utility, neighborhood area network)	X	X	X	X	X	X	X	X	—	P	P	P	—	P	P	P	—	—	—	—	X	X	X	X	X	X	X	X	—	—	P	X
WIDE-AREA NETWORK																																
Wide-area network (backhaul)	X	X	X	X	X	X	X	X	—	P	P	P	—	P	P	P	—	—	—	—	X	X	X	X	X	X	X	X	—	—	P	X

(continued)

SMART GRID CATEGORIES WITH POTENTIAL PRIVACY ISSUES	ENTITIES WITH INTERESTS IN SMART GRID DATA: CONSUMERS (EXPANDING UPON VERSION 1 OF NISTIR 7628)				COMMERCIAL/ INSTITUTIONAL (APARTMENTS, HOSPITALS, DORMITORIES, ETC.)				COMMERCIAL/ NONINSTITUTIONAL (OFFICE BUILDINGS, RETAIL STORES, DATA CENTERS, CAR RENTALS, ETC.)				INDUSTRIAL (STEEL MILLS, AUTO ASSEMBLY PLANTS, ETC.)				THIRD PARTIES (RESEARCHERS, VENDORS, SERVICE PROVIDERS, REGULATORS, MARKETERS, ETC., WHO ARE *NOT* UNDER THE SAME LEGAL AND CONTRACTUAL OBLIGATIONS AS THE UTILITIES)				UTILITIES				CONTRACTED AGENTS (ENTITIES THAT UTILITIES HAVE CONTRACTED TO DO WORK ON THEIR BEHALF AND MUST ABIDE BY THE SAME LEGAL AND CONTRACTUAL OBLIGATIONS AS THE UTILITY)				LAW ENFORCEMENT AND INVESTIGATIONS			
	Ph	Ad	Te	PD	Ph	Ad	Te	PD	Ph	Ad	Te	PD	Ph	Ad	Te	PD	Ph	Ad	Te	PD	Ph	Ad	Te	PD	Ph	Ad	Te	PD	Ph	Ad	Te	PD
COMMUNICATIONS PROCESSORS																																
Communications processors (head end)	X	X	X	X	X	X	X	X	—	P	P	P	—	P	P	P	—	—	—	—	X	X	X	X	P	P	P	P	—	—	P	X
BACK OFFICE SYSTEMS AND APPLICATIONS																																
Back office systems and applications	X	X	X	X	X	X	X	X	—	P	P	P	—	P	P	P	—	—	—	—	X	X	X	X	P	P	P	P	—	—	P	X
THIRD-PARTY APPLICATIONS																																
Third-party applications (including cloud apps)																																
Selected by consumer	X	X	X	X	X	X	X	X	—	P	P	P	—	P	P	P	X	X	X	X	X	X	X	X	P	P	P	P	—	—	P	X
Selected by utility	X	X	X	X	X	X	X	X	—	P	P	P	—	P	P	P	P	P	P	P	X	X	X	X	X	X	X	X	—	—	P	X

MARKETING																																
Use of consumer data	X	X	X	X	X	X	X	X	P	P	P	P	—	—	—	—	X	X	X	X	P	P	P	P	P	P	P	P	—	—	—	—
Sharing consumer data	X	X	X	X	X	X	X	X	P	P	P	P	—	—	—	—	X	X	X	X	P	P	P	P	P	P	P	P	—	—	—	—
RESEARCH																																
Use of consumer data	X	X	X	X	X	X	X	X	P	P	P	P	—	—	—	—	X	X	X	X	P	P	P	P	P	P	P	P	—	—	—	—
Sharing consumer data	X	X	X	X	X	X	X	X	P	P	P	P	—	—	—	—	X	X	X	X	P	P	P	P	P	P	P	P	—	—	—	—
ENERGY GENERATION (E.G., WIND, SOLAR, ETC.)																																
Energy plants/utilities	—	—	—	—	—	—	—	—	—	—	—	—	—	—	—	—	—	—	—	—	—	—	—	—	—	—	—	—	—	—	—	—
Consumer location generation	P	P	P	P	P	P	P	P	—	—	—	—	—	—	—	—	P	P	P	P	P	P	P	P	P	P	P	P	P	P	P	P
NSTIC AND TRUSTED IDS																																
NSTIC and trusted IDs	P	P	P	P	P	P	P	P	P	P	P	P	P	P	P	P	P	P	P	P	P	P	P	P	P	P	P	P	P	P	P	P
RFID ISSUES/RISKS																																
RFID issues	P	P	P	P	P	P	P	P	—	—	—	—	—	—	—	—	P	P	P	P	P	P	P	P	P	P	P	P	P	P	P	P
GOVERNMENT ACTIVITIES																																
U.S. local	P	X	X	X	P	X	X	X	—	—	—	—	—	—	—	—	P	X	X	X	P	X	X	X	P	X	X	X	X	X	X	X
U.S. state	P	X	X	X	P	X	X	X	—	—	—	—	—	—	—	—	P	X	X	X	P	X	X	X	P	X	X	X	X	X	X	X
U.S. federal	P	X	X	X	P	X	X	X	—	—	—	—	—	—	—	—	P	X	X	X	P	X	X	X	P	X	X	X	X	X	X	X
International	P	X	X	X	P	X	X	X	—	—	—	—	—	—	—	—	P	X	X	X	P	X	X	X	P	X	X	X	X	X	X	X
CONSUMER AND PERSONNEL ISSUES																																
CONSUMER AND PERSONNEL ACTIVITIES																																
Posting data on websites	X	X	X	X	P	X	X	X	—	P	P	P	—	—	—	—	X	X	X	X	X	X	X	X	X	X	X	X	P	X	X	X
Sharing with third parties	P	X	X	X	P	X	X	X	—	P	P	P	—	—	—	—	P	X	X	X	X	X	X	X	X	X	X	X	P	X	X	X

(continued)

Purpose of matrix:	The physical issues would include physical access to the following (add to this list as necessary):	The administrative issues would include the following (add to this list as necessary):	The technical issues would include the following (add to this list as necessary):	NSTIC and trusted IDs:
Provide a comprehensive way to identify and prioritize the areas for the NIST Smart Grid privacy subgroup work going forward. As a result of continuing work, provide recommended privacy guidelines for energy data, as well as identifying responsibilities for entities with access to energy data.	Smart meters Smart appliances PEVs Power plants Utilities facilities Data storage devices	Policies Procedures Breach identification and response Training and awareness Opt in/opt out/rescind opt in or out Consent and rescind consent (totally or by various collection, usage, sharing, transborder, and retention preferences) Giving access to individuals Data ownership Responsibility and accountability Purposes for collecting Limiting collection to only that which is necessary Limiting use of data Disclosure and sharing Data retention Data accuracy Ensuring appropriate safeguards Giving notice, openness, and transparency Correcting and updating data Laws, regulations, and standards Accounting for disclosures of energy data	Home area networks (HANs) and privacy networks (wireless and hardwired) Intranets and corporate networks (LANs) (wireless and hardwired) Field area networks (FANs and neighborhood area networks) (wireless and hardwired) Wide-area networks (WANs and backhaul) Public networks (Internet) Encryption Access controls Authentication Authorization Anonymization, de-identification, and aggregation Malware Data storage and backups	How would trusted IDs impact privacy in the Smart Grid? For example, trusted IDs as a means of providing individual choice to share/not/rescind sharing of PI or sensitive PI; could they lead to privacy incidents, etc.?

Appendix B: Example of One State's Actions for Smart Grid Privacy

There were many states that were considering rules to establish for Smart Grid privacy at the time this book was written. California is also frequently cited in this book for its privacy laws and policies regarding energy usage data since one of the authors, Christine Hertzog, resides in that state.

The actions of California could provide a good overview of the types of laws and rulings that other states may subsequently implement as a result of these precedents.

Here is a brief compilation of the most important California privacy rulings and laws impacting not only energy usage and production data, but also general privacy protections for all types of personal information, at the time of this writing.

California State Constitution. Article 1, Declaration of Rights, Section 1. "All people are by nature free and independent and have inalienable rights. Among these are enjoying and defending life and liberty, acquiring, possessing, and protecting property, and pursuing and obtaining safety, happiness, and privacy." (*Note*: Nine other state constitutions explicitly mention privacy.*)

Assembly Bill (AB) 1274. Privacy: customer electrical or natural gas usage data. This California law was approved on October 5, 2013, to address the role of businesses such as energy service providers (ESPs) as data managers. The bill aims to "prohibit a business from sharing, disclosing, or otherwise making accessible to any 3rd party a customer's electrical or natural gas usage data without obtaining the express consent of the customer and conspicuously disclosing to whom the disclosure will be made and how the data will be used. The bill would require a business and a nonaffiliated 3rd party, pursuant to a contract, to implement and maintain reasonable security procedures and practices to protect the data from unauthorized disclosure."† It also provides for a civil penalty for violations.

Senate Bill (SB) 1476. Public utilities: customer privacy: advanced metering infrastructure. This law was approved on September 29, 2010, and addresses consumer rights to their electricity usage data, and applies this law to IOUs and publicly owned utilities such as municipal and rural cooperatives.‡

Assembly Bill 1103. Nonresidential Building Energy Use Disclosure Program. This California law was approved on October 12, 2007, to provide whole building information about energy use.§ The California Energy Commission was conducting hearings at the time this book was written about how to implement this legislation, including guidance for utilities to comply with requests for building data.¶

* http://www.ncsl.org/research/telecommunications-and-information-technology/privacy-protections-in-state-constitutions.aspx.

† http://leginfo.legislature.ca.gov/faces/billNavClient.xhtml?bill_id=201320140AB1274.

‡ http://www.leginfo.ca.gov/pub/09-10/bill/sen/sb_1451-1500/sb_1476_bill_20100929_chaptered.html.

§ http://www.energy.ca.gov/ab1103/documents/ab_1103_bill_20071012_chaptered.pdf.

¶ http://www.energy.ca.gov/ab1103/.

Assembly Bill 531. This law was approved on October 11, 2009, to clarify the role of the State Energy Resources Conservation and Development Commission in setting a schedule for compliance in supplying the required building benchmarking data.[*]

Senate Bill 1386. Personal information: Privacy. This law was approved on September 25, 2002, and required businesses to disclose any breach of personal information (name) in combination with a variety of other data elements, such as social security number, credit card number, or driver's license or California ID number.[†] It also identifies that any breaches are civil code violations and can result in penalties.

D14-05-016. This CPUC decision issued rules regarding access to energy usage and usage-related data with safeguards for privacy of personal data. It provides for the availability of aggregated and anonymized data for research purposes to academic institutions and local governments.[‡]

D12-08-045. This CPUC decision extended the privacy and security directives for electricity usage data to natural gas data.[§]

D11-07-056. This CPUC decision issued directives regarding privacy and security of customer electricity usage data.[¶] It aligned its privacy rules with the Fair Information Practice Principles (FIPPs), and defined approval mechanisms for utilities to share this data with third parties.

---

* http://www.energy.ca.gov/ab1103/documents/2011-09-12_workshop/2011-09-12_Assembly_Bill_531.pdf.

† http://www.leginfo.ca.gov/pub/01-02/bill/sen/sb_1351-1400/sb_1386_bill_20020926_chaptered.html.

‡ http://docs.cpuc.ca.gov/PublishedDocs/Published/G000/M090/K845/90845985.PDF.

§ http://docs.cpuc.ca.gov/PublishedDocs/Published/G000/M026/K531/26531585.PDF.

¶ http://docs.cpuc.ca.gov/WORD_PDF/FINAL_DECISION/140369.pdf.

Index

S

Titre I

Champ d'application de la Convention de Bruxelles

Les trois chapitres de ce titre seront consacrés au champ d'application *ratione materiae* de la Convention (chap. 1), à son champ d'application dans l'espace (chap. 2), et dans le temps (chap. 3).

Chapitre 1

Champ d'application *ratione materiae*

26 – Principe. Le principe est que la Convention s'applique «en matière civile et commerciale» (section 1), mais l'art. 1 énumère limitativement certaines matières expressément exclues du domaine d'application de la Convention (section 2).

Section 1: La Convention joue «en matière civile et commerciale»

27 – Matière civile et commerciale. L'art. 1er énonce que la Convention s'applique «en matière civile et commerciale et quelle que soit la nature de la juridiction». Les auteurs de la convention ont donc visé les matières de droit privé, y compris les actions civiles jugées par les juridictions répressives (v. art. 5-4° *infra* n° 199). Les matières de droit public ne relèvent pas de la Convention. Mais, comme la distinction entre droit privé et droit public est parfois difficile et que, de plus, cette distinction n'a pas grand sens dans les pays de *Common Law*[1], il a été précisé lors de la Convention d'adhésion de 1978 que la Convention «ne recouvre notamment pas les matières fiscales, douanières ou administratives». Toutefois, même dans les pays de *Civil Law*, il ne sera pas toujours facile de savoir si la question en cause relève du droit privé ou du droit public, que l'on pense aux contrats passés par des opérateurs privés mais avec un fort encadrement de droit public, ou, au contraire aux contrats passés par des personnes de droit public mais semblables à des contrats de droit privé.

Une tendance se fait jour actuellement à vouloir étendre le domaine d'application de la Convention, mais il est trop tôt pour savoir sur quelles réalisations elle débouchera[2].

---

1. V. Fr. Knoepfler, La *House of Lords* et la définition de la matière civile et commerciale, Mélanges Grossen, Neuchâtel 1992, p. 9.

2. V. Communication de la Commission au Conseil et au Parlement européen (SEC (1992) 2277 final) où la Commission souhaite une extension à «d'autres domaines». V. aussi la Communication de la Commission relative à la coopération entre la Commission et les juridictions nationales pour l'application des art. 85 et 86 (JOCE C 39 du 13 février 1993) où, au point 44, la Commission dit qu'elle va étudier la possibilité d'étendre le champ d'application de la Convention de Bruxelles aux affaires de concurrence attribuées aux juridictions administratives et ajoute que, selon elle, «les jugements en matière de concurrence relèvent déjà de cette Convention lorsqu'ils sont rendus dans des affaires civiles et commerciales ».

28 – Précisions données par la Cour de justice. La Cour de justice a précisé ce qu'il fallait entendre par « matière civile et commerciale » dans deux arrêts *Eurocontrol* du 14 octobre 1976, aff. 29/76, et du 14 juillet 1977, aff. j. 9 et 10/77 et dans l'arrêt *Rüffer* du 16 décembre 1980 aff. 814/79. Dans les affaires *Eurocontrol* était en cause une action intentée par *Eurocontrol* (Organisation européenne pour la sécurité de la navigation aérienne) en recouvrement de créances dues par la Cie aérienne allemande L.T.U.. Dans l'arrêt *Rüffer*, le gouvernement néerlandais réclamait au sieur *Rüffer* le remboursement de frais d'enlèvement d'un bateau coulé dans la baie de Watum. La Cour posa dans ces arrêts deux principes d'interprétation importants

29 – Interprétation autonome. Tout d'abord, dans l'arrêt *Eurocontrol* de 1976, pour la première fois, la Cour admet que les notions utilisées par la Convention soient intepr étées « de façon autonome » et non par référence à un système national. La Cour déclare : « Pour l'interprétation de la notion de "matière civile et commerciale" aux fins de l'application de la Convention du 27 septembre 1968... il convient de se référer non au droit d'un quelconque des États concernés, mais, d'une part, aux objectifs et au système de la Convention, et, d'autre part, aux principes généraux qui se dégagent de l'ensemble des systèmes nationaux ». Ce principe constructif d'interprétation fût ensuite fréquemment utilisé par la Cour.

30 – Critère de distinction entre matières de droit privé et matières de droit public. En second lieu, dans l'arrêt *Eurocontrol* de 1976 et dans l'arrêt *Rüffer* de 1980, la Cour de justice pose un critère de distinction entre affaires relevant du droit privé et donc de la Convention et affaires relevant du droit public et donc exclues du domaine de ce texte : s'il y a « intervention d'une autorité publique agissant dans l'exercice de la puissance publique », l'affaire échappe à la Convention de Bruxelles. Et, dans les deux espèces, la Cour relève que l'organisme public en cause a exercé des prérogatives de puissance publique. Les indices retenus dans l'affaire *Eurocontrol* sont essentiellement les suivants : il s'agit de « recouvrement de redevances dues par une personne de droit privé à un organisme national ou international de droit public en vertu de l'utilisation des installations et services de celui-ci, notamment lorsque cette utilisation est obligatoire et exclusive... », de plus, « le taux des redevances, les modes de calcul et les procédures de perception sont fixées de manière unilatérale vis à vis des usagers... », « l'organisme a unilatéralement fixé le lieu d'exécution de l'obligation à son siège et choisi les juridictions nationales compétentes pour juger de son exécution. » Dans l'affaire *Rüffer*, il apparaît à la Cour que lorsqu'ils procèdaient à l'enlèvement des épaves, les gestionnaires des voies d'eau publiques intervenaient en exerçant leur autorité publique. Ainsi et dans l'affaire *Eurocontrol* et dans l'affaire *Rüffer*, la Convention de Bruxelles a été jugé inapplicable. Le critère de « l'autorité publique agissant dans l'exercice de ses prérogatives de puissance publique » n'est pas dépourvu de logique. Il appelle toutefois deux observations :

1) Ce critère est également utilisé en droit international privé pour décider des cas dans lesquels joue l'immunité de juridiction de l'État étranger : on sait que, s'il est

généralement approuvé, il ne supprime pas toutes difficultés d'application. On pourrait d'ailleurs discuter déjà la solution adoptée par la Cour de justice dans l'affaire *Eurocontrol*: le contrat entre *Eurocontrol* et la compagnie aérienne allemande débitrice des redevances évoque autant un contrat d'adhésion de droit privé qu'un contrat de droit public[3]. Il y aura sans doute encore des difficultés pour tracer la frontière entre droit public et droit privé et la Cour de justice aura peut-être du mal à répondre abstraitement aux questions posées et à ne pas qualifier *in concreto* les litiges (elle n'a d'ailleurs pas échappé à cet écueil dans les affaires *Eurocontrol* et *Rüffer*).

2) La seconde observation est qu'il parait nécessaire pour que la Convention soit écartée qu'au moins une des parties en cause soit une autorité publique. Si le litige s'élève entre deux personnes privées, il relève de la Convention (sous réserve des exclusions étudiées *infra*, n° 31 et ss.), quand bien même la règle de droit en cause serait une règle de droit public. La Cour de Paris en a décidé ainsi à propos de la législation française sur les spoliations en énonçant qu' «aucune exception tenant à l'ordre public n'est prévue quant à l'application des règles de compétence édictées par la Convention... il n'y a donc pas lieu de soustraire à son application les matières régies par les lois d'ordre public, ou par des lois de police et de sûreté[4] ». La Première chambre civile de la Cour de cassation a confirmé cette solution dans une autre affaire le 3 février 1987[5]. Il faut également citer l'arrêt de la Cour de justice du 21 avril 1993, *Volker Sonntag*, aff. C-172/91, qui indique qu'un enseignant d'une école publique poursuivi civilement et pénalement en raison du décès accidentel d'un élève n'était pas une «autorité publique agissant dans l'exercice de la puissance publique».

Si la Convention s'applique généralement «en matière civile et commerciale», l'art. 1er al. 2 exclut cependant diverses matières.

Section 2: Matières exclues

§ 1 : État et capacité des personnes, et droit patrimonial de la famille

31 – Principe. Selon l'art. 1er al. 2 1) sont exclus «l'état et la capacité des personnes physiques, les régimes matrimoniaux, les testaments et les successions». Il s'agit donc du statut personnel des personnes physiques (nationalité, nom, incapacités, début et fin de la personnalité, absence, etc.), ainsi que des rapports de famille extra-patrimoniaux (mariage, filiation, divorce) et patrimoniaux (régimes matrimoniaux, testaments, suc-

---

3. V. sur ce point G. Droz, RC 1977, 781 et ss.

4. Paris 16 déc. 1974, Gaz. Pal. 1975, 1, 179; D. 1975, 355; JDI 1976, 146, 1re esp. note D. Holleaux. Cet arrêt confirme Trib. gr. inst. Paris, réf., 7 juin 1974, RC 1974, 1reesp. note P. Lagarde; D.S. 1975, 339, 2e esp. note G. Droz; JDI 1975, 82, 4e esp. note D. Holleaux.

5. JDI 1988, 135 observ. A. Huet; RC 1987, 617, note Gautier.

cessions). On notera toutefois que des travaux sont actuellement en cours pour rédiger une Convention applicable au droit de la famille dont l'esprit serait analogue à celui de la Convention de Bruxelles.

La Convention s'applique aux obligations alimentaires; en effet, ces obligations donnent lieu à des décisions patrimoniales pour lesquelles il est particulièrement important de prévoir un système de compétence et de reconnaissance favorable au créancier d'aliments (v. *infra*, l'étude de l'art. 5-2°, n° 178 et ss.). Cette première catégorie a donné lieu à précisions de la part de la Cour de justice à propos de l'exclusion de la notion de régime matrimonial et de l'inclusion de la notion d'obligation alimentaire.

32 – Exclusion des régimes matrimoniaux: notion communautaire. Pour les régimes matrimoniaux, la difficulté est venue de ce que la notion de régime matrimonial n'est pas appréhendée de la même façon par tous les États contractants. Ainsi le concept de «régime primaire» (ou «statut fondamental») développé par les droits allemand, belge ou français, n'est pas connu partout; et même lorsqu'il est connu, on n'y trouve pas toujours exactement les mêmes règles. Bien plus, au Royaume-Uni et en Irlande, le concept global de «régime matrimonial» n'existe pas, même si ces droits connaissent diverses règles propres aux rapports patrimoniaux entre époux.

La Cour de justice a indiqué qu'il fallait adopter une définition communautaire de la notion de «régimes matrimoniaux» exclus du domaine de la Convention: à l'occasion d'une procédure de divorce opposant un français, M. de Cavel, à sa femme allemande au sujet de mesures provisoires ordonnées par le Tribunal de Paris sur des biens mobiliers situés en Allemagne, alors qu'on s'interrogeait pour savoir si ces mesures relevaient ou non de la Convention, la Cour déclare le 27 mars 1979, aff. 143/78: «... la notion "régimes matrimoniaux" comprend non seulement les régimes de biens spécifiquement et exclusivement conçus par certaines législations nationales en vue du mariage, mais également tous les rapports patrimoniaux résultant directement du lien conjugal ou de la dissolution de celui-ci»[6]. Il en résultait que les mesures provisoires en cause ne relevaient pas de la Convention. La motivation de la Cour dans cet arrêt de 1979 ayant laissé planer quelques doutes (les mesures provisoires étaient-elles exclues en raison de leur caractère accessoire par rapport à la procédure de divorce, ou en raison de la nature des droits dont elles assuraient la sauvegarde?), la Cour de justice devait préciser dans un second arrêt De Cavel, du 6 mars 1980, aff. 120/79, que la mesure provisoire en cause, l'apposition de scellés, ne relevait pas de la Convention de Bruxelles «non à cause de son caractère accessoire mais parce qu'il apparaissait que, par son objet propre, elle relevait en l'occurence du régime matrimonial des époux». Ainsi, il semble que les mesures provisoires prises à l'occasion d'une instance en divorce, dans la mesure où elles préparent d'une certaine façon la liquidation du régime matrimonial, doivent être exclues du champ d'application de la Convention.

---

6. V. aussi CJCE, 31 mars 1982, C.H.W. c ; G.J.H., aff. 25/81, Rec. 1189, concl. Rozès.

Un arrêt de la Cour de justice du 31 mars 1982, *C.H.W. c. G.J.H.*, aff. 25/81, vient à l'appui de cette conclusion; saisie à l'occasion d'une procédure de divorce, la Cour dit: «Une demande de mesures provisoires tendant à obtenir la remise d'un document afin d'empêcher son utilisation comme preuve dans un litige concernant la gestion des biens de la femme par son mari ne relève pas du champ d'application de la convention... si cette gestion se rattache étroitement aux rapports patrimoniaux qui résultent directement du lien conjugal». C'est cette notion de «lien avec les rapports patrimoniaux» qui semble importante, même si l'arrêt de 1982 relève aussi que c'est «en raison de son caractère accessoire» que la demande de mesures destinées à assurer la remise d'un document est à rattacher au régime matrimonial. Peu importe en réalité que la mesure en cause soit accessoire ou non, ce qui compte c'est qu'elle ait un lien étroit avec les rapports patrimoniaux entre époux résultant du mariage. Donc, seules les questions patrimoniales entre époux sans aucun lien avec le mariage ou le divorce relèvent de la Convention. Au contraire sont exclus, selon la formulation anglaise de l'art. 1er al. 2 de la Convention de Bruxelles les «*rights in property arising out of a matrimonialship*». L'expression est plus vaste que celle de «régimes matrimoniaux» dans la mesure où elle vise tous les droits patrimoniaux «résultant d'une relation matrimoniale».

33 – Non-exclusion des obligations alimentaires. Les obligations alimentaires relèvent de la Convention comme le prouvent l'art. 5-2° ainsi que l'art. V bis du Protocole annexé à la Convention, article ajouté en 1978. Ce dernier texte précise que «en matière d'obligations alimentaires, les termes "juge", "tribunal" et "juridiction" comprennent les autorités administratives danoises» (v. *infra* n° 316). Le second arrêt *De Cavel*, du 6 mars 1980, énonce clairement que les obligations alimentaires appartiennent au domaine de la Convention[7]. Ce même arrêt a, de plus, apporté deux précisions :

1) Dans les rapports entre époux divorcés, était en cause la «prestation compensatoire» de l'art. 270 du Code civil français. On sait que, en droit français, cette prestation a un fondement indemnitaire plus qu'alimentaire. Elle a un caractère forfaitaire et peut être payée en une seule fois sous forme de capital. Peut-on encore la qualifier d'«obligation alimentaire»? La Cour de justice a répondu affirmativement dans l'arrêt *De Cavel* du 6 mars 1980 au motif que cette prestation est fixée «selon les ressources et les besoins des intéressés». Même si l'analyse de la Cour gomme quelque peu les différences que le législateur français de 1975 a voulu faire entre prestation compensatoire et pension alimentaire, le résultat paraît satisfaisant. Il serait peu logique de distinguer entre les diverses formes de secours entre conjoints divorcés et d'en inclure seulement certains dans le domaine de la Convention.

2) Le même raisonnement doit guider la réponse à donner s'agissant d'une obligation alimentaire à caractère successoral. Certes, l'art. 1er al. 21) exclut de la Convention

7. V. aussi Civ. 1re 9 novembre 1983, RC 1984, 501, note B. Ancel.

les testaments et successions et le rapport Schlosser (n° 92) préconisait d'exclure aussi les obligations alimentaires à caractère successoral. Mais cette solution paraît condamnée par la jurisprudence De Cavel: en effet, si la prestation compensatoire entre époux relève de la Convention, alors que la définition extensive par la Cour du « régime matrimonial » aurait permis de l'inclure dans cette catégorie, on ne voit pas pourquoi on exclurait du domaine de la Convention une obligation alimentaire à caractère successoral, quand bien même la convention écarte les testaments et successions[8].

34 – Non-exclusion des donations et des trusts. Ni les donations, ni les trusts ne sont exclus par l'art. 1er al. 2 de la Convention.

Pour les donations, la Convention ne sera cependant pas applicable si les litiges qu'elles entraînent sont de nature successorale[9] ou sont directement liés à une question de régime matrimonial (par exemple s'il s'agit d'une donation entre époux)[10].

Pour les trusts, depuis la Convention d'adhésion de 1978, ils relèvent certainement de la Convention et on verra que plusieurs articles les mentionnent expressément. Toutefois, le trust échappera à l'application de la Convention s'il est utilisé en matière de régime matrimonial, de succession, ou encore de faillite, matières exclues de la Convention.

§ 2 : Faillites, concordats et autres procédures analogues

35 – Principe. L'art. 1er al. 2 2) exclut « faillites, concordats et autres procédures analogues ». Le motif des rédacteurs de la Convention était que ces procédures devaient être règlées par une convention spéciale qui était déjà projetée en 1968... mais n'a pas encore abouti en 1993.

Il s'agit des procédures concernant un opérateur économique insolvable. Au contraire, la dissolution d'une société solvable relève de la Convention (art. 16-2°, v. *infra* n° 94). Ainsi le « *winding up* » connu au Royaume-Uni et en Irlande relèvera-t-il de la Convention si la société est solvable et non si elle est insolvable[11].

La Cour de justice, dans l'arrêt *Gourdain c. Nadler*, du 22 février 1979, aff. 133/78, a donné une définition des procédures exclues: il s'agit des « procédures fondées, selon les diverses législations des parties contractantes, sur l'état de cessation de paiement, l'insolvabilité ou l'ébranlement du crédit du débiteur, impliquant une intervention de l'autorité judiciaire aboutissant à une liquidation forcée et collective des biens ou, à tout le moins, un contrôle de cette autorité ». Ceci inclut à coup sûr la procédure de redressement et liquidation judiciaire du droit français (loi du 25 janvier 1985).

---

8. V. en ce sens, J.P. Beraudo, Juriscl. Europe, fasc 3000, n°37.
9. En ce sens rapp. Jenard, p. 11 et rapp. Schlosser n°112.
10. Ceci résulte de la jurisprudence De Cavel précitée.
11. Ce qu'indique le texte anglais de la Convention, l'art. 1er al. 2 2) excluant: « ... *proceedings relating to the winding up of insolvent companies or other legal persons* ».

L'exclusion ne joue que si l'action «dérive directement de la faillite et s'insère étroitement dans le cadre d'une procédure collective[12] »: c'était le cas pour une action en complément de passif (art. 99 de la loi du 13 juillet 1987) en cause dans l'affaire *Gourdain*. Au contraire, s'agissant d'une procédure engagée pour le recouvrement d'une créance de fournitures et donc non directement liée à la faillite, la Cour de Paris a justement considéré que la Convention de Bruxelles devait s'appliquer[13].

§ 3 : Sécurité sociale

36 – Principe. L'art. 1er al. 2 3) exclut la Sécurité sociale, matière dont il est difficile de savoir si elle relève du droit privé ou du droit public. Toutefois le rapport Jenard précise qu'est »seul exclu de l'application de la Convention... le contentieux de la Sécurité sociale, à savoir les différends issus des rapports entre l'administration et les employeurs ou employés... Par contre, la Convention est applicable lorsque l'administration fait valoir un droit de recours direct contre un tiers responsable du dommage, ou est subrogée envers ce tiers dans les droits d'une victime assurée par elle, car elle agit alors selon les normes du droit commun»[14]. Si la Sécurité sociale est exclue, le droit du travail en revanche relève de la Convention (v. *infra* à propos des art. 5-1°, n°166 et ss., et 17, n°142)[15].

§ 4 : Arbitrage

37 – Principe. L'art. 1er al. 2 4) exclut l'arbitrage. Certes l'art. 220 du traité de Rome visait aussi la reconnaissance et l'exécution des sentences arbitrales, mais les auteurs de la Convention constatant que l'arbitrage était déjà régi par un important réseau de conventions internationales, on préféré l'écarter[16]. Il n'est effectivement pas très gênant que la Convention de Bruxelles ne s'applique pas aux litiges sur la désignation des arbitres, sur la fixation du lieu de l'arbitrage ou sur la procédure arbitrale. De même seule une décision judiciaire, à l'exclusion d'une sentence arbitrale, peut

12. CJCE 22 février 1979, aff. 133/78; v. aussi rapp. Jenard, p. 12.

13. Paris 16 mars 1979, RC 1980, 127, note Mezger; pourvoi rejeté par Civ. 1re 10 mars 1981, RC 1981, 553, note E.M., mais le pourvoi ne portait pas sur cette question. V. aussi Paris 14 juin 1979, Rev. Soc. 1980, 555, note De Bottini; 9 février 1983, Gaz. Pal. 1983, 1, 217, note Tandeau de Marsac; Trib. com. Paris 29 février 1984, Gaz. Pal. 1984, l, som. 185; Civ. 1re 12 nov. 1986, Bull. I n°257; Paris 13 mars 1991, Paris 30 mars 1990 et Douai 21 juin 1990, JDI 1992, 187, note A. Huet; Civ. 1re 13 avril 1992, D. 1992, inf. rap. 156; RC 1993, 67, note Rémery: jeu de la Convention pour une action en paiement de fournitures même si le débiteur est en faillite.

14. Rapp. Jenard, p. 13; rapp. Schlosser, n°60.

15. V. CJCE, 13 nov. 1979, *Sanicentral*, aff. 25/79; et les arrêts de la Cour de cassation dans cette affaire: Soc. 10 janvier 1979, RC 1979, 453, note P.L.; Soc. 4 juin 1980, JDI 1980, 896, note Tillhet-Pretnar.

16. Rapp. Jenard, p. 13; rapp. Schlosser, n°61.

faire obstacle à la reconnaissance dans un État contractant d'une décision émanant d'une juridiction d'un autre État contractant (art. 27- 3°)[17]. Mais en réalité, l'exclusion de l'arbitrage pose des questions délicates[18].

38 – Refus de recours préjudiciel par l'arbitre. La Cour de justice a indiqué dans l'arrêt *Nordsee* du 23 mars 1982, aff. 102/81[19], que, en droit communautaire en général et non pas spécialement pour la Convention de Bruxelles, un arbitre ne pouvait lui poser une question préjudicielle en interprétation dans le cadre de l'art. 177 du Traité CEE. Cette solution vaut certainement pour la Convention de Bruxelles: le protocole de 1971 ne mentionne pas l'arbitre parmi les instances qui peuvent saisir la Cour de justice d'un recours en interprétation.

39 – Contestation de la convention d'arbitrage. La Convention n'a rien prévu pour le cas où une juridiction de la Communauté, compétente selon la Convention de Bruxelles, est saisie alors que l'existence ou la validité d'une convention d'arbitrage est contestée. La Cour de justice a pris position dans une hypothèse particulière, dans un arrêt *Marc Rich* du 25 juillet 1991, aff. C 190/89: la *Court of Appeal* demandait essentiellement si l'exclusion formulée par l'art. 1er al. 2 4) s'appliquait à un litige ayant pour objet la désignation d'un arbitre et où se posait la question incidente de l'existence initiale d'un accord d'arbitrage. Suivant les conclusions de M. l'avocat général Darmon[20], la Cour conclut à l'inapplicabilité de la Convention de Bruxelles: «L'art. 1er al. 2 4) doit être interprété en ce sens que l'exclusion qu'il prévoit s'étend à un litige pendant devant une juridiction étatique qui a pour objet la désignation d'un arbitre, même si ce litige soulève au préalable la question de l'existence ou de la validité d'une convention d'arbitrage». En effet, comme l'avait clairement démontré M. Darmon, le système créé par la Convention de Bruxelles est totalement inadapté à l'arbitrage, et ce serait aller à l'encontre de toutes les tendances récentes en matière d'arbitrage international (délocalisation de l'arbitrage, souci d'efficacité maximum de

---

17. V. *infra* n° 318; et sur ce que cet état du droit peut parfois être regrettable en pratique, v. Beraudo, Juriscl. Europe, fasc. 3000 n° 34, qui parle à ce sujet de «lacunes qui pourraient aiguiser l'imagination de plaideurs de mauvaise foi».

18. Pour un examen complet de ces questions, v. B. Audit, *Arbitration and the Brussels Convention*, in *Arbitration International*, vol. 9, 1/1993, p. 1 à 25; v. aussi, Collins, *The Marc Rich Case and Actions for Negative Declarations*, Mélanges Grossen, Neuchâtel 1992, p. 385; et Schlosser, *The 1968 Brussels Convention and Arbitration*, Riv. di dir. int. priv. e proc. 1989, 545 qui, contrairement à l'opinion exprimée dans son rapport sur la Convention d'adhésion de 1978, estime que la Convention de Bruxelles doit s'appliquer à toutes les instances judiciaires étatiques ayant trait à une question d'arbitrage.

19. Rec. 1095, concl. Reischl; Revue de l'Arbitrage 1982, 473. V. aussi A. Mc Clellan, Le rôle de l'arbitrage commercial et le droit communautaire, Rev. de dr. internat. et de dr. comp. 1990, 301.

20. V. les très riches conclusions de M. Darmon, et en particulier ses observations sur le cas où l'on est en présence d'une sentence arbitrale «fusionnée» dans un jugement («*awards merged into judgments*»), situation relativement fréquente au Royaume-Uni, (points 67 à 70 des conclusions); v. aussi P. Mayer, *L'autonomie de l'arbitre international dans l'appréciation de sa propre compétence, RCADI, 1989, t. 217, p. 323 et ss.*